CREATING THE FUTURE OF **WebWe**

THROUGH STRATEGY

AND COMMUNITY BUILDING

LEADERSHIP

IN THE

METAVERSE

CAROL A. POORE, PH.D.

FC

**FAST
COMPANY**
Press

Fast Company Press
New York, New York
www.fastcompanypress.com

Distributed by River Grove Books

Design and composition by Greenleaf Book Group and Mimi Bark
Cover design by Greenleaf Book Group and Mimi Bark

Grateful acknowledgment is made to the following sources for permission to reproduce copyrighted material:
International Futures Forum: Graphic "IFF Community Hub: What Do We Hope to Create Together?" Copyright © by the International Futures Forum.
Winnipeg Public Library: Graphic "Our Strategic Priorities." Copyright © by The City of Winnipeg and Sam Bradd. All rights reserved.

Publisher's Cataloging-in-Publication data is available.

Paperback ISBN: 978-1-63908-027-4

Hardback ISBN: 978-1-63908-029-8

eBook ISBN: 978-1-63908-028-1

First Edition

CONTENTS

PREFACE

WHEN I FIRST HEARD THE WORD "metaverse" in late 2021, I cringed.

I envisioned people escaping into a digital fantasyland, never to fully return to real life.

I gasped at the idea of buying digital real estate or virtual designer handbags. How awful to create a fake, digital-world image when there's plenty of that in real life. The metaverse sounded like a complete breakdown of the human race.

Looking back now, I find this initial paradigm of the metaverse was uninformed. I had *a lot* to learn.

As you read this, billions of dollars are being invested into the metaverse—a virtual environment projected to contribute *trillions* of dollars in annual commerce to the world's economy. That's trillions, with a capital "T."

The metaverse, which is also referred to as Web3 and WebMe, is the next phase of the internet. In it we will be able to connect with countless shared, persistent, and 3D virtual worlds. We will jump in and out of various virtual worlds using eyeglasses, headsets, phones, digital contact lenses, and anything designed to connect digital worlds with human beings.

We'll gather for birthday parties with loved ones across the world. We'll conduct business, attend school, watch sports, visit museums, and enjoy live music concerts.

In the metaverse, we'll meet up in work teams, plunge ourselves into virtual travel across numerous universes, and present ourselves as a variety of avatars. Our avatars will mimic our facial expressions, represent our styles, and exude our personality based on the occasion.

The metaverse is impossible to clearly define at this early stage, because of its vast, unknown potential. As immersive technology is developed by many during the next ten years,[1] we will see the metaverse gradually unleashed. Life as we know it will be forever changed. For us, and for future generations.

You could say we are living in the calm before the storm. Urgency is in the air.

I've written this book for people who want to be prepared to effectively lead, work with teams to shape strategy, and build cohesive communities in the metaverse.

Now is the time to fine-tune leadership, strategy, and community-building skills in anticipation of the greatest digital culture shift the world has ever seen.

Many argue that we're already living in a metaverse world. We live much of our lives through our smartphones, using filters and hashtags to curate our virtual appearance and interests. We stare at our computers, working, attending meetings, paying bills, making reservations, and so much more.

Within the next decade, metaverse technology is expected to bring 3D holograms into our digital social experiences, along with the haptic sensations of touch. Early adopters such as Nike have created 3D metaverse-like experiences. Today, people already are experiencing the benefits of virtual travel. And yes, the metaverse is a place where we will continue to play video games and visit fictitious worlds just for fun.

As I wrote this book, I had two very different reactions from colleagues.

Most knew nothing about the metaverse. They were curious, leaned in, and wanted to know more.

The other reaction was dramatically different. A few people physically backed away as I spoke, as if they were nauseated. Several even plugged their ears. They didn't want to hear about the metaverse. One walked away, citing her opinion about the evils of social media.

Fascinating!

No matter what you may know or think about the metaverse, one thing's certain: we're clearly living digital–physical hybrid lives, and innovation waits for no one.

As the metaverse evolves, the way we relate to each other as human beings will no doubt change, and it will not be all good.

We need to develop an evolving playbook of principles and practices for building effective, human-focused, kind, caring, and productive leadership—leaders who foster participative strategy and build communities of people who join together to make a difference—to make a positive impact on planet Earth.

It's been said that leadership is a practice, not a position. Leaders can be found at all levels of an organization, as well as within volunteer initiatives. Leaders connect people with a unified purpose, and inspire them to live the vision, mission, and values of their organization. Leaders instill shared ownership of goals, whether at the team or project level, the department level, or the enterprise level.

Most important for our discussion about the metaverse: leaders lead change. Effective leaders provide the urgency and context for why change is needed, developing the vision, buy-in, and action plan to support the change.[2]

Those who long with nostalgia for the "old normal" prior to the COVID-19 pandemic that arrived to the globe in early 2020 know in their hearts that we are never going back.

With this book, I will connect early metaverse principles to the practices of leadership, community building, and strategy-making. I've examined the metaverse based on what is known at this time, and I intend to update this information as the metaverse evolves.

I hope to help leaders be better prepared to create a world of Web*We*—instead of a worldview solely focused on Web*Me*.

While the technology world is busy creating the metaverse and working on the protocols, it's worth examining, from a human perspective, how we will live together, work together, and build our future together on planet Earth.

I explore the metaverse with three social-science lenses:

- **Strengthening leadership skills for a permanent hybrid world.** What principles and practices will be needed for people and organizations to thrive in a seamless physical/digital metaverse world?

- **Developing open and agile strategies to connect people with their organization's future.** How will the metaverse impact the shaping of your company's strategy and decision-making? How will multiple worlds influence our ability to think clearly, develop long- and short-term foresight, and shape strategies for future success? Will leaders be distracted or empowered by virtual scenarios and altered realities?

- **Defining and building "Big C" human communities that make an impact in our physical and real-life world.** We really do have a choice: Will the metaverse create an individualistic environment where people live their lives through a headset and become indifferent to each other, isolated and lost in a world of 3D animation? Or can the metaverse bring us closer, and create new types of physical-world community relationships?

My investigation cannot possibly answer every question or solve every issue concerning our metaverse world to come. However, if you're reading this book, you are already a potential early adopter. We will be discussing leadership, strategy, and community building in the metaverse. We'll explore how this new frontier creates an early, evolving conversation and the opportunity to tackle the issues that lie ahead for every leader and every organization.

As an executive in corporate America who has led for-profit, non-profit, and higher education institutions, I understand how to help organizations thrive through times of growth, innovation, and turnaround. My career has focused on building leaders who are skilled at leading change.

I've witnessed the negative impact of our constant online world on the faces of leaders, students, and community builders. People are overwhelmed. Community leaders struggle to show up either in person or on-screen. Event no-shows are at an all-time high, even as we recover from the pandemic. Human interaction skills seem to be at an all-time low.

As the world's biggest technology companies such as Microsoft, Meta, Roblox, Apple, and Epic Games are spending billions of dollars to create their metaverse visions, few nontech leaders really understand it. More than 60 percent of online adult consumers in the United States and United Kingdom don't know what the metaverse is. They say they have no need for it in their lives.[3]

While other metaverse authors have discussed technical, marketing, and cryptocurrency topics, I want to focus on the human side of what's to come. We don't really understand the impacts of the metaverse on the next generation of leadership, strategy, and community building.

This is a book for anyone who is curious about the metaverse. You may be an executive helping your organization become more agile to constant, volatile change. You may be a community leader concerned about declining volunteerism. You may be a policymaker or involved in research.

If you are interested in how the metaverse might change the future, and your role in it, this book is for you.

CHAPTER 1

METAVERSE BASICS FOR NONTECHS

AS I PUT THE GOGGLES ON, I fought self-doubt.

I wasn't an experienced gamer.

But there I was, standing tall and buff as a shiny metallic avatar, waving at two avatar teammates at Arizona State University's Dreamscape Learn center, where students become explorers, scientists, and learners. We were about to take off into a virtual reality mission, traveling into an endangered biological ecosystem to save a lizard-like reptile from a mysterious cancer.

We climbed into separate travel pods equipped with hand-held devices to control the flight. I could choose my flight speed, direction, and altitude.

My pod got stuck over a euphoric group of ponds filled with bright-green lily pads and colorful lizards unlike anything found on Earth. One was struggling, almost dead.

The narrator pointed out that the lizard was struck with a mysterious illness, very contagious. Our mission was to find a cure for the illness before the reptiles became extinct.

Our pods shrunk to a molecular level. We traveled into the lizard's cells to discover what was making the creature sick. We took a biopsy and soon diagnosed the problem, saving the reptile population from extinction. This activity was designed to fulfill the learning objectives of a conventional introductory biology lab. The experience was developed to deliver a rigorous set of learning outcomes where students return to the classroom and discuss the data collected from the virtual reality biopsy.

At the end of my metaverse mission, I was ready for another adventure. I soaked up this colorful new world of imagination and adventure. Why return to real life?

If you're thinking that this new metaverse world sounds like Steven Spielberg's movie *Ready Player One*, you're only on the front porch of a new, unchartered journey. The metaverse movement is already underway, and it's about to explode.

The Metaverse Is Being Described As

real-time

3D

persistent

large-scale

virtual worlds (plural)

environments where people and companies will spend an enormous amount of time and money

---

The metaverse is referred to as Web3, WebMe, and a more immersive, next generation of the internet. It's where physical and digital worlds collide—or, better put, are *seamlessly connected.*

As I introduce the metaverse, it would be a mistake to describe the metaverse as an "imaginary" or "fake world" as compared to "real life." This would not be an accurate way to think about the metaverse.

Real life will become an integration of physical and digital lives. It seems odd to think of it this way, but those who aren't participating in the metaverse will miss out on what will be considered as the *new* real life.

The metaverse will be a very real place, a digital representation of real-life transactions.

Throughout this book, when I refer to life "in the metaverse," I'm referring to the integrated combination of physical human life—our "biological life"—with our "digital internet life" as a seamless, hybrid experience.

Most of us are already living our lives in the metaverse. The merging of physical and digital worlds already plays a big role in our everyday real lives. From the moment we wake up, we communicate through a series of screens and apps, from smartphones to computers, even in our vehicles.

Some may believe that the *metaverse is evil*. I disagree. Similar to the internet, the metaverse on its own isn't evil. We know that evil is performed by bad human beings; it's the *bad actors who are evil*. Many significant issues will coexist, such as security and privacy at all levels of life, driven by bad actors and their evil intentions.

On a brighter note, the metaverse brings limitless possibilities for innovation, connection with each other, and productivity.

Participants in the metaverse will be people—human beings—most of whom are good people. We will explore new requirements for effective leadership, community building, and strategy in this early stage of metaverse development.

The metaverse will not produce better leaders, community builders, and strategists. The metaverse cannot give what it doesn't have. It will be up to real humans—us—to identify and cultivate needed skills to bring together physical and digital worlds so that life in the metaverse leads to a better life on planet Earth.

THE METAVERSE IN A NUTSHELL

Loosely defined, the metaverse is a network of 3D virtual worlds focused on social connection,[1] often described as a sort of next generation of the internet as a single, universal virtual world that is facilitated by, *but not defined by*, the use of virtual reality (VR) and augmented reality (AR) headsets.

It's a virtual realm and place of "being" introduced in the 1992 science fiction novel *Snow Crash*, combining "meta" and "universe." Author Neal Stephenson envisioned the metaverse as a collective, physically persistent virtual shared space *connected to* the real world rather than existing only in cyberspace.[2]

The metaverse as a "place" was first realized in 2003, with the online video game *Second Life*.

Second Life is a vast, 3D-generated virtual world and platform filled with user-generated content, where people can interact with each other in real time. It also hosts a thriving in-world economy. The platform was officially launched to the public by Linden Lab on June 23, 2003, but its development dates back to at least the late 1990s.[3]

In *Second Life*, virtual avatars known as "residents" interact with one another in a virtual world known as "the grid." In this virtual world players can interact with other residents, socialize, trade, and participate in group activities.

Similarly, the metaverse is a persistent, interconnected, virtual environment where we work, shop, trade, play, socialize, and are entertained. The metaverse's melding of virtual and real worlds was accelerated by changing consumer behavior throughout the pandemic.[4]

While this world may be digital, the money being exchanged is *very* real.

According to a Citibank report, the metaverse now represents a potential total addressable market of up to $13 trillion by 2030, made up of five billion users. The bank's broad definition of the metaverse goes far beyond gaming and applications in virtual reality to include smart manufacturing technology, virtual advertising, online concerts and events, and digital forms of money such as cryptocurrencies.[5]

The metaverse—

- Connects our physical and virtual worlds through virtual and augmented reality, enabled by 5G infrastructure.

- Requires cross-industry collaboration for interoperability.

- Advances us toward a richer, more connected digital life across virtual platforms.

- Will eventually move us from the smartphone we use today to access web-based services and connect with people, to potentially everyday eyewear that overlays digital information on top of the physical world.

- Will present human beings as avatars—cartoon-like 3D figures that depict the person behind the avatar.

- Will support business transactions, just as we conduct business online today. Transactions may provide much more immersive experiences, such as being able to see objects in three dimensions or taking an adventure to explore a product and test it virtually before making a decision to purchase.

Billions of dollars today are being invested by companies such as Microsoft and Meta, with anticipation that people will be working, playing, learning, and entertaining in this virtual environment.

"The metaverse will be the biggest disruption to how we live that the world has ever seen," announced investment bank Jeffries. Jeffries is a diversified financial services company engaged in investment banking, capital markets, asset management, and direct investing. "Financial firms are looking at the metaverse as a huge potential opportunity."[6]

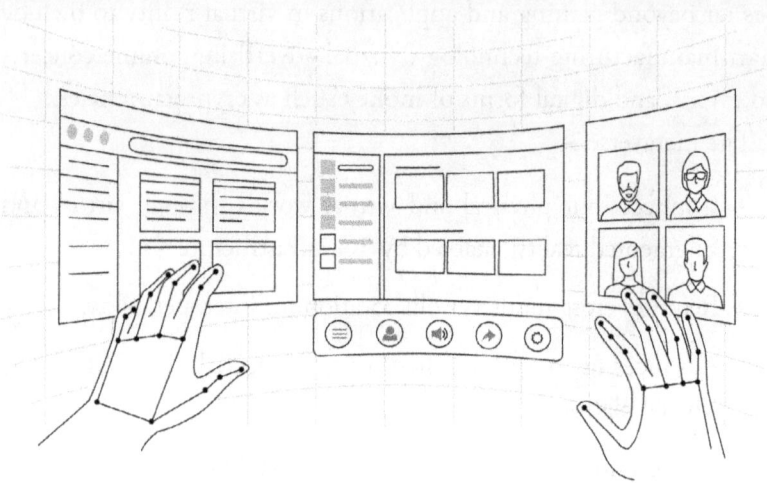

The gaming industry was an early metaverse accelerator.

Gaming company Roblox has dominated the US iPhone gaming industry, with more than $3 million in daily revenue, attracting more than 54.1 million daily active players across various platforms such as smartphones, tablets, desktops, and Xbox.[7] Roblox moved from a gaming-only company to a cocreating company empowering anyone who wants to create metaverse experiences.

Metaverse thought leaders say we're a decade away or less from a full-blown, functional metaverse. There are interoperability bugs to work out. That is, the various worlds still need to sync up, powered by compatible technology that allows a person to travel from universe to universe seamlessly, without technical hiccups.

Interoperability means that we will be able to travel, personified as an avatar, from one world to the next, owning our digital representation, including clothing and belongings. Currently, "metaspaces" operate as separate places owned by organizations, where the avatar assets are confined to the space, such as becoming a player on a gaming site.

While the metaverse is revolutionary, it's also *evolutionary*, and we've been acclimating for three decades.

THE GREAT ACCELERATOR REVVED US UP

The COVID-19 global pandemic that began in 2020 propelled us toward the metaverse, like a foot on the pedal.

We quickly acclimated to a world of remote, distributed work and life. Use of remote conferencing and telepresence tools such as Zoom and Webex soared.

In 2020, approximately 40 percent of US workers worked from home all or most of the time. While the transition was difficult for many, workers enjoyed the flexibility and advantages of working remotely.

Today, perceived work value and productivity is no longer tied to being physically present in the office. Many organizations such as Dropbox, Slack, Zillow, and Twitter permanently closed down most offices, reducing operating costs, only keeping corporate headquarters for in-person meetings and the core executive team.

Whether you work at home or in person, the big, corporate corner office has lost its luster. Power structures have shifted.

Today's symbol of prestige is autonomy—the ability to work whenever, and wherever, in virtual and hybrid settings. The executive suite has been replaced by a new type of individual power, fueled by technology.

"What employees are saying they want in their work environment going forward is a lot more important than a bunch of senior executives at the top of an organization determining what that will be," says Andi Owen, chief executive of MillerKnoll, the maker of the Aeron chair and office furniture.[8]

The Great Resignation was a major wake-up call. According to the US Bureau of Labor Statistics, more than 47 million Americans voluntarily quit their jobs in 2021.

The hybrid workplace model is not going away. More than 90 percent of employers planned to adopt a hybrid model for their knowledge workers in 2022.[9] This is not a temporary working solution—it's the norm. Employees want the option of working remotely and only coming into the office when needed, if at all.

However, 60 percent of US workers have jobs that must be performed in person, interacting face-to-face with others. In-person human contact is essential for teachers, healthcare workers, first responders, bankers, and in hospitality and retail, for example.[10]

The work from home movement doesn't come without drawbacks. Working remotely has taken a toll regarding organizational social capital. Nearly two-thirds of today's remote workers say they feel less connected to their coworkers than when they worked together in person, but they prefer to continue working remotely.

Metaverse goggles, glasses, or sophisticated headsets may become the new corner office.

AND THEN, IT HAPPENED

In 2021, the metaverse became a thing when three notable events occurred.

First, the word "metaverse" exploded when Facebook rebranded to Meta in October of 2021. Meta's founder, chairman and CEO Mark Zuckerberg, released a descriptive video announcing the rebrand from Facebook to Meta, and introducing his vision for the metaverse, complete with 3D holograms and avatars. It is a must-watch for anyone interested in conceptualizing what's to come.[11]

Zuckerberg's prelude of life in the metaverse spanned life from work to personal life at home. This includes socializing with friends at our imaginary digital homes, showing up as avatars or holographic beings.

Second, the massive gaming platform Roblox became a publicly traded company. The price point of $64.50 per share put Roblox's valuation at more than $41 billion, more than double the size of private competitor Epic Games. Roblox's platform is made up of user-generated games, many created by children and teens, some of whom have made millions of dollars for themselves. About 54 percent of Roblox users are under the age of thirteen, according to the company.[12]

In summer 2020 when the first wave of the COVID-19 pandemic was in full swing, *more than three quarters* of American children were reported to be on Roblox, a popular gaming universe. Roblox reported that its 164 million players spent three billion hours on the platform that July.[13]

Third, metaverse exchange-traded funds (ETFs) were launched. Fidelity was the most high-profile fund being offered, bringing credibility to the metaverse as a mainstream investment.

Bloomberg and other analysts estimate a potential metaverse global market size of $800 billion and predict $80 billion invested in ETFs by 2024.[14]

The Fidelity Metaverse ETF portfolio includes the following top ten holdings as of 2022:

1. Meta Platforms Inc. Class A

2. Apple Inc.

3. Tencent Holdings Ltd.

4. Adobe Inc.

5. Alphabet Inc. Class A

6. NVIDIA Corp.

7. Nintendo Co. Ltd.

8. Activision Blizzard Inc.

9. NetEase Inc. ADR

10. Electronic Arts Inc.

The Roundhill Ball Metaverse ETF,[15] which trades on the New York Stock Exchange, cites the top ten holdings in the exchange as of 2022:

1. NVIDIA Corp.

2. Microsoft Corp.

3. Roblox Corp.

4. Facebook Inc.

5. Unity Software Inc.

6. Snap, Inc.

7. Autodesk Inc.

8. Amazon Com Inc.

9. Tencent Holdings Ltd.

10. Sea Ltd.

Trivia question: How long did it take to put novel technology into the hands of fifty million users across the globe?[16]

- Telephone: fifty years

- Electricity: forty-six years

- Radio: thirty-eight years

- Television: twenty-two years

- Mobile phones: twelve years

- Internet: seven years

- Metaverse: zero years

Why zero for the metaverse? Because the internet already exists.

The metaverse is considered to be the third stage of internet development. The history of the internet can be summarized as Web 1, 2, and 3.

The Metaverse and the Evolution of Web 1, 2, 3

- **Web 1.0**   The internet was introduced as a vast, online information resource.

- **Web 2.0**   The internet evolved to become a two-way tool for commerce, communication, and social exchange. Large communication platforms such as Facebook, Instagram, LinkedIn, YouTube, and huge commerce platforms such as Amazon are centralized, with user data they acquire being owned by the companies.

- **Web 3.0**   The internet will become a persistent virtual place featuring many worlds or universes.

  - The internet is operated as many DAOs (decentralized autonomous organizations) where members in DAOs (a global union) decide the future of their organizations.

  - Participants own the digital content they create.

  - Participants live and operate in a virtual world, creating virtual-world identities displayed as avatars, with the ability to own digital possessions or digital assets that may include physical-world benefits connected with the assets.

  - Persistent worlds, similar to websites today, offer nonstop engagement opportunities and resources for visitors at any moment, with no respect to time zones.

  - Metaverse persistency creates an immense global resource, allowing people to jump in and out of virtual worlds round the clock.

THREE BRIGHT, SHINY OBJECTS

There are three bright, shiny objects that make digital and physical convergence possible. They are—

Virtual Reality

Virtual reality (VR) immerses you inside an entirely made-up world designed for VR headsets and goggles, allowing you to explore new worlds and experiences designed exclusively for VR devices. The newest headsets projecting digital imagery are sleek, similar to putting on a pair of glasses.

While VR is used extensively in the gaming world, the technology is helping businesses achieve competitive advantage through new product development. VR is used for immersive training sessions, presentations, and virtual conferences. The technology is used in the real estate industry to showcase properties and to offer potential buyers a more immersive experience.

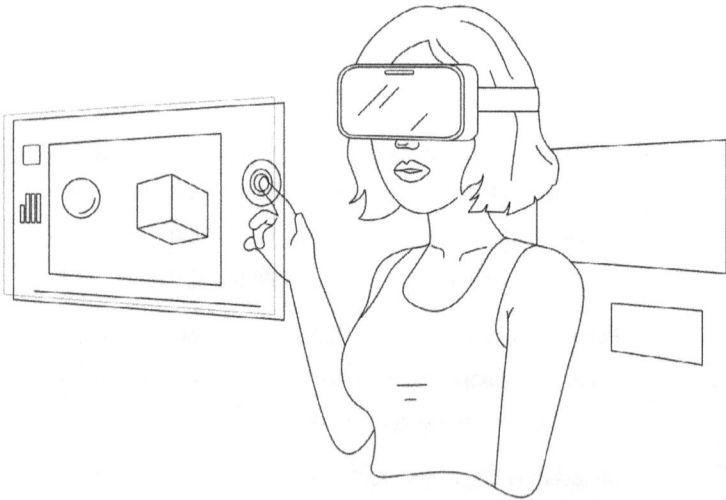

Augmented Reality

Augmented reality (AR) combines virtual images on top of the real world, augmenting your senses to create new experiences. AR is often combined with VR.

For example, with more than 200 million Snapchat users playing with more than six billion augmented reality lenses each day, Snap is using its technology to let users dress up and apply filters that track your facial expressions. In 2021, the company made advancements in body tracking, clothing simulation, and object recognition. The company assessed that users are more than two times more likely to buy products with Snap's AR try-on technology. This allows users to try on clothing and other products.

In 2021, Google announced new AR features for Google Maps accessed through smartphones. The Live View feature overlays digital guides on top of real-world images on a user's phone, to provide directions while indoors at places such as shopping malls and airports. Users search in Google Maps and markers guide with arrows and other digital indicators. This feature could assist travelers in airports, for example, to expedite finding a gate, restaurants, restrooms, and transportation pick-up.

Holograms

Holograms produce 3D physical structures that diffract light into an image perceived as a real object and can create lifelike social interactions online. Examples include the ability to project holograms of colleagues from around the world in one virtual room, or to be able to travel in time to meet a loved one from prior generations via a simulated dialogue.

The term "hologram" can refer to both the encoded material and the resulting image. A viewer's eyes perceive virtual images as if they were real objects: a high-resolution image in full color and three dimensions.

Easy-to-incorporate holograms will be the next big metaverse innovation.

India-based market research firm BIS Research estimates the global holographic imaging market will jump 2.7 times by 2025, growing from $607.6 million to more than $1.8 billion by 2025.

Holographic video techniques are being developed by companies such as DoubleMe, headquartered in Seoul, South Korea, now operating in the United States and England, to transform the future of media and communication.

WHAT ARE METAVERSE PIONEERS SAYING?

After months of research, as I scoured articles, listened carefully to podcasts, and attended online metaverse events, common themes emerged—themes such as ownership of your own digital persona and work, coupled with having your own unified digital identity on blockchain. I became acquainted with the prevailing metaverse thought leaders. I could then begin to think deeply about how Web3 will require new leadership, strategy, and community-building insights and skills.

For example, in their book *Navigating the Metaverse: A Guide to Limitless Possibilities in a Web 3.0 World*, authors Cathy Hackl, Dirk Lueth, and Tommaso Di Bartolo state that the metaverse presents three paradigm shifts:[17]

- **Experience:** People don't just want to consume. It's far more engaging to have gamified, contextual experiences.

- **Identity:** People value their digital persona and want to carry it with them across the metaverse and even into the real world.

- **Ownership:** Wherever people choose to spend their time, they want skin in the game.[18]

My metaverse research will continue on a daily basis for decades to come, providing fresh insights for leadership, strategy, and community building, as well as future editions of this book. Here are striking descriptions to date of what the metaverse is, and its implication on organizations and people.

WIRED writer Eric Ravenscraft says that defining the metaverse is a "bit like having a discussion about what 'the internet' meant in the 1970s."[19]

No one would have dreamed of sitting in front of a computer screen—a small TV screen—that would aggregate and deliver information about any topic within seconds. Prior to the internet, research required visits to libraries in search of physical books and stored resources.

Rev Lebaredian, NVIDIA's vice president of Omniverse & Simulation Technology, says, "The scale and the exact shape and feeling of it we can't predict, but one thing I think we can be sure of is that the metaverse is going to be bigger than anything we've ever known. It's not VR headsets. It's connecting the physical and the digital."[20]

Mark Zuckerberg, founder, chairman, and CEO of Meta, says that "the metaverse is the next big chapter of the technology industry. The metaverse is an embodied internet where you're in the experience, not just looking at it."[21]

Elsewhere, he describes this in more detail:

> I think that this is a persistent, synchronous environment where we can be together, which I think is probably going to resemble some kind of a hybrid between the social platforms that we see today, but an environment where you're embodied in it. So that can be 3D—it doesn't have to be.

You might be able to jump into an experience, like a 3D concert or something, from your phone, so you can get elements that are 2D or elements that are 3D . . . think about things like community and creators as one, or digital commerce as a second, or building out the next set of computing platforms, like virtual and augmented reality, to give people that sense of presence.[22]

Matthew Ball, metaverse thought leader, investor, and author, suggests that most uses of the metaverse will be for productivity at the enterprise level, including government and industry. The metaverse is a series of interconnected virtual worlds that link together content, information, and people. You can explore an infinite number of worlds by going to a web address or by logging into a network. He believes that with companies such as Google and Facebook investing in the space, the popularity of the metaverse will continue to grow.[23]

"Whether you're a metaverse believer, skeptic, or somewhere in between, you should be comfortable with the fact that it is too early to know exactly what a 'day in the life' might look and feel like when the metaverse arrives," Ball says. "But the inability to precisely predict how we'll use it, and how it will change our daily life, is not a flaw. Rather, it's a prerequisite for the metaverse's disruptive force."[24]

The metaverse "is the internet but in 3D," he explains. "Without 3D, we might as well be describing the current internet."[25]

His definition of the metaverse is "a massively scaled and interoperable network of real-time rendered 3D virtual worlds that can be experienced synchronously and persistently by an effectively unlimited number of users with an individual sense of presence, and with continuity of data, such as identity, history, entitlements, objects, communications, and payments."[26]

Ball offers seven defining core attributes for the metaverse:

1. **Persistent**. It never "resets" or "pauses" or "ends," but it just continues indefinitely. The metaverse is a space that connects virtual worlds together so that people can enter and exit those worlds as they please.

2. **Synchronous and live.** The metaverse will be a living experience that exists consistently for everyone and in real time.

3. **Without any cap to concurrent users—no limit to users—while also providing each user with an individual sense of "presence."** Everyone can be a part of the metaverse and participate in a specific event, place, and activity together, at the same time— and yet with individual agency.

4. **A fully functioning economy**. Individuals and businesses will be able to create, own, invest, sell, and be rewarded for an incredibly wide range of "work" that produces "value" that is recognized by others.

5. **An experience that spans both the digital and physical worlds**, private and public networks/experiences, and open and closed platforms.

6. **Unprecedented interoperability**. This includes interoperability of data, digital items/assets, and content across experiences or user platforms.

7. **Populated by content and experiences created and operated by a wide range of contributors**. Creators could include independent individuals, informally organized groups, or commercially focused enterprises.[27]

Author Cathy Hackl, chief metaverse officer and cofounder at Journey, says that "while defining the term is not easy, one thing is probably true. The term will not be defined by one single person or company, it will be defined by many, and it will evolve."[28]

> You cannot enable the open decentralized metaverse that many of us dream of without blockchain . . . Blockchain is the underlying component. NFTs [nonfungible tokens] are a bit of a stepping-stone into the metaverse when it comes to ownership of digital assets and digital identity. How do you actually enable that? NFTs are a big part of that equation.[29]

CNET tech editor at large Scott Stein says that "the metaverse isn't a destination—it's a metaphor. It's a new way of conceptualizing the way that we interconnect. It's philosophical. It's not escaping into another place—it's rethinking what it means to connect and communicate and build the internet. It will keep changing. How do you keep it consistent? It's unclear if there'll be a single metaverse ('the metaverse'), multiple metaverses ('a metaverse') or a combination of both. Maybe it's best thought of as a metaphor for the internet's continual change."[30]

According to David Baszucki, CEO and cofounder of Roblox Corporation—

> We think of the metaverse as a human co-experience category that supports people coming together to socialize, to learn, to play, someday to work to experience entertainment and amazing brands.
>
> We're actually in the middle of it right now. There are over 200 million roughly monthly people on the Roblox platform every month. They do a lot of things. They have an identity; they have an avatar. They do stuff together. Sometimes when they can't be together in person, they'll

go to a birthday party together or graduate from high school together.

You can either overlay onto the physical-world digital attributes, like when you look at a building, like a restaurant it shows you on your AR glasses what time does it open what time does it close or you can go completely into the digital world and actually have a virtual reality experience.

We're really early in this. This amazing opportunity. I think it's going to change the way people both communicate the way we share stories. I think ultimately it's going to allow people to learn together in interesting new ways. As more people are working remotely, it's going to power that as well.[31]

Tech writers Liz Harkavy, Eddy Lazzarin, and Arianna Simpson have said that "the metaverse is just another name for evolving the internet: to be more social, immersive, and far more economically sophisticated than what exists today."[32]

They go on to cite two competing visions for the metaverse. The first is a decentralized model based on generous property rights, interoperability, and an open system owned by those who build and maintain it. The second is a centralized vision and closed system subject to the "whims of corporations; and often extracts painful economic rents from its creators, contributors, and inhabitants."

They discussed seven defining metaverse characteristics:[33]

- **Decentralization**. The metaverse is not owned or operated by one single entity or "at the mercy of a few powerbrokers."

- **Property rights**. People can buy and own their own digital assets, especially in gaming environments.

- **Self-sovereign identity** focuses on people owning their own identity in the metaverse. This focuses on authentication of a person's identity: proving who a person is, what they have access to, and what information they share. The cryptography at the core of Web3 enables people to authenticate without relying on intermediaries. People can control their identity directly or with the help of services they choose.

- **Composability.** This is the ability to mix and match software components similar to building blocks, where every software component only needs to be written once and can thereafter simply be reused.

- **Openness and open source.** This is the practice of making code freely available and able to be redistributed and modified at will. This promotes universal standards and interoperability.

- **Community ownership** emphasizes the coordination and alignment of builders, creators, investors, and users to strive for the common good.

- **Social immersion** allows people to remotely hang out, work together, mingle with friends, and have fun.[34]

Tim Sweeney, Epic Games Inc. CEO, says that "over the coming decades, the metaverse has the potential to become a multitrillion-dollar part of the world economy. The metaverse is a term like the internet. No company can own it."[35]

He goes on to explain:

> The metaverse is going to have purely digital manifestations, places that don't exist in the real world. If you want to go up to a space station or another planet, that's going to be purely digital. And there will be real-world

manifestations, too, which integrate virtual overlays on top of it, like Pokémon Go does.

Imagine the entire world being a beehive of different activity. In some places, there are Pokemons running around. In some places, there are other game assets . . . I think there's a lot of magic to be had by converging both parts of this, so sometimes you're in the physical world with virtual enhancements and sometimes you're in the purely virtual world.[36]

Sweeney believes the next three years are going to be critical for all of the metaverse-aspiring companies such as Epic, Roblox, Microsoft, and Meta. "It's a race to get to a billion users, whoever brings on a billion users first, would be the presumed leader in setting the standards."[37]

According to CoreAxis, a learning and development company—

The metaverse is a shared online space where virtual reality, augmented reality, and physical presence can exist together. Users can interact as avatars with benefits of digital tools such as digital whiteboards and 3D drawing capacity.

Avatars and information can coexist across multiple metaverses, meaning everything can be shared and is interoperable. Therefore, many metaverses can be created by users themselves and everything they generate can be shared while maintaining the fidelity of the items and information created.[38]

Yat Siu, cofounder and executive chairman of the gaming and blockchain company Animoca Brands, has this to say:

Reality will exist on a spectrum ranging from physical to virtual, but a significant chunk of our time will be spent somewhere between those extremes, in some form of augmented reality.

Augmented reality will be a normal part of daily life. Virtual companions will provide information, commentary, updates and advice on matters relevant to you at that point in time, including your assets and activities, in both virtual and real spaces. These facets of reality will not compete, but instead will enhance each other.

For example, VR will involve you in physical-world activities, while products and events in the real world will direct you to virtual environments. These new technologies will require fundamental shifts in thinking.

For example, today we see AR as a link to a virtual world, perhaps as a way to escape or enhance the physical world. But in the future, AR will serve as a pathway back to the real world, allowing users to take breaks from full virtual immersion—maybe to eat or exercise—without completely disconnecting.[39]

According to Terry Winters, author of *Metaverse: Prepare Now for the Next Big Thing!*—

These parallel virtual environments and the convergence of the online and offline worlds will allow us to experience and communicate in the digital world through avatars— the user's chosen persona—and feature many elements from physical reality including buildings, work and leisure locations, and other different landscapes.

Many of these metaverse worlds will consist of limited land that you can build on, lease, and socialize with other avatars. The ultimate goal of the metaverse is to look and feel like physical reality, allowing your avatar to move around freely, interact with others, and access information within a 3D environment, just like in the real world. Interactions will affect both your own state of being and that of others in the metaverse.[40]

David Chalmers, author of *Reality+* and philosopher at New York University, argues that virtual worlds can be as real as our everyday reality. In an interview with Scott Stein, Chalmers says, "Community is really important for building meaningful social worlds, actually building communities where people feel invested, like we're building something here."[41]

Sam Hamilton, creative director for The Decentraland Foundation, a decentralized virtual reality platform powered by the Ethereum blockchain, tells us this:

> We can expect self-contained virtual social worlds but also service layers and tools that unlock opportunities for creatives and entrepreneurs that the physical world can't or won't provide. It will be immersive and all-encompassing, but at the same time impact the physical world across finance, goods, and services, play, education, governance, and more.
>
> What it won't be is a centralized experience. A centralized metaverse is not a metaverse, it's a video game. A curated entertainment. You can't empower creators and residents of the metaverse to shape its future without giving them ownership and the right to govern. So, the authentic metaverse will be a shared, collaborative space, backed by a decentralized structure. We are witnessing world-building as it happens. The old rules don't apply.[42]

Finally, Nicolas Pouard, vice president of Ubisoft's Innovation Lab and the head of the company's blockchain initiatives, states that "without global infrastructure, and without global currency, you don't have a metaverse. There is no global currency except crypto. There is no global infrastructure except blockchain infrastructure."[43]

BASIC METAVERSE TAKEAWAYS

To make sense of the metaverse as envisioned, here are five common themes.

The metaverse is going to bring **prolific changes to societal culture and daily life** on planet Earth—perhaps one of the biggest cultural shifts humankind has experienced.

The metaverse offers a **persistent virtual environment** much different from the static websites of the past—places that will be available for consistent, continual engagement or activity.

Interoperability is a key necessity to ensure developers and users can travel or operate seamlessly throughout the metaverse. For example, an avatar should be interoperable—that is, it should have the ability to cross through all metaverse platforms. You are able to be identified by your avatar or multiple avatars.

Human beings will be personified in the digital world as avatars. People will create one or more personas in the form of avatars to display personality and uniqueness as a person in the metaverse. Assuming one or more avatars seems to be a given. Experts agree that participants can choose to create multiple metaverse identities as one or more avatars. Relevant to leadership, community building, and strategy includes the challenge of interacting not only with people in the physical world, but to sustain the intellect and emotional poise while interacting with numerous versions (or avatars) of people in the metaverse world, as well.

Blockchain, cryptocurrency technologies, and NFTs create the financial foundation for metaverse transactions.

There are many other themes and issues, but this gets us started. The glossary of innovations at the end of this book includes some of the most important innovations leading up to life in the metaverse.

REFLECTION QUESTIONS

1. What facet of the metaverse do you find most intriguing, and why?

2. How do you envision your life changing as the metaverse evolves? Do you predict that you'll spend more time online, less time, or about the same?

3. How might your organization benefit from the metaverse?

CHAPTER 2

MEET ME IN THE METAVERSE

HOW DOES A PERSON GET TO the metaverse? In this chapter we'll discuss a few things you'll need to get started. You do not need to be an experienced gamer to enjoy 3D websites and companies that are experimenting with early metaverse events, shopping, and other experiences. Read on to discover how to meet me in the metaverse.

YOU NEED EQUIPMENT

The metaverse works by connecting multiple virtual environments. Each environment is accessed through apps that you download for your VR or AR device. So you'll need either a VR or AR headset—or gear that features both—to see the virtual content.[1]

Today, you can access early versions of the metaverse through your smartphone or computer. For example, you can go to Nike's metaverse, NIKELAND, hosted on Roblox, to jump into a free metaverse experience. Also, *Fortnite*, a free-to-play metaverse game available on the EpicGames.com website, can be accessed through PCs, game consoles, and phones.[2]

To enter augmented and virtual reality 3D worlds today, you need special headgear for vision.

Vision tools—headgear—will evolve over time, in ways we cannot yet imagine. Today, the typical vision tools include a headset, as well as hand and feet gear called "trackers."

Headsets used by gamers today are equipped with self-aware sensory systems influenced by robotics and AR/VR—similar to the technology being tested for self-driving cars. The headsets are bulky, strapped on, and secured in order to produce the ability to see 3D objects and become fully immersed in new worlds. In the future, you may be able to wear stylish glasses, a metaverse contact lens, or other technology not yet developed.

For example, Mojo Vision announced a smart contact lens prototype called Mojo Lens that creates a digital display within a user's own field of vision. Built into the lenses are motion sensors, battery power, and wireless radio to stream content to your eyes. People would wear one in each eye, and the lens would communicate with an accessory on their body that can talk with a smartphone to get content.

"We're inventing the next generation of computing," says Steve Sinclair, the senior vice president of product and marketing at Mojo Vision. "We're trying to take us out of our smartphones and looking down at screens and bringing that information up into the big world."[3]

Tiffany Rolfe, chief creative officer at the global branding and marketing firm R/GA, foresees different layers of reality we can simultaneously experience while being in the same physical space environment.

"We're already doing that with our phones to a certain extent— passively in a physical environment while mentally in a digital one. But we'll see more experiences beyond your phone, where our whole bodies are fully engaged, and that's where the metaverse starts to get interesting—we genuinely begin to explore and live in these alternate realities simultaneously," she notes.

"Once we are comfortable wearing our powerful phones over our faces, it's game over. Or rather, game on."[4]

YOU NEED AN AVATAR

Think of your avatar as a highly personalized, digital representation of you. Your avatar, whether static or animated, will be your digital persona.

An avatar in the metaverse will be a user's identity in that digital space or universe. We likely will adopt multiple avatars to represent different moods and purposes, such as for shopping, socializing, learning, and working in metaverse environments.

"If you're going to be in these virtual worlds, you have to find a way to show up with a visual representation of who you are," says head of Instagram Adam Mosseri.[5]

At this very early stage of the metaverse, you can choose to design your own avatar, or you can hire creative expertise. Or, you may prefer to select a ready-made avatar from a creator website.

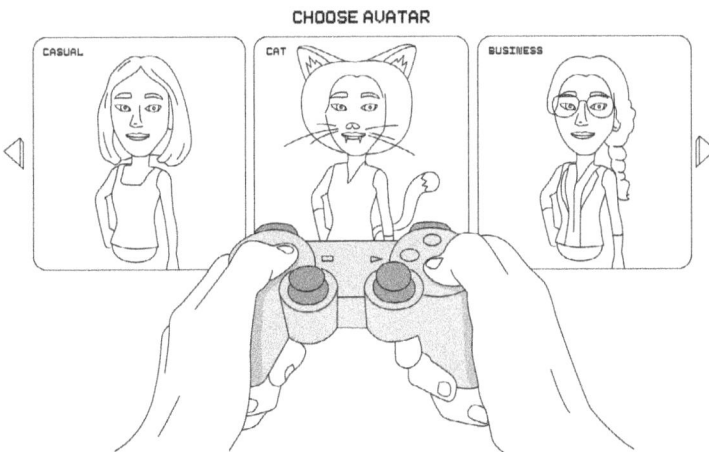

Owning your own avatar's identity is closely related to property rights. Metaverse thought leaders assert that you can't own anything if you don't own yourself. As in the real world, people's identities must be able to persist throughout the metaverse without complete reliance on a small set of centralized identity providers.[6]

According to Mark Zuckerberg, "Avatars are going to be as common as profile pictures today, but instead of a static image, they're going to be living, 3D representations of you—your expressions, your gestures—that are going to make interactions much richer than anything that's possible online today. You'll probably have a photo-realistic avatar for work, a stylized one for hanging out, and maybe even a fantasy one for gaming."[7]

But there's more. Not only will you buy clothing and belongings for your physical life as a human being—you will also determine whether to invest in digital wardrobe and belongings in your virtual world. Brands such as Gucci and Nike already are selling digital apparel.

In mid-2022, more than $14 million has been spent on Nike shoes purchased as NFTs, with crypto holders spending between $10,500 and $12,500 for a pair.[8]

"You're going to have a wardrobe of virtual clothes for different occasions, designed by different creators, and from different apps and experiences. Importantly, you should be able to bring your avatar and digital items across different apps," Zuckerberg adds.[9]

People will be continually asking themselves questions, such as, "How do I want to show up?" and "Can I afford to buy expensive digital clothing to maintain an image in the metaverse?" This could lead to a digital world of "haves" and "have-nots," no different than the physical world.

Supersocial founder and CEO Yonatan Raz-Fridman speculated that he might have "five to ten different Avatars that live and exist and interact in the metaverse." The result? "The metaverse could have potentially 100 billion personalities that live, interact, engage and conceal in the metaverse. The metaverse could have a size of economy in the trillions, not as real people but with multiple identities that are manifested as avatars."[10]

An avatar in the metaverse is more than just a user's created face. It will likely become that user's entire manifestation in the metaverse. Therefore, whatever actions the avatar undertakes are directly driven by the user. Apart from just playing a few games, all types of other activities, including important business and financial ones, will also be reflected onto the avatar and therefore the user. The metaverse relies on this specific principle of "user equals avatar," and therefore cannot exist without it.[11]

"In the near future, I believe our online identities *will* be our identities. Our avatars are already our way of expressing ourselves to an ever-growing segment of our global-local society," notes Kwasi Amaning Asare, cofounder, chief marketing officer, and board member at ESAIYO, a company aimed at creating social identity and virtual-world connections around the concept of objects.[12]

More About Avatars

There are currently two types of avatars: VR avatars, and full-body avatars.

VR avatars see the world from the avatar's point of view. Other participants of the world can see the upper torso part of the avatar, along with arms, but without the lower limbs.

Full-body avatars require sensors to replicate and recreate the full body's movements through a kinematics system. This requires hardware that is capable of full-body tracking. The user has greater freedom of mobility inside the virtual world and can use all limbs to interact with digital assets.

Avatars can be changed to fit your aesthetic, such as skin tone, height, hair, and apparel. Many of the most famous brands from the real world offer clothing and accessories in the metaverse in the form of NFTs.[13]

There will be multiple dimensions and purposes for avatars. People's identity in the metaverse may be congruent or incongruent with their physical identity. Each identity could have multiple, separate connections based on the world or universe a person is entering. This may include a new pathway to creating human empathy, providing the ability to step into another person's shoes to experience their life.[14]

How will people with numerous avatars be verified, for example, for financial transactions? No doubt blockchain will play a role in verifying identities and preventing fraud. We live in a world where fictitious characters are becoming celebrities and brand icons on social media channels, such as Lil Miquela.

Trivia

Lil Miquela was the first nonhuman, computer-generated digital avatar operating as social influencer. Today, this cartoon avatar has more than three million Instagram followers. The avatar generated an estimated $10 million to $12 million for its creators through paid promotions with brands in 2020.

Source: Yvonne Lau, "You'll Soon Be Able to Put Your Metaverse Avatar to Work—and Make Actual Money from It," *Fortune*, February 7, 2022, https://fortune.com/2022/02/07/metaverse-avatar-work-make-money-nft/.

Blogger Tony Jones has said, "If the metaverse is an extension of reality, the users should own their avatars . . . just having the avatars be open source and on multiple platforms could create a sense of ownership. Having an avatar that feels like it belongs to you will create a new dynamic with users of the metaverse."[15]

Chief artificial intelligence officer of eBay Nitzan Mekel-Bobrov, in an interview with *Fast Company*, explains the importance of AI to avatar efficacy by saying that "it wouldn't be an exaggeration to say that without AI, the metaverse won't exist; as carbon is to the organic world, AI will be both the matrix that provides the necessary structural support and the material from which digital representation will be made."[16]

He believes that of the many ways AI will play a role in shaping the form of the metaverse, perhaps most essential is how it will affect the physical–digital interface. He says, "Translating human actions into digital input—language, eye movement, hand gestures, locomotion—these are all actions which AI companies and researchers have already made tremendous progress on. Understanding what a physical object is in order to represent it digitally starts with its correct identification, the beginning of which we already see in current computer vision applications."

Avatars, Egos, and Personal Reflection

All participants in the metaverse, including leaders, will show up as avatars, metaverse thought leaders say. At a company, for example, there may be the large company universe and smaller departments or smaller worlds within the corporate universe.

For example, employees could show up to department meetings as their "department avatar," in casual attire. When they attend larger company events, perhaps some employees will show up as a completely different avatar character. People will be able to select how they show up based on personal factors such as their mood and the purpose of the metaverse context, such as a special event or work meeting.

As mentioned earlier, avatar status symbols in the metaverse may lead to the haves and have-nots syndrome with which we're familiar on physical planet Earth. Avatars will show up in clothing purchased as NFTs—clothes owned by the avatar. Here are some questions to ponder:

- Will the metaverse create virtual snobbery and metaverse exclusion rather than inclusion? For example, will avatars in designer clothing shun or intimidate those who cannot afford to purchase the latest digital shoes, purse, or clothing?

- To conform to peer pressure, will people buy digital possessions at the expense of their physical, human lives?

- Will the use of avatars help or hurt a person's sense of authenticity and identity? How will avatars impact a person's sense of self-esteem and ego? What role will fake or fictional identities play when people show up in avatar skins?

- Will leaders—such as the boss—hide behind their avatar masks?

- In the metaverse, will avatars create a loss of personal identity? Or will personal identity be enhanced? Will avatars reduce bias and create more openness to others with different points of view and different backgrounds, including age, race, and ethnicity?

- How will leaders be perceived in a world of avatars? Might they appear intimidating, egotistical, power-hungry, or comical versus authentic and credible?

- We live in a digital society where online gaming has attracted millions of participants across the globe and is a multibillion-dollar industry. People want to be entertained. What does this mean for leaders who want to lead with charisma, but also be taken seriously?

- Will avatars have rules to abide by to govern conduct, promote ethical behavior, and prevent abuse and intimidation? In an avatar's body, will this game-world way of showing up in the metaverse be simply a complicated add-on to reality versus reality itself, causing chaos and dystopia?

YOU NEED METAVERSE DESTINATIONS OR WORLDS

Billions of dollars are being invested to create virtual worlds for gamers, consumers, education providers, government, businesses, entertainment, sports, and even nonprofit organizations.

For example, the nonprofit Habitat for Humanity of Central Arizona says it became the first charitable organization in the world to create a metaverse for conducting an online gala in 2022, raising funds through cryptocurrency using the Decentraland platform.[17]

Brands such as Nike, Ralph Lauren, Louis Vuitton, Tommy Hilfiger, Balenciaga, Burberry, Gucci, Vans, Zara, and Forever 21 are taking experimental approaches with metaverse marketing, exploring the impact of VR and AR both online and in person.

Prominent gaming virtual worlds are attracting millions of participants, where you can create an avatar and socialize with other players. (We'll talk about some of those popular gaming worlds at the end of this chapter.)

Embodied in your personal avatar, you could travel to a virtual pub, and then head to a concert venue to see a virtual live performance. Or you could join a meeting with remote employees. You wouldn't be going anywhere in the physical world—instead, you would move across virtual worlds.

A number of worlds, also referred to as universes and cyberspaces, exist today where you can interact with others, transact business, and be immersed in topics of interest. A few consulting firms have been swift to create a client focus aimed at helping businesses define their business strategy in the metaverse.

For example, information technology consulting firm Accenture says, "We design, build and operate metaverse capabilities for our clients, including world-building and engagement, content management, marketplace development, blockchain, 3D commerce, extended reality, digital twins, trust and safety and ecosystem and community development."[18]

YOU OWN VIRTUAL PROPERTY THROUGH NFTS

NFTs or nonfungible tokens are digital assets owned by the owner. NFTs can be bought, sold, and traded as if the NFT is real property. NFT sales grew to more than $17 billion in 2021—a 21,000 percent increase from 2020's total of $82 million.[19] (See the glossary in appendix 1 for more information.)

In the metaverse, NFTs are designed to be unique and have a variety of different characteristics, such as rarity and brand quality. Digital assets could include digital homes, digital land, or digital art. They can be bought, sold, and traded using a decentralized digital market, called the Metaverse Digital Asset Exchange.[20]

You can then sell your NFTs (assets, or content) or exchange NFTs with other users to acquire other digital assets. NFTs can be created in a limited edition of a physical product with a certain number of units attached to it. With NFTs, each unit is completely unique, and has a different level of rarity.

"We should absolutely consider crypto and the metaverse as one and the same thing," says Jamie Burke, Sys Outlier Ventures founder and CEO. "The metaverse makes our physical and digital spaces indistinguishable. The metaverse will eventually connect every platform, virtual world and game into a single permissionless peer-to-peer economy native to the internet, most importantly underpinned by crypto and Web3 technology."[21]

The blockchain-based economy is the key attribute needed to decentralize ownership. Blockchain secures and verifies the transactions. This means users can create their own digital assets, own them, and trade them with other users.[22]

Epic Games CEO Tim Sweeney was candid in his opinion of NFTs in this early stage of the metaverse. He said, "I firmly believe there's going to be a multi-trillion-dollar economy around digital goods in the future. But I think so much of the crypto currency effort, especially touching the gaming space, doesn't address that problem of utility. They're showing you digital goods you can't do anything with except to say that you own it. You can cryptographically prove that you own it, but who cares?"[23]

By 2022, the most expensive collage of NFT art pieces ever sold was called *The Merge*—for $91.8 million. Created by Pak, a prominent, anonymous artist or collective, *The Merge* is the most expensive NFT ever sold as of this writing.[24]

Within a three-day window, purchases were made by 28,983 collectors snapping up 312,686 total NFTs, known as "units of mass." Previously, the highest price achieved by a digital artwork was *Everydays: The First 5000 Days* by Mike Winkelmann, professionally known as Beeple. It fetched $69.3 million at a Christie's online auction in March.[25]

NFTs are big in the entertainment and sports sectors, featuring connection to physical-world experiences.

Digital sports cards in the form of NFTs are being sold by the National Basketball Association (NBA). The NFTs feature clips of memorable game plays. NFT owners receive special perks such as premium seating, NBA T-shirts, and backstage tours at in-person games.

Famous NFTs existing on OpenSea, the world's first and largest Web3 marketplace for NFTs and crypto collectibles, are CryptoPunks, Bored Ape Yacht Club, and The Sandbox, where you can buy digital real estate. Rapper-songwriter Snoop Dogg owns real estate in The Sandbox. He's also made investments in CryptoPunks NFTs, featured prominently on his Twitter profile.

Briefly, here's how it works. If you wanted to sell a limited edition of a physical product with a certain number of units attached to it, you would create a new NFT with your product's details on it. This would include the number of units available for sale and the price per unit. In addition to this information, you would also add the date the NFT will be available for purchase and the date it will expire.

You can create an NFT from digital art without coding. The process of creating them is called minting—the act of publishing a unique instance of the token on the blockchain.

NFTs are minted once they are created, similar to how metal coins are created and added into circulation. After this procedure the particular piece of digital art becomes secure and tamper-proof, as well as hard to manipulate. Once your digital item becomes an NFT, it can be bought, sold, and digitally tracked when it is resold or recollected.[26]

This is where you would set your token's metadata. You would set its name, description, and image to help prospective customers learn more about your NFT.

Those well versed in crypto admit that it's not easy for those even in the gaming world to understand how to jump into the metaverse. How does one purchase an NFT—and what is a wallet? What is cryptocurrency? Where and how does one buy crypto? How does one evaluate an NFT project, and what is a good project versus a bad one? These are just some of the questions to consider. I recommend that you research these topics. Many articles are available online from reputable sources such as *U.S. World and News Report*.[27]

THE METAVERSE WILL BE CREATED BY MANY

Who are the future metaverse creators? Gamers. Teachers. Anyone interested in storytelling—which means potentially everyone.

Rory Abovitz, founder of Magic Leap AR wearable headsets, believes the metaverse will be a "wild, organic, and amazing outgrowth of what we think of today as the internet and web." He predicts, "No one entity will, or should control the metaverse, although many will try."[28]

Abovitz's hopes for the metaverse include creator participation—something that everyone can do such as building a webpage or blog—to be able to "share richer parts of their external and inner lives at incredibly high-speed across the planet."

Creator sites have geared up for mass creator use, including Fortnite, Snap AR, NVIDIA, Roblox, and Unity AR. In Roblox, for example, creators can monetize their games. Some game developers have earned up to $1 million annually. The system also has an entire digital economy and currency called Robux. This currency is often used in-game for an avatar's clothing.

For example, in 2010 Alex Hicks released his first video game on Roblox. By 2020, he made more than $1 million a year as the owner of his game development studio RedManta, creating games for Roblox that have generated nearly one billion plays.[29]

The Metaverse Strategy of Epic Games

There are two prongs to the metaverse strategy of Epic Games.

First, Epic Games aims to expand *Fortnite* from a game with sixty

continued

million monthly active users to an experience that in the future could reach a billion. *Fortnite* has rapidly evolved from a popular multiplayer game into an online space where people socialize and big-name musicians host virtual concerts.

Second, the company wants to capitalize on its content-creation tools like the Unreal Engine for 3D graphics, "enabling all of the companies throughout the industry to have a real-time 3D presence."*

*Source: Sohee Kim, "Metaverse Is a Multitrillion-Dollar Opportunity, Epic CEO Says," Bloomberg, November 17, 2021, https://www.bloomberg.com/news/articles/2021-11-17/metaverse-is-a-multitrillion-dollar-opportunity-epic-ceo-says.

POPULAR VIRTUAL WORLDS

To get a sense of some of the noteworthy metaverse virtual worlds available for creators and gamers on the internet today, have a look at the following examples.[30] I encourage you to visit these to see how virtual worlds are being developed.

Decentraland

Decentraland (https://www.decentraland.org) is one of the metaverse virtual worlds that emphasizes ownership. Decentraland's website says that it is the first fully decentralized virtual world, or DAO.

The Decentraland DAO owns the most important smart contracts and assets that make up Decentraland—the LAND Contract, the Estates Contract, Wearables, Content Servers, and the Marketplace. MANA is Decentraland's fungible, ERC-20 cryptocurrency token limited to a total original supply of 2,805,886,393, according to the Decentraland website, which allows it to be truly autonomous, as well as subsidize various operations and initiatives throughout Decentraland.

The website notes that the original vision is "to hand over control to the people who create and play in this virtual space. In short—you, the users. Through the DAO, you are in control of the policies created to determine how the world behaves: for example, what kinds of wearable items are allowed (or disallowed) after the launch of the DAO, moderation of content, LAND policy and auctions, among others."

Some believe that advances in technology will deliver virtual worlds that rival and surpass the physical realm. Decentraland is filled with lush forests, beautiful skies, thriving cities, and vast oceans.

Decentraland also consists of individual virtual land plots and has 90,601 plots of land in the form of the LAND NFT. Each plot is its own metaverse world. Because Decentraland is tied to the blockchain, every new plot of land also becomes a crypto world.

When you own LAND, you can develop it as desired. With the LAND Estate feature, users can merge multiple plots into a single whole. Groups with similar themes can be linked together as districts to form shared communities around a single shared theme.

Meta's Horizon Worlds and Arena Clash

Horizon Worlds (https://www.oculus.com/horizon-worlds/) is the virtual reality experience provided by Meta. It's one of the metaverse virtual worlds that heavily emphasizes gaming. Users can choose to play, attend events, or hang out and socialize. Users create their own environments, such as the popular Wand & Broom, Mark's Riverboat, and Pixel Plummet worlds. Meta created a similar environment with a laser game called *Arena Clash*, a world featuring a heavy emphasis on socialization.

Roblox

Roblox (https://www.roblox.com/) is a metaverse world focused on game creation. All Roblox games are made by users, rather than by the Roblox company.

Roblox reports that an estimated twenty million games have been made within its metaverse. Many of the games are free to visitors. Roblox makes creating games easy, fun, and potentially profitable for its creator community, as noted earlier.

Fortnite

Created by Epic Games, *Fortnite* (https://www.epicgames.com/fortnite/en-US/home) features three modes: Save the World, Battle Royale, and Creative. Save the World was the original version of the game, in which you play as a survivor in a zombie-like apocalypse.

Players gather resources and focus on surviving missions filled with challenging elements and enemies. Battle Royale is the most popular game mode, where groups of up to a hundred players compete against each other to be the last one standing.

To win, you must defeat the other ninety-nine online players in the game. This competitive element adds urgency to the game. Gamers also need to avoid being caught in the eye of the storm to remain in the game, and there are countdowns when the storm is approaching.[31] The Creative mode is a game in The Sandbox, where players are allowed to design and create their own *Fortnite* games and experiences.[32]

Somnium Space

Somnium Space (https://somniumspace.com/) is a VR-based, blockchain-connected metaverse world and open-source platform. Users can purchase digital land, build homes and buildings, play hyperrealistic video games, start businesses, and offer concerts and live events.

Somnium Space consists of five thousand land parcels that support full ownership. As with most metaverse virtual worlds, space for land isn't limited. New land can be added as needed.

It is a full-crypto world with easily defined asset ownership. Its economy is based on a native ERC-20 token called Somnium Space CUBEs.

CUBE tokens also make it easy to publish or buy avatars. Avatars are usable in a wide variety of other metaverses. Somnium Space also makes it easy to buy land parcels (PARCELs). Land parcels can additionally be purchased and sold as standard NFTs on other systems. PARCELs also support new NFT placement within the land, for building additional assets.[33]

The Sandbox

The Sandbox (https://www.sandbox.game/en/) is a game and virtual world where you can buy, sell, and trade virtual plots of land. The Sandbox's world consists of a large number of land plots on a grid. Users can combine properties to create a singular whole. Land is limited. Land plots are typically sold on Binance, a cryptocurrency exchange, using its Ethereum-based cryptocurrency, SAND.[34]

The Sandbox is notable because rapper Snoop Dogg bought land and a metaverse mansion within the system. He released his first metaverse video in 2022 and plans to offer metaverse concerts. Virtual land near his estate sold for US $450,000.

Voxels

Voxels, formerly Cryptovoxels (https://www.voxels.com/), is a virtual world and metaverse powered by the Ethereum blockchain. Players can buy land and build stores and art galleries. Editing tools, avatars, and text chat are built in.

Ethereum is used to buy land and assets. Voxels users can embed audio, video, standard images, or any number of other media within their landscapes. Collectibles representing real-world objects are also available.

Spatial

Spatial (https://spatial.io/) was one of the earliest metaverse world projects to focus on the workplace. It was released in 2018 as an "infinite desktop" and collaboration tool for augmented reality. The system makes it easy to wander through virtual landscapes with full 3D avatars and provides gallery and hosting space for NFTs.

Gather

Gather (https://www.gather.town/) was created as a way to emphasize humanity in virtual interaction. The creators designed this virtual world to create positive social connections.

Second Life

Second Life (https://secondlife.com/) is a platform released in 2003 that first popularized the concept of metaverse virtual worlds. It was created by Linden Lab, and users can create custom avatars, pets, and other items, and can purchase land in Second Life for their activities. The website notes, "With thousands of virtual experiences and communities, you'll never run out of places to explore and people to meet—music clubs, roleplaying communities, virtual cinemas and more." This includes sharing stories or connecting with others who are going through similar experiences.

HyperVerse

HyperVerse (https://thehyperverse.net/) is a virtual metaverse featuring millions of planets or universes. In the HyperVerse, players (voyagers) connect with friends, experience cultures and lifestyles, create tokenized items, start businesses, and explore the universe.[35]

Planets are not owned by any single entity. Voyagers generate tokens, engage with one another, and explore planets as a group.

Star Atlas

Star Atlas (https://staratlas.com/) is a VR game set in the year 2620. Conquest, political dominance, and resource gathering are all aspects of *Star Atlas*. Humans, aliens, and androids are in an ongoing struggle for resources, territorial conquest, and political domination. Players have the ability to influence the outcome of this intergalactic conflict while creating the opportunity to earn rewards for contributions. Tokens can be earned throughout the game.

Matrix World

Matrix World (https://matrixworld.org/home) is a decentralized, open virtual world that lets users interact with immersive, 3D applications simultaneously running on different blockchains. The world consists of Lands, issued as NFTs, which permanently persist on blockchain networks such as Ethereum and Flow. Matrix Lands are tradable and transferable via blockchain networks. Owners retain control over the creations on their Lands.[36]

NFT Worlds

Operating from its Minecraft decentralized metaverse platform, NFT Worlds (https://www.nftworlds.com/) allows users to create games, experiences, venues, concerts, community hangouts, and more. Each world is its own fully flexible metaverse interconnected with other worlds in the NFT Worlds ecosystem.[37]

NFT Worlds is a collection of 10,000 virtual worlds that exist as NFTs on the Ethereum blockchain. Each world is a limitless universe that can be built into anything a user can imagine. Each land plot is unique as its own metaverse, and visitors are free to explore. NFT owners design their environments as desired, and can create new game modes, such as role-playing games.

Substrata

Substrata (https://substrata.info/) is a multiuser metaverse where each user also hosts their own personal world where metaverses, graphics, avatars, and NFTs can be created. Players can chat with other users or explore objects and places that other users have created. Players can create a free user account and add objects to their worlds. Land parcels in Substrata are for sale and can be minted as Ethereum NFTs.

Worldwide Webb

Worldwide Webb (https://webb.game/) is a massively multiplayer online role-playing game (MMORPG) in the metaverse using NFTs for in-game avatars, pets, lands, items, and quests. It was created to support crypto-native game developers, artists, coders, and marketers who are rapidly pushing out new technologies and apps.

Worldwide Webb aims to "create a template for metaverses with the core values to keep the space open to all, and to incorporate other NFT projects into the world, giving tools to build and create their own communities inside our world. While there are many 3D projects, we feel that there needs to be a 2D verse too! We aim to push the limits and innovate on this frontier. The end game . . . is a fully interoperable metaverse game with a flourishing play-to-earn and create-to-earn economy for players, creators, and collectors alike."[38]

REFLECTION QUESTIONS

1. Do you think humans in the metaverse, embodied by avatars, will create a physical world environment, such as in work groups, with more empathy and inclusion, or less empathy and inclusion? If so, how? If not, why not?

2. How will multiple avatars impact a leader's sense of self-identity and style of leadership brand? How will you choose to show up? What style of avatar will you create? Do you prefer a realistic avatar in your photo likeness, or an animated avatar? Will you create multiple avatars, or do you prefer a single avatar?

3. How will the rise of gaming popularity impact life on planet Earth?

CHAPTER 3

THE GOOD: INNOVATION

DRIVEN BY THE GAMING AND ENTERTAINMENT industries, the metaverse will bring transformation, creativity, and innovation to planet Earth. This chapter features examples of innovation currently at work in the metaverse.

The metaverse will change our lives forever, starting with three fascinating words: *immersive, persistent,* and *interoperable*.

Immersive describes the experience itself—being completely immersed into a scenario, a situation, or a world.

Imagine buying a car. You're in the metaverse, test-driving the vehicle on a racetrack of your choice, accelerating the car as if it were a racecar—much more exciting than observing cars in a stationary showroom.

Picture yourself consulting with a metaverse beauty expert in the comfort of your metaverse living room at a time that works for *you*, such as midnight on Thursday. These examples illustrate why retailers are rethinking the meaning of what a "store" is, as well as the customer experience, during this premetaverse time period.

Persistent means that the world stays put after you leave, identical to life in our physical world.

Interoperable means you, the avatar, will be able to jump in and out of worlds as the same, recognizable person, unlike today's environment where websites operate as separate systems.

MY FIRST CONFERENCE AS AN AVATAR

I recently attended a mesmerizing global "Meta Festival."[1] The event featured a metaverse conference welcome area, speakers, a conference arena, and a beautiful metaverse world of natural wonders such as mountains, an ocean, and a jungle where you could wander around as an avatar.

Upon arrival to the Meta Festival, I was invited to select an avatar from several options. I selected a space suit and entered the conference welcome area. I decided to explore the wilderness, pushing various buttons on my computer to walk, run, or fly.

I flew over the jungle, veering upward, sailing over the mountains. From there, I visited the ocean. I swiveled around to see the festival conference center in the distance. I lowered my avatar to the ground and tried to make my way back to the conference—but got stuck in between some rocks. After a few jumps, I freed myself from my precarious situation and decided it would be easiest to fly back, as I was clearly lost in the jungle.

Back at the conference entrance, other avatars were walking around. I waved repeatedly at the others, but no one waved back. Finally, one of the avatars saw me and returned my wave.

The metaverse space was on the right side of my computer screen. The presentations and other resources were shown on the left side of the screen. This allowed visitors to watch the live presentations at scheduled times. The presentations were recorded, and the festival allowed visitors to come and go for twenty-four hours.

The Meta Festival was a thrilling learning experience and great use of my three hours. The adventure taught me three things:

The virtual encounter was captivating. Even when my avatar got stuck in the jungle several times—a bit of a technical difficulty—the opportunity to explore the beautiful landscape, mountains, and ocean inspired my curiosity and amazement. This was my first time flying around as an avatar, exploring a "conference world."

I saw how conference experiences can be innovated—and this is just the tip of the iceberg. A series of metaverse panels were offered within three separate global time zones. This provided a customized agenda and well-known panelists tailored for each global region. The customized approach was impressive and showed the possibilities for creating entertaining and specific global conferences. The live panels were recorded and available to conference attendees for a twenty-four-hour period.

It was clear that metaverse technology is in nascent stages. For example, my avatar's movements were a bit clunky, although admittedly operator error played a role. For example, I had big challenges in figuring out how to leave the jungle and enter the conference sites. I took many leaps, backflips, and jumps to finally enter the conference arenas. Also, I noticed that it didn't feel like we were attending as a group of avatars, but rather, it was a very individual experience. As the technology improves, I expect that socializing with other avatars will become more fluid and interactive.

HEALTHCARE INNOVATION

Doctors were one of the first groups to use AR for medical procedure collaboration. For example, Microsoft's mixed reality headsets are enabling medical professionals from around the globe to virtually collaborate during surgical operations.

Surgeons can operate Microsoft's HoloLens with hand gestures and voice commands to bring up 3D images from scans, access patient data, and contact other specialists. This hands-free control is a significant benefit to the hardware for doctors and other healthcare professionals.[2]

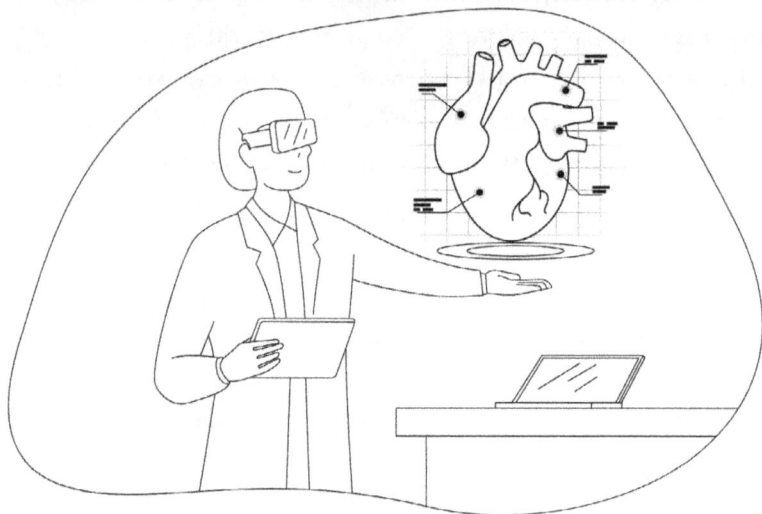

The Organic Robotics Corporation is beta testing its Light Lace wearable sensors with sports programs.[3] The soft, stretchable sensors track motion, muscle fatigue, and respiratory levels to prevent injuries and boost physical performance. The sensors produce an artificial skin that creates a digital twin of the tactical biometric information. The sensor is equipped with a light that warns the user of high fatigue levels.[4]

IMMERSIVE BUSINESS EFFICIENCY

The metaverse is expected to enhance business efficiency beyond today's online commerce. One early adopter launched a global business in the metaverse as an industry disruptor, even before the word "metaverse" became popular.

eXp Realty entered the real estate industry in 2009 as the world's first cloud-based brokerage. Today eXp supports more than 80,000 licensed real estate agents worldwide who work remotely in the metaverse.

eXp agents show up as their personal avatar. Agents can move throughout the virtual eXp World just as if they are in an office. They meet with colleagues within their local brokerages, as well as meet as avatars with other eXp agents across the globe, speaking through computer microphones.

eXp agents and staff have worked virtually using eXp World, a persistent online campus where business is transacted.[5] eXp's business model and metaverse strategy is an industry disruptor, allowing the firm to reduce office infrastructure costs while improving agent productivity.

"The experience and level of online engagement is just like meeting in person, however the difference is the incredible efficiency, without the expensive overhead costs of a brokerage office," explains Matt Battiata, eXp's No. 1 individual agent worldwide since 2020, based in Southern California.[6]

Hosted by Matt, I jumped into the eXp World. We visited eXp's central support office. We stood in line, only waiting a few moments behind another eXp agent avatar before being greeted by the eXp staff member.

eXp's metaverse contains virtual meeting rooms, an auditorium for conferences, and a virtual administrative support center with live support staff appearing as avatars, ready to help with accounting, human resources, brokerage operations, legal aspects, and technical support on a persistent 24/7 basis.

In eXp World, agents can rent and brand their own virtual offices and conference rooms equipped with presentation tools and tech support.

They have their own social media platform hosted by Facebook called "Workplace," where eXp agents can connect across the world, conduct private chats, and post announcements.[7] eXp World provides a virtual beach and soccer field for fun and socialization with other agents.

IMMERSIVE LEARNING

According to CNET author Scott Stein, "VR is not a game anymore—it's a real necessity."[8]

For years, gaming has been used to provide hands-on learning through simulation, used for military and in-flight pilot instruction, manufacturing and healthcare practice, energy sector forecasting, first responder and transportation training, and for many other e-learning applications.

Early evidence has shown that immersive experiences add value to traditional classroom learning.

Research has proven the efficacy of taking a virtual field trip. A study was conducted of 102 middle school students who took a nearly ten-minute virtual field trip to Greenland to examine the impacts of climate change.

One group of students used 3D headsets, while the second group took the field trip watching a video projected on a 2D screen. Findings proved that the 3D group scored significantly higher on immediate and delayed post-tests regarding presence, enjoyment, and interest in the subject material, linking immersive lessons with the potential for positive long-term learning effects.[9]

In a classroom setting, a college student cited that showing up as an avatar could be a confidence booster.

"It can be stage fright sometimes, where some people have a hard time talking in front of a bunch of people. When you're in a virtual space, it's a lot easier to have a suspension of belief that the audience is not really real, where you're able to speak more freely," he said.[10]

At Sandwell College in the West Midlands, England, VR is being used to help students learn core communication skills for job interviews at their own pace, in a safe virtual environment free from the judgment of peers and the social inhibitions that the shy or inexperienced find especially intimidating.

Sandwell College is partnering with Bodyswaps, an immersive learning platform designed to mirror behaviors. Students see, hear, and assess themselves as avatars following mock interviews. Students then reflect on how they would come across in real interview situations.

The college is expanding the Bodyswaps experience due to its success.

"Working with Sandwell, we've seen first-hand not only great engagement from students but actual improvement in their skills and confidence," says Christophe Mallet, CEO and cofounder of Bodyswaps.[11]

Arizona State University (ASU) created a VR platform named Dreamscape Learn within a space called the creativity commons. Students are using Dreamscape Learn to understand and address the complexities of climate change by experiencing it through a time travel scenario. VR tools include headsets, hand and foot trackers, and haptic sensations such as a shaking floor and blowing wind.

Dreamscape Learn is a partnership between ASU and Dreamscape Immersive, a VR entertainment and technology company cofounded by film producer Walter F. Parkes (e.g., *Gladiator* and *Men in Black*). The technology was first used to create experiences in malls and airport lounge waiting areas.

Lisa Flesher, ASU's chief of Realm 4, Project Acceleration, helps guide unique, technology-enhanced projects to advance immersive learning in higher education and K–12.

"At Dreamscape Learn, we wanted to make students the scientists and explorers. Then they go back to class, analyzing and graphing the data, forming a hypothesis and testing it," she explains. "The process of investigation, inquiry, failing and trying again are skills learned in real life that can be fostered in a VR environment in the metaverse."[12]

She is helping to build VR curriculum content, as well as connect faculty members to become cocreators, supported by the university's technical team. ASU hopes to offer faculty no-code creator solutions with an education asset library.

In 2020, Michael Angilletta, ASU professor and associate director of Learning Innovation in the School of Life Sciences, integrated VR into his biology curriculum.

"This VR way of learning will prepare students because what they're doing is discovering and solving problems in this novel world. The only way for them to solve the problem is to actually get engaged and do the work. And we hope that the fact that it's a narrative drives them to be emotionally connected . . . doing the work, learning what you need to know, and acquiring very specific skills along with very generic ones," Angilletta says.[13]

For medical education, Magic Leap innovated a lightweight, wearable computer headset with hand-held controllers to improve image quality for surgeries, as well as manufacturing and defense applications. A 70-degree field of view delivers an expansive digital workspace environment.[14]

For example, surgeons at UC Davis Children's Hospital used Magic Leap technology to help plan for the separation of rare, craniopagus twin babies. 3D reconstructions of MRI and CT scans were uploaded and viewed on the Magic Leap headset using a mixed reality viewer.

The AR wearable headset technology allows collaboration and "copresence." Teams around the world can wear headsets and collaborate on projects as if they were in the same room.[15]

Level Ex creates video games for doctors that capture the challenges of practicing medicine. The company aims to bridge gaps in the healthcare industry through state-of-the-art video game technology and design. For example, its *Top Derm* game is played by dermatologists.

The free, online mobile game is made by dermatology experts for dermatologists, covering a wide variety of dermatology topics.

Level Ex notes that "Top Derm is packed with incredible, medically accurate, computer-generated derm imagery in quick-burst challenges pulled from evidence-based research. Built on neuroscience-based game mechanics, Top Derm is a unique medical resource that also happens to be a ton of fun."[16]

Visible Body is a Boston-based team of biomedical visualization experts who created 3D animated teaching tools in multiple languages. The interactive learning content is used by more than a thousand learning institutions worldwide. Content is accessible by smartphones, computers, and other digital devices.[17]

Life science and medical students can take virtual, 3D tours through a human heart. Walkthroughs feature the heart's basic anatomy, including the four chambers, the heart's conduction system, and myocardium followed by a virtual dissection of the heart.

Visible Body helps teachers and students to "turn any room into an anatomy lab" with its VR and AR videos. The 3D anatomy tours require the interdisciplinary knowledge of biomedical visualization experts, software developers, editors, writers, and anatomy and medical professionals.

Digital information then is placed in that environment. For example, Visible Body added an augmented reality functionality to its *Human Anatomy Atlas* product. Viewers can place a virtual human organ or complete human body model on any flat surface, view it, and step through a virtual dissection.[18]

Cocreating in classrooms by teachers, students, and work teams will become a standard learning practice. Today, video games such as *Roblox*, *Fortnite*, and *Animal Crossing: New Horizons* equip players to build their own worlds. As the metaverse develops, it's very likely that the teachers of the future will learn how to build metaverse worlds offering immersive content and experiences that support academic learning.

TRAINING IN THE METAVERSE: VIRTUAL REALITY, MIXED REALITY, AND AUGMENTED REALITY

Digital technologies are helping industries such as healthcare achieve precision and improve outcomes. Mixed reality, where doctors view holograms but still use their own vision, is being used in complicated surgeries to improve patient outcomes.

Dr. Brian Rebolledo, an orthopedic surgeon at Scripps Health, is using mixed reality for shoulder replacement surgeries. He wears a headset showing holographic surgery models in three dimensions. The technology was created by Stryker, a medical technology and device company. Patients must first have a CT scan to create the hologram.

Virtual reality training has taken learners into imaginative and engaging environments to support technical and human-focused people skills training and performance improvement.

For example, a maintenance worker can learn how to fix a mechanical component without having to risk damaging equipment. A human relations manager can practice giving in-person interviews where body language and facial expressions are critical to making an employee feel at ease.

Augmented reality is similar to virtual reality in that both can leverage digital imagery and assets to provide information and simulations in a realistic space. AR can give access to key information by overlaying digital assets on a user's field of view, such as a smartphone or wearable device including AR-enabled headsets.

Trivia

The virtual training and simulation market size was valued at $204.41 billion in 2019. By 2027 the market size for AR is expected to triple, reaching a market size of more than $600 billion.

Source: "Virtual Training and Simulation Market Expected to Reach $601.85 Billion by 2027," Allied Market Research, August 2020, https://www.alliedmarketresearch.com/press-release/virtual-training-and-simulation-market.html.

Immersive Onboarding, Career Development, and Skills Training

Gone are the days of classroom-based onboarding. New hires can quickly become familiar with their workplaces and develop a community of support from coworkers within a metaverse experience. This reduces training time by more than 80 percent and creates memorable first impressions.

Technical Skills Training

Whether employees are on an assembly line, loading or unloading packages, or repairing an engine, metaverse training using a VR headset can provide an efficient and effective training solution. Learners can gain hands-on experience to improve operational efficiencies and speed up productivity.

Safety and First Responder Training

Learning proper lifting techniques or identifying hazards in the workplace requires situational awareness and critical thinking skills. An immersive safety training experience allows learners to become more familiar with their work setting and identify threats and risks, while being completely safe.

For example, SightCall is an enterprise-grade video cloud platform providing live, visual support. SightCall's AR technology is helping service leaders improve remote-assistance medical service calls without deploying unnecessary staff to the field.

The company blends digital and physical worlds into a real-time collaborative environment that empowers technicians to resolve emergencies more efficiently, save money, and improve the customer experience without unnecessary travel.

Customer Service Training

Immersion training programs can allow learners to practice realistic customer interactions, whether it's at a hotel lobby, call center, or store. Using scenario-based learning to build empathy, associates can take on the role of a customer and learn what drives their needs and concerns.

Sales Training

Sales simulations can allow a sales representative to role-play and negotiate with customers. Business simulations using storytelling and branching scenarios help to prepare sales associates for all contingencies, including managing resistance from prospective clients.

Leadership Development

Metaverse immersive training can help leaders develop people skills to improve team performance. This includes role-playing where avatars have difficult conversations, learn how to build a culture of listening and empathy, and create opportunities to address diversity, equity, and inclusion.

ENTERTAINMENT IN THE METAVERSE

In August 2021, pop star Ariana Grande partnered with the video game *Fortnite* to host a virtual reality concert. An astounding seventy-eight million players participated, signaling to entertainers that one virtual concert could be more profitable than an in-person tour by a huge margin, reducing venue, travel, and other costs.[19]

IMMERSIVE BRANDING AND MARKETING

The metaverse allows the customer to choose how and when to interact with brands. Customers will receive personalized product and service experiences while avoiding a trip to a physical store.

"While no one understands now how the metaverse will look and feel when it fully evolves, we can anticipate one thing: The metaverse will become a crucial new access point for brand experiences. Eventually, it will affect everything from virtual stores . . . to demonstrations and product collaborations," says Daniel Langer. A Pepperdine University professor, Langer is CEO of Équité, a luxury, lifestyle, and consumer brand strategy firm.[20]

In this current nascent stage, companies are experimenting, testing, and learning, rather than expecting a huge revenue generation from the metaverse. Expectations should be tempered because of the newness of this new frontier. Brands are aiming to create moments of surprise and delight for customers and audiences.

SPORTS

At the game company Unity, Peter Moore is the head of the sports and live entertainment and recently launched Unity Metacast. This platform will mirror professional sports in 3D in real time.

Cameras capture athletes on the field and the data is used to create digital twins. The first 3D broadcast was a match between two mixed martial arts fighters filmed in a small arena with 106 cameras. Moore told the *Financial Times* that he expects to expand the technology to fewer cameras and bigger playing spaces. Capturing live action and digitizing it immediately could make it easier to create NFTs from memorable game moments. The NBA's approach to Top Shots cards could expand to other sports.[21]

IMMERSIVE RETAIL

Founded in 1937, Procter & Gamble (P&G) entered the metaverse in 2020. P&G launched a 2020 Tokyo Olympics metaverse experience. The company developed a metaverse game for its Crest toothpaste brand based on its 1970s ad cartoon, the "Cavity Creeps." Participants travel in the metaverse as superheroes, arriving to gigantic teeth where they learn how to prevent tooth decay.[22]

FOOD/BEVERAGE AND RESTAURANT

McDonald's is one of the brands most actively exploring NFTs and the metaverse. In late 2021, it used the fortieth anniversary of its McRib to launch its first-ever NFTs—a collection of digital artworks representing the sandwich.[23] The image NFTs were won during a sweepstakes.

In 2022, McDonald's filed a trademark application hoping to eventually provide entertainment services, "namely, providing on-line actual and virtual concerts and other virtual events," the application read.[24]

The online gaming world is providing new opportunities for companies to grow revenue. Chipotle created a Halloween-themed corn maze on Roblox and offered $1 million worth of free burritos to users who successfully navigated their way through. Chipotle's gamified rewards strategy attracted five million players and Chipotle grew revenue by 26 percent in 2021, reaching $7.5 billion in sales.[25] In 2022, more than 45 percent of its sales were digital.[26]

Chipotle launched its Chipotle Burrito Builder on Roblox. The fast-food chain launched a new simulation experience that challenged players to roll burritos in the metaverse to earn Burrito Bucks, the brand's in-experience currency. The first 100,000 Roblox players who successfully rolled a burrito earned enough Burrito Bucks to exchange them for an entrée code that can be used on the Chipotle app.[27]

Gaming technology is offering brands unique opportunities to debut products and social spaces. For example, Ralph Lauren created a winter wonderful landscape with ice-skating, and Vans built a virtual skate park.

VIRTUAL TRAVEL

Interest in virtual immersive travel is growing following the COVID-19 pandemic. Metaverse travel will allow people to see the world, as well as travel through time via storytelling and creating digital worlds that replicate the past or the imagined future.

Will this include time travel? Yes!

The metaverse will be a 4D world where you will be able to travel into any past timeline. You will be able to create an ancient city, for example, or develop other places in your own space. You'll be able to study almost any topic in the past, present, and future, such as learning about a geographic region or a country.

A virtual tour in the metaverse will give users the sensation of being on location. It's a simulation of an existing location, usually composed of a sequence of videos or still images. It may also use other multimedia elements such as sound effects, music, narration, and text.

Virtual travel brings the added benefit of sustainability, shifting the demand toward low-carbon journeys where automobile and plane fuel is reduced, as well as the travel footprint on protected wildlife areas such as national parks.

IMMERSIVE MEETINGS

Virtual meetings save time and money, and technology continues to advance. Someday soon, we may be able to meet as lifelike holograms.

For example, Mesh for Microsoft Teams is offering its trademarked virtual meeting program Holoportation to "project yourself as your most lifelike, photorealistic self in mixed reality to interact as if you are there in person."[28] A Mesh VR headset, app, and equipment are required.

Why are so many event planners excited?

1. The metaverse can easily accommodate attendees all around the world.

2. With avatars, attendees can present themselves as they prefer.

3. It allows for unique event experiences and new opportunities for engagement.

4. You aren't limited by venue and vendor availability.

5. It could open up revenue streams from a new type of event attendee.[29]

Speakers appreciate the ability to interact more personally with virtual, metaverse audiences, too.

"When I'm speaking in person, I can't ask a question and have every single audience member answer it," says researcher Amanda Kaiser. "But online, I can ask a question, and every participant can answer. I can see their answers and respond, and every participant can learn from and talk to every other participant in the chat. What was once a one-way lecture can now inspire a delightful community of co-creation."[30]

IMMERSIVE JOURNALISM AND REPORTING TECHNIQUES

Immersive journalism is a form of journalism production that provides a first-person experience of news events or topics of interest.

Immersive journalism puts an audience member directly into the event. By accessing a virtual version of the location where the story is occurring as a witness/participant, or by experiencing the perspective of a character depicted in the news story, the audience gains unprecedented access to the sights, sounds, feelings, and emotions of the story.[31]

Recent examples include "Inside Xinjiang's Prison State," an immersive website experience revealing China's persecution campaign of its Uighur population, published by the *New Yorker*.[32]

The metaverse is expected to provide an audience engagement platform for a new era of immersive and experimental storytelling methods, including VR- and AR-powered documentaries, AI-supported data journalism, and visually intense digital stories.

MILITARY AND GOVERNMENT

The metaverse is expected to provide unprecedented opportunities to increase military readiness and capacity. In a military metaverse, service members could collaborate, train, and conduct any number of activities, described Lisa A. Costa, chief of technology and innovation of the United States Space Force (USSF), the newest branch of the Armed Forces, established in 2019.[33]

Costa notes that 86 percent of US airmen and guardians from the ages of eighteen to thirty-four view themselves as gamers—and the USSF wants to take advantage of those skills.

A metaverse is appealing to the Space Force because guardians normally rely on digital representations of the space domain to do their jobs, Costa says. Virtual reality, as well as augmented reality that combines the digital and physical worlds, could provide Space Force guardians with situational awareness and understanding about decision-making options. Space Force guardians could digitally engineer satellites, for example.[34]

"We are the only U.S. military service that was established during the information age," Costa says. "And so the Space Force has this unique opportunity to be born digital. And we're seizing on that opportunity."[35]

NASA uses AR and VR aboard the space station for remote control of robots or to complete maintenance tasks with an AR assist. In one particular project, astronaut Scott Kelly used a Microsoft HoloLens headset to conduct ISS training and do future mission prep. During these tests, a member of mission control on Earth streamed Kelly's field of view via the headset and also drew images rendered in 3D on the astronaut's HoloLens display.[36]

METAVERSE PERSISTENCE MEANS INNOVATIVE LEARNING

Learning and development is a function focused on empowering employee knowledge, skills, and capabilities to drive better business performance. Whether the function is organized centrally or decentralized throughout an organization, the opportunity for asynchronous, persistent learning in the metaverse is immense.

The persistent metaverse provides an asynchronous *and* synchronous online opportunity for learners to enter metaverse worlds when convenient for the individual, and to work at their own pace.

Asynchronous online learning allows students to complete work individually outside of live class sessions, on their own time and at their convenience. Group work is scheduled outside of the live classroom when students meet online for team interaction.

Table 1: Types and Benefits of Online Learning

Asynchronous online learning (independent work outside the scheduled classes)	Shared benefits from both modes of online learning	Synchronous online learning (during real-time classes conducted online)
Students complete work each week on their own schedule. Students receive immediate feedback on quizzes. Students schedule group work when most convenient for the team.	Students can attend class from anywhere, as long as they have a connected digital device. Students communicate regularly with instructors. Students can network and make connections with classmates.	Students attend class virtually each week with classmates and instructors who are teaching live and online. Students participate in real time during class. Students gain the benefit of improving their online presentation skills during real-time presentations.

Synchronous online classes allow students to attend class virtually each week with live, real-time instructors and classmates. Students participate in real-time discussions during class time, which helps them to sharpen their virtual presentation skills.

Both online learning modes provide opportunities for students to attend class remotely—similar to meeting up in a metaverse environment. Students communicate regularly with instructors and network with each other to make real-life connections with classmates.

"Asynchronous online classes mean that you don't always need to be online at the same time as your instructor or classmates," says instructional designer John Muir, who works with faculty to develop classes for Ohio State's online programs. "We know that students who are looking to take an entire program online are partially looking for that flexibility."[37]

Online asynchronous classes might include short videos teaching key concepts that you can watch over and over again, if necessary. In some classes, students can also complete homework assignments and receive immediate feedback, as opposed to waiting for instructors to grade them.

Asynchronous classes are just as rigorous as their synchronous or on-campus counterparts.

PERSISTENT AND INTEROPERABLE: DIGITAL TWIN INNOVATION

The metaverse someday will be interoperable. Interoperability is the ability to unify economies, avatars, and systems across platforms. That is, all of the platforms will be connected in a seamless system, where we can easily jump from one world into another, embodied by an avatar that we securely own and that represents our unique identity.

Digital twin technology is one of the metaverse's core building blocks. While the metaverse can help us create virtual worlds, it will also be useful in constructing exact replicas of reality. With inherent features and functionalities, digital twins can bring realism to the digital world.[38]

A digital twin is "a virtual representation of real-world entities and processes, synchronized at a specified frequency and fidelity."[39] Also, a digital twin could be a digital replica of a physical process or asset.

Digital twins collect data from sensors to offer improvements. For communities, this could mean improvements to reduce heat islands or improve traffic flow.

For example, Google's Nest Learning Thermostat uses sensors paired with the building's heating and cooling system. It detects the room's temperature and humidity and programs the heating, ventilation, and air-conditioning (HVAC) system to adjust appropriately—in real time.[40]

Ernst and Young forecasts that digital twins can help commercial property and infrastructure owners cut emissions by 50 to 100 percent, reduce operating costs by 35 percent, and improve productivity by 20 percent.[41]

The convergence of AI, AR/VR, Internet of Things (IoT), and satellite-generated data in the metaverse is rapidly advancing digital twins. Digital twins could help propel sustainability at the planetary level, from supply chains and manufacturing assets to individuals.

The European Space Agency is working toward a digital twin of Earth that will help visualize and forecast the impacts of human activity on the planet, such as changes in the ocean, forests, and climate, simulating different scenarios to inform policymakers.[42]

REFLECTION QUESTIONS

1. What metaverse innovations are most exciting to you, and why?

2. How might the metaverse support your work or your organization's work?

3. What metaverse innovations make you skeptical about the future of the metaverse, and why?

CHAPTER 4

THE BAD: THE FIVE DS

THE WORLD "METAVERSE" SEEMS TO EVOKE two extreme images: either utopia or dystopia.

A utopia is a place of ideal perfection: a theoretically perfect realm where everyone is content, and where all the problems that have plagued our world since the beginning of time no longer apply.

A dystopia is an imagined world or society where people lead wretched, dehumanized, fearful lives—where everything has gone wrong in the attempt to create a perfect society.

Either of these extremes tend to cause some concern for most people.

However, when people hear the term "a more immersive internet," they tend to relax a bit and seem to comprehend Web3 as being based on what they know, and their existing internet knowledge.

When you think of how much more time people will—without a doubt—spend in digital worlds connecting their eyeballs with their devices, it's not difficult to understand the permanent impact the metaverse will have on the human race, and the way we relate to each other.

Worldwide internet use is at 63 percent as of 2022, which equates to more than five *billion* internet users across the globe. This rate is rapidly growing.[1]

Now that we've scratched the surface and explored metaverse good in the form of innovation, here are "five Ds"—the anticipated bad aspects—of the metaverse. These Ds are like five pots that have been boiling for decades: distraction, distrust, disinterest, disconnection, and disenfranchisement.

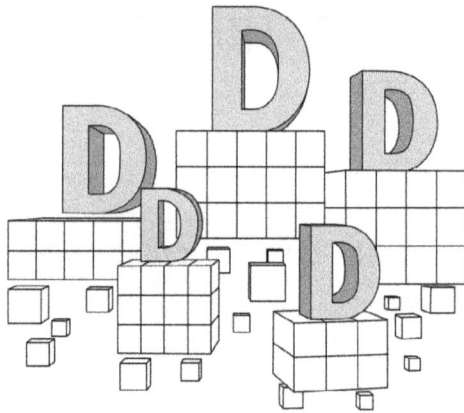

How can we minimize these five Ds in the metaverse? We clearly need effective leadership and a new level of strategy and community building to prevent the decline of human relationships and societal decay in our escalating, hybrid world.

DISTRACTION

Have you ever talked with a friend, loved one, or perhaps your boss and as you were speaking, they continued to look at their phone or watch? How did that make you feel?

The metaverse will bring bells, whistles, and a new level of infatuation with technology. Will it bring decay of the human connection—the reason it was created in the first place?

Imagine a world where people will put on their streamlined glasses and transcend physical and digital worlds until the glasses are taken off. No wonder we will need driverless cars—no one will be paying attention.

Another potential source of distraction is social media.

More than half of the world's population are users. In the United States, 72 percent of the public uses some type of social media. The average daily use per person across the globe is two hours and twenty-seven minutes.[2]

With this amount of social media use, and without guardrails, it can create major distraction as we switch back and forth between apps and accounts, fluidly checking email, social accounts, online meetings, and work messages.

Hours later, it's no wonder we may feel—

- Overwhelmed, unfocused, and paralyzed by information overload.

- Constantly bombarded by unsolicited messages from bots, robocalls, and political texts.

- Isolated—we're connected, but lonely; we're together online but separated by distance, as well as multiple priorities and agendas.

- Impatient—the average attention span is less than eight seconds.

- Like everyone's talking—but no one's listening.

- Like we cannot talk fast and loud enough to get our point across.

- Like we must continually entertain to keep people's attention.

German futurist Gerd Leonhard calls the metaverse a "bicycle for the brain, but bullets for the soul."[3]

He discusses the need for, *yet the challenge of,* processing information and turning it into deeper understanding, wisdom, and purpose.

This takes time and reflection, he says. Information overwhelm distracts humans from deeper thinking.

In efforts to attract attention and *keep people's attention*, some believe the metaverse is just a stepping-stone to a new level of narcissism.

The academic Yuval Levin recently argued that social media has "turned large swaths of our personal lives into platforms for pseudo-celebrity performance, where we display ourselves and observe others without really connecting. And they have elevated expression over action in ways that have mangled our civic and political cultures."[4]

Tristan Claridge, director of the Institute for Social Capital, attributes the decrease in empathy and increase in narcissism to the rise of social media use.

"So many of our employees are now empathy-challenged . . . we could describe them as sociopaths—not the type that would come into work next week and murder everyone. Since sociopathy is a continuum of severity, we simply mean someone who has some difficulty understanding or sharing another person's feelings," he says. "Social media encourages self-promotion and fame seeking—the attention economy—that results in narcissism—an inflated sense of our own importance, a deep need for admiration and a lack of empathy for others."[5]

Distraction leads to brain exhaustion. This leads to people who want to be constantly entertained rather than working through tough problems.

Studies have shown that students and adults are spending less time reading books.[6] Sadly, because of the shorter attention spans due to multiple sources of digital distraction, some teachers are offering abbreviated material with quick links rather than full texts.

What happens when we get distracted while at work? It takes twenty-three minutes and fifteen seconds to return to the original task on average, and for some, the mental impact can last as long as a half hour. Then we try to compensate for interruptions by working faster, but this comes at the price of more stress, higher frustration, time pressure, and effort.[7]

Here's what tech experts have to say about their *own* distraction, *pre*metaverse, according to data from a survey of 1,150 people who are active in global internet business, policy, governance, and research activities.

- "Digital technologies have made it more difficult for me to stay on task and devote sustained attention. This interferes with my work productivity."

- "I can't seem to get my brain to calm down and focus. It is all over the place. I can't concentrate. I just start thinking about what I'm going to do next."

- "I am becoming increasingly aware of the way constant access to digital forms of communication can be overwhelming."

- "We are distracted and addicted to our devices, making it challenging for students to pay attention in class, and people to pay attention to each other when having conversations."

- "It has become an ever-present overhang on all aspects of life. There is no escape."

- "One major impact is the overall decrease in short-term memory."[8]

But to be disconnected from the metaverse would mean that critical everyday information would not be at your fingertips. We will be dependent on the virtual layers of information projected in our glasses or contacts, and without it we could be disadvantaged socially, economically, and intellectually.[9]

Distraction also leads to living life in shallow waters. When we are distracted and lack deep focus, we may be more vulnerable to believe the quick and easy—the hearsay. And this can blaze a path to the second D: distrust.

DISTRUST

Because of bad actors, the metaverse most certainly will be a more immersive place for breeding lies, cybersecurity, fraud, and other evils that will continue to threaten security and erode trust.

"We don't understand what we can trust anymore," says one cyber-security expert.[10]

In the metaverse, critical concerns include information privacy, hacking, deception, user addiction, escapism, preferring life in fake/fabricated worlds, safety/protection against harmful egos, and cyberbullying.

For example, we will all be using virtual avatars to navigate the metaverse, so protecting our identities will be critical. How will avatars be verified? How will metaverse worlds verify their users?

The metaverse will be an enhanced platform for predators, scammers, political agitators, and manipulators. Metaverse users must stay on guard to protect themselves—and especially children—from harassment and abuse.

Recent data reveals that roughly two-thirds of adults under thirty have been harassed online.[11] Women are targeted twice as much as men, and Black, Hispanic, and Asian adults are targeted even more than whites.[12]

There are a number of serious threats to trust in the metaverse. As we traipse from one world to the next suited up as avatars, there will be multiple universes promoting multiple truths. And just as creepy, there will be those whose multiple avatars represent complex identities, all wrapped up into one person.

Continual vigilance will be needed to protect ourselves.

In late 2022, CNN, *Wall Street Journal* and other news sources reported that Epic Games, maker of *Fortnite*, will pay $520 million to resolve US Federal Trade Commission allegations that the company invaded children's privacy and tricked players of all ages into making unintended purchases. This illustrates the types of privacy and ethical dilemmas to be addressed as online gaming and metaverse worlds evolve.

Misinformation, Disinformation, and Fakes

Misinformation is *any* wrong or false information, whether it is shared knowingly or unknowingly.

In contrast, disinformation is false information that is deliberately shaped and spread. The false information is deliberately misleading. As propaganda, the disinformation could be biased, or may be a manipulation of facts or narratives.

Fake news is false or misleading information presented as news. Fake news often has the aim of damaging the reputation of a person or entity or making money through advertising revenue.[13]

Algorithmic bots are specially designed programs that use computer processing power to spread misinformation, disinformation, and fake news through fake user accounts. The bots have increased the spread of fake news to targeted audiences through algorithms.

Furthermore, algorithms are designed to keep people together with the same philosophies and interests, to keep people's attention and focus. This puts us together with people who think the same way, as opposed to having a community dialogue—being able to agree, disagree, and have a conversation together.

"Influence operations, whether launched by governments or non-state actors, existed long before social media, but what is new about contemporary influence operations is their scale, severity and impact, all of which are likely to grow more pronounced as digital platforms extend their reach via the internet and become ever more central to our social, economic and political lives," explains Eric Jardine, assistant professor of political science at Virginia Tech who researches trends in cybercrime using blockchain data.[14]

Influence operations represent a clear cybersecurity challenge. Yet democracies, which depend on the open and free sharing of information, are particularly susceptible to the poison of influence operations that spread fake news, disinformation, and propaganda.

Jardine notes that fake news and other influence operations are made more powerful by filter bubbles—algorithms leading to online information ecosystems.

"Once within such a bubble, people tend to get more of what they like, based on their earlier online choices, whether those are funny YouTube videos of cats or ideologically infused podcasts and posts. The troubling part is that the commercial aim of platform filters—namely, to give people what they want to encourage consumption of content—tends to play out badly in the political space," he says.

People hear their own messages played back over and over, rather than hear other points of view. The echo chamber is reinforced by algorithms. While democracy requires the free exchange of information and ideas, filter bubbles isolate users. In a filtered environment, information does not circulate widely and freely.[15]

Worldwide concern about algorithm-driven fake news and its influence on political, economic, and social well-being is growing. A study completed by Massachusetts Institute of Technology (MIT) scholars revealed that lies spread faster than the truth.[16]

False news reached more people than the truth; the top 1 percent of false news cascades diffused to between 1,000 and 100,000 people, whereas the truth rarely diffused to more than 1,000 people.[17]

The degree of novelty and the emotional reactions of recipients may be responsible for the falsehood to spread faster, farther, deeper, and more broadly, the study found. False stories inspired fear and disgust. True stories inspired human emotions of anticipation, sadness, joy, and trust.

Deepfake technology uses digital photo and video imaging techniques to create convincing but entirely fictional photos from scratch. The fake representations of real people—including celebrities and elected officials—could be used to discredit leaders, organizations, and governments, and disrupt societies.

Audio can be deep-faked to create voice clones of public figures. The chief of a UK subsidiary of a German energy firm paid nearly £200,000 into a Hungarian bank account after being phoned by a fraudster who mimicked the German CEO's voice. The company's insurers believe the voice was a deepfake, but the evidence was unclear.[18]

Shallow fakes are videos presented out of context, with altered reality, or are doctored with simple editing tools. Programs such as Adobe's AI-powered Smart Portrait enable users to alter photographs, such as aging faces, changing expressions, and editing backgrounds. Even crude, shallow fakes such as altering a photo background or editing a person's voice can be destructive.

Conspiracy theories are explanations for an event or situation that invoke a conspiracy by sinister and powerful groups, often political in motivation, when other explanations are more probable.[19]

Privacy and Security in the Metaverse

Privacy is a long-standing internet issue. Through internet locations and specific devices we use, the metaverse will continue to collect and store personal data about every user, including eye-tracking, physical reactions, and haptics.

Computer scientist and AR expert Louis Rosenberg believes that if used improperly, AR in the metaverse could be more divisive than social media, and an insidious threat to society and even reality itself.

"The fact is, we now live in dangerous times, and AR has the potential to amplify the dangers to levels we have never seen," Rosenberg says. He continues:

> Imagine walking down the street in your hometown, casually glancing at people you pass on the sidewalk. It is much like today, except floating over the heads of every person

you see are big glowing bubbles of information. Maybe the intention is innocent, allowing people to share their hobbies and interests with everyone around them.

Now imagine that third parties can inject their own content, possibly as a paid filter layer that only certain people can see. And they use that layer to tag individuals with bold flashing words like "Alcoholic" or "Immigrant" or "Atheist" or "Racist" or even less charged words . . . Those who are tagged may not even know that others can see them that way. The virtual overlays could easily be designed to amplify political division, ostracize certain groups, even drive hatred and mistrust. Will this really make the world a better place? Or will it take the polarized and confrontational culture that has emerged online and spray it across the real world?[20]

With more than three hundred awarded patents in AR, VR, and AI, Rosenberg serves as CEO of Unanimous AI, a California company focused on amplifying human intelligence using AI algorithms modeled on biological swarms. Rosenberg is known for developing the first functional augmented reality system at Air Force Research Laboratory.

Distrust also could be connected to avatar identity issues. We don't fully understand the impact of people appearing as animated characters versus seeing—and verifying—the real human behind the avatar.

When people distrust each other, they shut down. They insulate themselves to create safety. Distrust fosters the third and fourth Ds: disinterest and disconnection.

DISINTEREST AND DISCONNECTION

Disinterest and disconnection go hand in hand.

Disinterest is the loss of interest in things that once brought joy and happiness. Disconnection is the distancing or severing of relationships.

A deep loss of interest is a main symptom of depression leading to being disconnected, distancing oneself. Loss of interest can be an overwhelming and far-reaching symptom that impacts relationships with friends and family, work and school productivity, hobby enjoyment, and more.

Some distancing is purposeful. We can block people on social media. We can snooze our so-called friends when we want to take a break from people with whom we may suddenly disagree.

We are alone together—distanced by disconnection—with the average American spending roughly 5.4 hours per day staring at a mobile phone screen.[21]

The average person checks a smartphone approximately *every ten minutes* and touches it 2,600 times a day.[22]

Because of information overload, we disconnect. We're less apt to join clubs or service organizations. We narrow our networks so we can maintain focus.

Disinterest and disconnect result in the loss of community and civic engagement. In research discussed by Robert Putnam decades ago, he addressed the topic of collective "community loneliness." In his bestselling book *Bowling Alone*, he notes television's devastating impact on civic engagement and social capital—long before the advent of smartphones.[23]

The metaverse of today and the foreseeable future is the equivalent of Putnam's TV. We cannot deny our addiction to our digital devices and tether to the internet.

The metaverse has the potential to create disinterest and disconnection if people become addicted to living life in the virtual world—similar to gaming addiction. In virtual worlds, it's easy to lose track of time. People who are exposed to the metaverse for too long might lose interest in reality and may go beyond that, to not wanting to acknowledge the existence of a world besides the virtual one.

"Increased isolation is a negative effect I feel in my life; the time I spend using digital technologies could well be spent in other more creative and productive ways," says one tech leader.[24]

Time spent in the metaverse could mean further disconnection from health and wellness, including disconnection from exercise, the outdoors, and the beauty of nature. It's been said that sitting is the new form of smoking. VR hangovers, post-VR sadness, and cyberaddiction are real. How will our society combat the physical and mental health challenges of an immersive world?

We're saturated by smartphone information but are starving for human community. Our technology comes at the opportunity cost of relationships, interests, and connections.

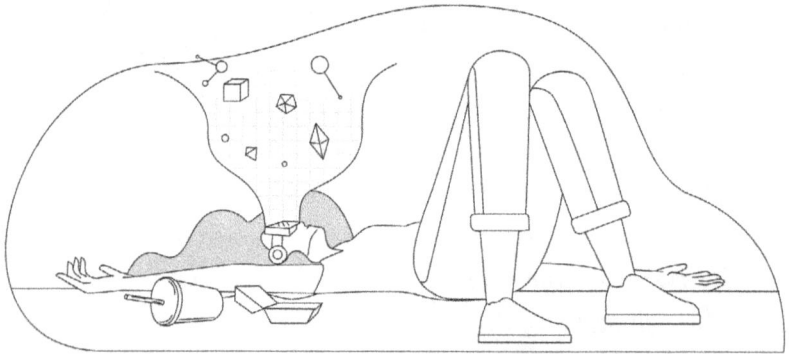

When metaverse headsets become sleek and streamlined, people may wear these all day, distracted with metaverse activity and becoming further disconnected from the human race. Will the convergence of our digital and physical lives in the metaverse turn us into avatars with little empathy, divorced from reality, with few meaningful, human relationships?

According to Vanessa Mason, author and research director of the

Institute for the Future, "If we really hope to save democracy, we need to save ourselves from the pull of loneliness, disconnection, and disaffiliation. That will require reminding ourselves of what we hold in common—values, aspirations and hopes—while embracing the creative, but often uncomfortable friction that results from how we differ."[25]

DISENFRANCHISEMENT

The fifth D acknowledges the divide between those with technology, and those without.

How can technology providers support people having equal access to the technology needed to join the metaverse, including handsets, headsets, and connectivity?

According to the Close the Gap Foundation, the digital divide is a multifaceted issue of disenfranchisement. Two main characteristics define this gap: access to high-speed internet and access to reliable devices. Many of the individuals who struggle with the digital divide face both challenges.

WebMe promotes a highly individualistic digital world geared to the individual and his or her unique experiences. However, we need to have a candid conversation about how to expand access to all who desire to have basic connection to the internet.

Digital inequity may divide and separate us even further as a global society. Some see the metaverse as exclusionary. For example, owning an NFT meme probably doesn't rank among the top concerns for a household that couldn't secure a working Wi-Fi connection or laptop for their children during the worst days of the pandemic.[26]

In some areas internet access is either limited, unavailable, or unaffordable for those who might be equipped. Even with a reliable internet connection, access to certain digital spaces can remain a challenge, always just out of reach for those who can't afford costly tools including laptops and software.

This leaves countless students and professionals to rely on public computers or their mobile devices as their only tools to exist in an increasingly digital world. It leaves many more, such as those in rural areas or living under the poverty line, without even that.

Finally, negative environmental impacts associated with metaverse technology are being examined. A recent study estimates that training just one AI model could generate 626,000 pounds of carbon dioxide, which is more than *five times* the amount of greenhouse gases emitted by a car in its lifetime.

Cloud gaming, which is necessary for VR, could also raise carbon emissions by 2030, increasing the need for high-resolution images. This increases the need for more energy. Moreover, the continuous development of VR will encourage people to buy new technology, which means an influx in e-waste—polluting our soil, groundwater, and landfills.[27]

REFLECTION QUESTIONS

1. While most discussion has focused on technology and how to make money using cryptocurrency, from a social science perspective, how might the metaverse impact leadership, community building, and strategy?

2. What are the changing leadership skills needed to thrive in a blended physical and metaverse-digital world?

3. Do you think humans will prefer living digital lives—some in the world of gaming and fantasyland—over our physical lives?

CHAPTER 5

THE UGLY: THE LONELINESS EPIDEMIC

AS THE METAVERSE EVOLVES, MANY EXPECT it to be *less of a place* and more about *how people will be communicating*. In theory, immersive tools and experiences will enhance the way we connect, transact business, and build community.

No doubt the metaverse will provide endless places of immersive escape on a persistent, 24/7 basis. Meeting with work colleagues and friends as 3D holograms will be fun and fantastical, but is unlikely to replace the need for human, in-person time together.

Whether the metaverse develops as predicted, a *human social recession* already exists across the globe, a crisis—and it's called the loneliness epidemic.

The loneliness rate in the United States is greater than 50 percent,[1] with the highest rates among young adults according to a recent study. Multinational resources found that one in five people are lonely.[2] And an unprecedented 70 percent of teens say depression and anxiety are major issues.[3]

Loneliness is the absence of caring, kind, and compassionate relationships in a person's life.

Loneliness is a serious health and mental health problem. Feelings of loneliness and social isolation are associated with increased risk for inflammatory disease and death.[4]

How can we ensure the metaverse contributes to the quality of human connections? To date, metaverse enthusiasts have acknowledged the potential for metaverse addiction.

Will the metaverse prevent loneliness by connecting us in new ways? Or will the metaverse create even more loneliness, alienation, and anger—people feeling pushed to the margins, not feeling seen or heard? It will require a variety of disciplines, including mental health experts, creatives, and leaders far and wide, to work together to pilot and scale early interventions and support systems to address the avalanche of loneliness to come. Human intervention is key.

THE SCOPE OF LONELINESS

Loneliness is normal—all of us can feel lonely from time to time.

"Loneliness," as defined by one study, "is a lack or loss of companionship when there is a mismatch between the quantity and quality of relationships we have, and those we want."[5]

People can live solitary lives and not feel lonely because of quality relationships in their lives.

Conversely, people can have many acquaintances and live ostensibly busy social lives, and yet feel profoundly lonely due to their lack of quality human conversations and interactions.[6]

Our human communities—family, friends, coworkers, neighbors, and people who share our interests—help to nurture our sense of belonging. Our human relationships help us feel loved, safe, and supported. We feel understood—listened to, heard, and valued for who we *already* are.

Researcher Stephanie Cacioppo notes that feelings of being alone equate to a *perception* of social isolation—of being disconnected from others. She believes the *mind* is the most important factor helping us feel connected or disconnected.

"Lonely people don't see reality as it is but as they *think* it is," she says.[7]

During the pandemic, people felt isolated after weeks and months of social distancing. Going for a drive or visiting a grocery store became a welcomed relief, just to be able to see other human beings. The masks, much needed for survival, blocked our ability to see facial expressions and fully connect with others.

The pandemic stole time away from family, friends, school, work, and so much more. Death, isolation, and fear took a huge mental toll.

Vivek Murthy, physician and former surgeon general of the United States, authored a book about the impact of loneliness on human health.[8] Care, compassion, and human connection is key to a healthy life, Murthy says, adding that simply showing up—being present—is a lost art.

His research revealed that loneliness is prevalent in the lives of young adults. Murthy advocates for the quality of relationships rather than the quantity of social media connections.

"Social media provides an illusion that a people's 'friend' count and likes is equivalent to having thousands of friends. The research points out that close-knit relationships requires steady human investment," Murthy says.

He cited loneliness as the No. 1 health crisis in the United States, leading to anxiety, depression, lack of sleep, mental health concerns, and lack of coping mechanisms.

Soon after your mid-twenties, your social circle shrinks.[9] To avoid the progression of loneliness, a lifetime of active relationship building is needed to promote physical and mental health. Recent studies have connected loneliness with health decline, as well as the COVID-19 pandemic.

- Findings from seventy studies found that loneliness increases the chance of premature death by 26 percent.[10]

- Loneliness is as deadly as obesity and smoking—physically as harmful as smoking fifteen cigarettes a day.[11]

- Loneliness contributes to cognitive decline.[12]

- At least one in five, or 22 percent of adults in the United States, United Kingdom, and Japan, struggle with loneliness.[13]

- The rate of loneliness has jumped in the United States since the COVID-19 pandemic. In 2018, 35 percent of people over the age of forty-five said they were lonely.[14] In 2020, in the US, loneliness among *all ages* was greater than 50 percent, with highest rates among young adults. Americans of all ages, from teens to older adults, often feel alone, left out, and lacking a meaningful connection with others.[15]

As a university faculty member for more than a decade, I've noticed the increase of students who constantly look at their phones, rather than take the time to get to know their classmates. Without faculty who serve as a catalyst for creating classroom bonding, students might attend a course and not know any names of fellow classmates by the end of the semester.

Teachers skilled in classroom community building—from early childhood through adulthood—are the vital academic support system students will need as the metaverse expands.

"The problem is when loneliness persists for a long period of time. And when it is chronic, then we enter into a chronic stress state," Murthy says. "And that is what has dramatically consequential impacts on our health. Because in chronic stress, we also increase our levels of inflammation in the body, which damage tissues and blood vessels and increase our risk for heart disease and other chronic illnesses."[16]

A massive society of lonely people will weaken problem-solving resources for governments and communities.

"Just as a strong economy bolsters all of us against losses, social connection is a renewable resource that helps us address the challenges we face as individuals and as a society," Murthy says.[17]

Columnist George Will of the *Washington Post* opined that "Americans are richer, more informed, and are so-called more connected than ever, yet are unhappier, isolated and unfulfilled."[18]

For the first time in the United States, life expectancy is declining, while the numbers of "deaths of despair" (from suicide, drugs, and alcohol abuse), especially among white males, is on the rise.[19] The chances of dying from an opioid overdose or suicide are now higher than the odds of dying in a motor vehicle accident.[20]

Relationship Churn

Under normal circumstances, our networks don't simply shrink; networks tend to churn. As we lose touch with friends during transitions, we usually forge new relationships to replace the ones we've lost.

continued

Research published in 2021 proved that without face-to-face contact, our emotional attachment to friends and family deteriorates quickly.

After two months without an in-person gathering, feelings of closeness between friends and family members drop by more than 30 percent. After that, friendships go frigid.

After five months, feelings of closeness between friends plummets by 80 percent.

Source: Marissa King and Balazs Kovacs, "We're Losing Touch with Our Networks," *Harvard Business Review*, February 12, 2021, https://hbr.org/2021/02/research-were-losing-touch-with-our-networks.

ONLINE GAMING ADDICTION

Online gaming shows no signs of slowing down. Gamers are the early adopters. There were almost two billion video gamers across the world in 2015. By 2024, the number of online gamers is expected to reach 3.3 billion.

Globally, the average time gamers spent online each week is 8.45 hours. China ranked as No. 1 in gaming time, with gamers averaging 12.39 weekly hours. Vietnam ranked second, with an average of 10.16 weekly gaming hours.[21]

The Oxford Internet Institute completed a 2022 research report linking six weeks of 38,935 players' objective game-behavior data, provided by seven global game publishers, with three waves of self-reported well-being. The study found little to no evidence for a causal connection between game play and well-being.

However, the Oxford Internet Institute study reported a distinct difference in the experience of gamers who *want to* play, versus the gamers who can't stop—the gamers who feel like they *have to* play.[22]

Three to 4 percent of gamers are addicted to video games, according to a 2021 global research study. For youth ages eight through eighteen, the percentage of addicted gamers is 8.5 percent. The meta-analysis extracted data from fifty-three studies conducted between 2009 and 2019, across seventeen countries.[23]

Today, that equates to at least sixty million people across the globe who are addicted gamers.[24]

The average age of a gamer is thirty-five years old, while the average age of a gaming addict is twenty-four years old. The majority of gamers are within the age bracket of eighteen to thirty-four years old.[25] In the United States, more than 90 percent of American children play video games.

While the social benefits of playing online video games has been documented in research, there are profound social and mental health downsides.

"Video games of today are quite literally designed to be addictive," notes Cam Adair, founder of Game Quitters.[26] "They fulfill so many of our basic human needs such as social connection, escape, growth and challenge. Nothing else in the world accomplishes this as effectively as gaming."

In 2019, the World Health Organization added "gaming disorder" as a mental health condition to its International Classification of Diseases, ICD-11.

Gaming disorder is defined as "a pattern of gaming behavior (digital-gaming or video-gaming) characterized by impaired control over gaming, increasing priority given to gaming over other activities to the extent that gaming takes precedence over other interests and daily activities, and continuation or escalation of gaming despite the occurrence of negative consequences."[27]

With gaming disorder, the mental and physical impacts are significant. Too much screen time has been linked to the following:[28]

- Obesity

- Poor sleep or insomnia

- Behavioral problems, including impulsive actions

- Loss of social skills

- Violence

- Less time for play

- Eye strain

- Neck and back problems

- Anxiety

- Depression

- Difficulties with work or school

Addiction to gaming also is described in the American Psychiatric Association's *Diagnostic and Statistical Manual of Mental Disorders* (*DSM-5*), which is used by mental health professionals to diagnose mental disorders.

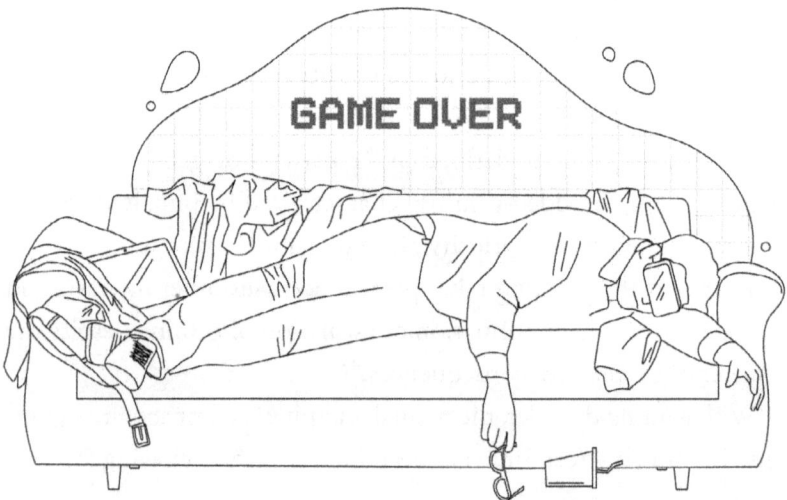

The *DSM-5* diagnostic guide for gaming disorder notes that gaming must cause "significant impairment or distress" in several aspects of a person's life. This condition is limited to gaming. It does not include problems with general use of the internet, online gambling, or use of social media or smartphones.

The symptoms of internet gaming disorder include the following:[29]

- Preoccupation with gaming

- Withdrawal symptoms when gaming is taken away or not possible (sadness, anxiety, irritability)

- Tolerance, the need to spend more time gaming to satisfy the urge

- Inability to reduce playing time, unsuccessful attempts to quit gaming

- Giving up other activities, loss of interest in previously enjoyed activities due to gaming

- Continuing to game despite problems

- Deceiving family members or others about the amount of time spent on gaming

- The use of gaming to relieve negative moods, such as guilt or hopelessness

- Risk, having jeopardized, or lost a job or relationship due to gaming

GAMING AND VIOLENCE

Excessive use of gaming screens can result in long-term or permanent changes in the brain that require extensive behavioral and medical treatment to reverse—urges that take over a person's life, blocking out other thoughts.[30]

Research conducted by the US Federal Bureau of Investigation's Behavioral Science Unit links fantasy-world isolation with the rise in mental health issues and violence.

The FBI reported active shooter data for the period of 2017 to 2021, revealing an upward trend. The number of active shooter incidents in 2021 represents a 52.5 percent increase from 2020, and a 96.8 percent increase from 2017.[31]

In 2021, there were sixty-one active shooters in the United States. Sixty were male, and one was female. Shooters under the age of thirty-five comprised 56 percent, with the largest group ranging from age twenty-five to thirty-four—young angry men.[32]

Scott Bonn, criminology professor and bestselling author, explains that isolation and feelings of anger and resentment often become part of a cyclical process in the lives of fledgling serial killers. Fantasies of violence prompt their isolation from society, which in turn creates a greater reliance on fantasy for pleasure and relief from anxiety. Serial killers often fantasize about murder and sexual violence for years before claiming their first victim.

"Serial killers program themselves in childhood to become murderers through a progressively intensifying loop of fantasy," Bonn notes. "The definition of fantasy in this context is an elaborate mental thought with great preoccupation that is anchored in the daydreaming process. Fantasy can be experienced through mental images or feelings. Fantasy serves to relieve anxiety or fear and most people have them to one extent or another. Although some fantasy in childhood is normal, it can become a compulsive form of escapism in children who are abused, neglected, or otherwise traumatized."[33]

Addictive metaverse behaviors leading to fantasy-world isolation might include these:

- Spending money on metaverse digital clothing, games, or land in a fantasy world, even though you can't afford it.

- Cutting back on social or recreational activities because of a preference for being present in metaverse worlds as an avatar.

- Continuing to spend excessive amounts of time in metaverse worlds, even though you know it's causing problems in your life, such as poor performance at school or work, or letting household responsibilities go.

- Displaying signs of irritability, anxiety, or anger when forced to leave metaverse worlds, even for brief periods of time.

- Lying to others about the extent of your metaverse use.

- Needing more metaverse time to get the same level of enjoyment.

- Neglecting your appearance, including lack of interest in physical-world grooming or clothing.

WILL THE METAVERSE *CAUSE* A LONELINESS PANDEMIC?

Clinical psychologist, author, and professor at MIT Sherry Turkle says, "Technology is seductive when what it offers meets our human vulnerabilities. And as it turns out, we are very vulnerable indeed. We are lonely but fearful of intimacy. Digital connections and the sociable robot may offer the illusion of companionship without the demands of friendship. Our networked life allows us to hide from each other, even as we are tethered to each other. We'd rather text than talk."[34]

Turkle is deeply concerned about the human cost of being disconnected in our real, physical human lives. Networks such as the metaverse will be seductive, she believes.

"If we are always on, we may deny ourselves the rewards of solitude. As we distribute ourselves, we may abandon ourselves," she notes.

She goes on to describe the impact of technology on human dialogue and relationship building. She advocates that the societal issue of lost conversation be recognized and restored.

> There's been an assault on conversation. Our children are less likely to be willing to sit at a dinner table and talk to us.
>
> I think that this metaverse thing plays into, maybe I could just meet friends in this place where I'd have a perfect body and a perfect face. And if I said the wrong thing, I could just leave. It plays into this feeling of fragility.
>
> So I think it's playing into exactly what's going to make us feel ultimately *more* lonely, because in the end, this friendship without the demands of real intimacy is not really what makes people feel less alone . . . it isn't the same as sitting across the table from someone and saying, how are you? What's been going on? Even a telephone call where someone can hear the catch in your voice.
>
> I'm interested in why are we letting ourselves get fascinated by going to space, going to the metaverse? Time to be interested in our children, ourselves, our agency, our earth, our relationships.[35]

While the metaverse may be the gateway to an even more lonely existence for some, for others, it could be a tool for new and innovative ways to enhance communication with other humans. The difference resides in people who care about each other and mindfully put human relationships first—using metaverse technology as an innovative tool, rather than allowing it to foster isolation and inattention.

THE METAVERSE MAY *PREVENT* LONELINESS

On the brighter side, in 2020, Nextdoor released results from global scientific research partnered with universities.[36] The most promising finding is this: knowing *as few as six of your neighbors* reduces the likelihood of feeling lonely and is linked to lower depression and social anxiety.

The study examined how meaningful connections and small acts of kindness help to combat feelings of loneliness, quality of life, and well-being.

The metaverse may help combat loneliness among the elderly, disabled, and those who are not able to leave their homes for any reason. VR will enable virtual travel, meetups, exercise, watching movies together, providing a new level of immersive connection, bringing together friends, neighbors, and experiences across the globe—but only *if people have access* to the metaverse and its required tools.

SIMULATED HUMAN HUGS UNDER DEVELOPMENT

Touch is an important part of the metaverse, to communicate emotion, creating a sensation to enhance human communication and a shared experience. From wearable devices to deviceless solutions, the opportunity for metaverse haptics will significantly enhance the opportunity for human connection.

For example, innovators are working on a device—not yet on the market—that emits a force field to create a simulated human response without devices being required.

Cox Communications rolled out "The Hug Project," helping loved ones to embrace with a virtual hug no matter the distance. Partnering with technology innovator CuteCircuit, Cox manufactured an innovative wearable "HugShirt" programmed to simulate a human hug. Haptic sensors in the shirt connect two people. Isolated individuals will be able to feel the touch of a person just as if they are there with them.

The shirts were designed after analyzing dozens of hugs—and mapping hand positions with sensors and haptic actuators designed to give and receive the sensation of touch.

When the HugShirt connects to a Bluetooth-enabled phone running the HugShirt app, a connection forms, allowing users to send custom-made or preset hugs in real time from anywhere in the world.[37] Each hug is unique, driven by the user.

LEADERS WILL COUNTER THE LONELINESS EPIDEMIC

The loneliness epidemic, combined with the five Ds, provides a wake-up call for leaders, and everyone concerned with the quality of human life on planet Earth. Leaders are human beings, not avatars. As such, leaders *never* are perfect and *always* have lots to learn. Our burgeoning metaverse presents exciting learning opportunities as we journey together into the unfamiliar.

To conquer the five Ds and loneliness, leaders can and *must* foster human connectivity, moving us forward in the metaverse:

From	To
Distraction	Purpose, focus, and full attention
Distrust	Trust, credibility, and truth
Disinterest	Engagement
Disconnection	Participation
Disenfranchisement	Belonging and empathy
Loneliness	Being part of a community

Effective leadership, strategy, and community building are critical for fostering human relationships on planet Earth. We have *a lot* to explore.

REFLECTION QUESTIONS

1. How can leaders *and* organizations use the metaverse in a positive way for good, to overcome loneliness throughout the world, at all levels of society?

2. As the metaverse evolves, how can leaders cultivate a sense of belonging within their teams, organizations, and community groups?

3. What mental health and safety boundaries need to be created for the metaverse, as well as taught to people of all ages, starting at early childhood? How can *you* make a difference?

A QUICK BREATHER

ARE YOU STILL WITH ME? I know I've thrown a bunch of new terminology and concepts your way. It's a lot to take in. It may even be a bit scary or overwhelming, figuring out how the metaverse fits within your organization or leadership strategy.

If it's any consolation, I too was a bit overwhelmed as I began my journey into the metaverse. What I've found is that like any social technology, it's not a one-size-fits-all. The metaverse will provide a sliding scale of purposes and immersion.

For some organizations, it will be this large immersive world where employees put on VR headsets and go to work in a completely virtual office. For others it might simply be weekly virtual meetups where 3D and VR features are incorporated.

It will be up to you and your team to discover if—and when—a metaverse will support your organization's purpose and goals.

But now that we've taken a breather, let's strap back in and get a bit more specific. Up to this point we have been focused on defining key terms and establishing where we are today regarding the digital world around us. Let's now shift our focus and talk specifically about the metaverse, but through the lens of leadership.

We'll review classic leadership theories, examine leadership styles, and explore three leadership skills needed for success in our evolving metaverse world. I'll share how you can grow these much-needed leadership skills as you prepare for the metaverse.

Here we go!

CHAPTER 6

LENS 1: EFFECTIVE LEADERSHIP IN THE METAVERSE

IF YOU ARE GOING TO BE an effective leader, you'll need to be a metaverse early adopter.

If you've made it this far, you are well on your way. By mastering three leadership capacities, you'll be prepared for the sea change ahead. Or at least you'll be at the top of the metaverse iceberg.

In just a few years, the metaverse is expected to be in full force.

In fact, the word "hybrid" does not really capture the immersive realm of the metaverse, and how we will fluidly transcend physical and digital worlds.

Most leaders today say they don't know much about the metaverse. They're certainly not anticipating the daily impact of this brave new seamless, immersive, always-on hybrid world. Instead, they're coping with lingering fallout from the pandemic, including workforce and supply chain shortages.

The remainder of this book is dedicated to helping you create your own blend of metaverse brilliance as a leader, strategist, and community builder. Whether your organization develops a metaverse presence or not, you will need to be prepared to foster a new level of trust, engagement, participation, belonging, empathy, and community—and fight the loneliness epidemic and five Ds.

ON YOUR MARK . . .

The metaverse *will* change the way we engage with one another in ways we don't yet understand.

Still, you may scoff. You may think the metaverse is pure nonsense—a fantasyland full of avatars and holograms. While you may be skeptical, I challenge you to be open-minded. Think big picture and don't dismiss the winds of change. Remember, evidence to date makes it clear that—

- Our world is volatile, uncertain, complex, and ambiguous.

- Global companies and people are investing billions of dollars into the metaverse.

- Our world *is* becoming *more* digital.

- Hybrid is *not* going away.

- People are spending more time online, for work, information, and social interaction.

- The metaverse is expected to provide a more immersive internet experience filled with visual data. As a result, the metaverse will become a critical information lifeline, seamlessly integrated into everyday life.

- Research shows that visualization works from a human perspective because we respond to and process visual data better than any other type of data. The human brain processes images 60,000 times faster than text, and 90 percent of information transmitted to the brain is visual.[1]

GET SET: *YOUR* LEADERSHIP MATTERS

Your effective leadership is needed in the metaverse.

Effective leadership—or the lack of it—always impacts how followers navigate change. With metaverse technology being so new, you should aim to be effective, not perfect.

Leadership is not considered to be a position, but a *process* that occurs through organizations, communities, and societies. Leadership mobilizes people toward a common purpose.[2] Leadership is *not only* about doing things right, but leadership is also about *doing the right things.*[3]

In the metaverse, you must be human-focused, able to bring together people from physical and digital worlds. Effective metaverse leaders will help humans create purposeful and strong human bonds that lead to real-world impact on planet Earth.

Humans will hunger for meaningful human interaction—the one thing that even the most mesmerizing 3D fantasy worlds won't be able to fully satisfy.

The metaverse will expose old-model, inept leaders who fail to engage their communities in new ways. If you are operating under the old corner-office model of hierarchy, you will miss opportunities to fully engage in the metaverse with people who need you, and your human presence.

Take heart—most of us are metaverse beginners. You will need to relearn how to become an effective leader at three levels: leading yourself, leading others, and leading a community.[4]

In the metaverse, when you lead yourself, you're learning how to monitor your own leadership behavior. You're also discovering how to take the physical "you" and translate this persona in the virtual worlds. While that may seem like a no-brainer, creating an online personality that is authentic and personable isn't always intuitive. You will learn how to monitor your own virtual leadership behavior, such as how you behave when you're embodied by an avatar.

When you lead others, you're learning how to create a community environment that motivates participants and helps them realize *their* potential. You're learning how to give effective feedback and how to engage people when they may be hundreds or thousands of miles away. Sometimes, this will require you to conduct difficult, constructive conversations.

When you lead a community, whether it is digital, or in person, or hybrid, you're learning how to create effective group collaboration, action, and results. You're bringing together people who otherwise might not have come together in the same digital or physical space, including people who may come from different backgrounds, cultures, and societal norms.

In the metaverse, people will expect communication to be immersive, entertaining, and proficient. *You* will make the difference.

GO! LEADERSHIP SKILLS NEEDED IN THE METAVERSE

The integration of physical and digital worlds creates urgency for a sharpened leadership mindset and skills. This is a metaverse learning journey, not a quick accomplishment or overnight sensation. The journey requires you to personally invest time into this new medium.

Effective leaders in the metaverse will build and demonstrate the following three capacities:

1. **Create purpose and focus by leading with strategy and agility.**

You will need strategy plus agility to navigate constant change, adjust the course when needed, and help people cope with a persistent, hybrid metaverse environment.

- Strategy focuses on combining purpose and big-picture thinking with bringing many pieces of an organization's puzzle together. Strategy provides purpose and focus.

- Agility results in swift decision-making at the operational level. Strategy plus agility unifies and quickly mobilizes a distributed group, or scattered workforce.

2. Earn and build trust by being authentic.

You, the trusted leader, will seek, speak, and live the truth—in both the physical and digital worlds.

- Trusted leaders build healthy, truthful, and participative communities. They build people up, rather than tear people down.

- Trusted leaders are ethical, bona fide leaders who build credible records of service to others.

- You, the trusted leader, will demonstrate transparency and authenticity.

3. Develop community within your groups, clubs, work teams, departments, companies, and boards by nurturing kind, compassionate human relationships, and by growing your hybrid community building, bonding, and bridging skills.

People-focused leaders build participative communities and a culture of people who care about their fellow human beings, connecting physical and digital worlds in a meaningful way.

- You build shared purpose, values, and goals. Your bonding skills are important for creating a cohesive community. Your bridging and linking skills are vital for creating new resources and teamwork with external organizations.

- You are growing your capacity to care about humans, taking deliberate steps such as welcoming people into your community and helping them feel like they belong and have a purpose there.

- You are upskilling your capacity to be a hybrid facilitator of people, content, and technology. This is a tall order, because it means you're eliminating wasted minutes of fumbling around with technology glitches. You are facilitating productive, inclusive conversations that build civil discourse. You are encouraging respectful, constructive dialogue and debate while welcoming different points of view, and helping people refuse polarization, isolation, and opinion echo chambers prevalent on social media.

- You are providing kind, compassionate, and human-focused leadership rather than being solely technology-driven.

A LEGACY OF LEADERSHIP THEORIES

Leaders throughout history have shaped our planet, and a rich legacy of leadership theories, based on years of research, provides a solid foundation of understanding from which to update principles, practices, and skills needed for the metaverse.

Leadership icon John W. Gardner, who served as president of the Carnegie Corporation and US secretary of health, education, and welfare from 1965 to 1968, spoke these profound words to describe the impact of leaders:

> Leaders have a significant role in creating the state of mind
> that is the society. They can serve as symbols of the moral
> unity of the society. They can express the values that hold

the society together. Most important, they can conceive and articulate goals that lift people out of their petty preoccupations, and carry them above the conflicts that tear a society apart and unite them in the pursuit of objectives worthy of their best efforts.[5]

Here are a few important lessons learned during the past two centuries of leadership study:

- Leadership is a complex, interactive process involving behavioral, relational, and situational elements.

- Leadership is not found solely in the leader but occurs at individual, two-way, group, and organizational levels.

- Leadership is bottom-up (promoted upward from lower organizational levels) as much as it is top-down (promoted downward from higher levels).

- Leadership occurs internally in an organization, with internal stakeholders, as well as externally with community stakeholders.[6]

The topic of leadership has been formally studied since 1841. Numerous theories and styles have been researched and articulated in an attempt to understand leaders and their complex behavior. These leadership theories do not operate in isolation, but most often are found in combination.

Our understanding of what makes an effective leader continues to evolve. We know that leaders must be change-oriented.

Harvard professor and bestselling author John Kotter emphasizes that *navigating change is the primary function* of leadership—that is, being able to set direction and ensure alignment. Change, by definition, requires creating a new system and then institutionalizing new approaches.[7]

The metaverse will certainly bring the need for leaders to create new systems and approaches.

Scholar Kurt Lewin paints a mental picture of this by describing organizational change as an ice block frozen in time, until leaders melt the old ways, create a new culture, and refreeze the changes, establishing the new norm.[8] Lewin envisions change as a continuous process, not static.

To help us understand where leadership is going in the metaverse, let's briefly look back at the prominent leadership theories that brought us to today.

Pre-1900s

Great man theory was introduced in the nineteenth century. The great man theory promoted the philosophy that history was shaped by the leadership of influential great men.[9] Sadly, it's notable that there is no mention of great women during this nineteenth-century time period.

1900-1940s

Environmental theory focused on the relationship between the emergence of a great leader and the environment—being in the right time, place, and circumstance.[10]

Trait theory posited that leaders are endowed with superior qualities, or traits that differentiate leaders from followers. These traits are evident and are able to be identified.[11]

Behavioral theories focused on leadership behaviors and the interactive effect of leaders and followers on each other. Behavioral theories suggest that leaders can be developed, based on learnable behaviors.[12]

Psychoanalytic leadership theories focused on the interaction of leader personalities and situations, such as the "leader as a father figure" example, where the leader provides the follower with a source of love or fear, as an embodiment of the superego.[13]

Situational leadership and contingency theories focused on the situational context of a leader. Similar to environmental theory, these theories examine how a leader's effectiveness, success, or failure is directly determined by the specific situation.[14]

Laissez-faire leadership is defined as a hands-off style of empowering individuals, groups, or teams to make decisions. Laissez-faire is a French phrase for "let it be." This style of leadership provides followers with individual freedom of choice and action. For example, construction of the US transcontinental railroad serves as a laissez-faire type of project. No single leader was responsible for building the North American railway system. However, the combination of presidential directives, congressional support, and private enterprise collaboration resulted in a monumental project. The track extended thousands of miles from coast to coast and to this day remains unprecedented.[15]

1950s–1970s

Exchange theories include transactional leadership and leader-member exchange, or LMX. These theories see social interaction as a form of exchange in which group members make contributions at a cost to themselves and receive rewards at a cost to the group or other members.[16]

Interaction-expectation theories examined action, interaction, and expectancy reinforcement with followers.[17]

Humanistic theories examined the development of effective and cohesive organizations. Human beings, by nature, are motivated.[18]

Perceptual and cognitive theories (including **attribution theory**) posited that in order to understand a leader's behavior, we must go inside the person's head. Related theories include leadership as human problem-solving, in which shared problem spaces exists;[19] systems analysis, which focuses on the leader's role in the larger organizational context, embedded in a systems point of view;[20] and the rational-deductive approach, helping a leader determine if participative or directive leadership is most rational for the situation.[21]

Transactional leadership theory was first discussed by sociologist Max Weber and later expanded upon by Bernard M. Bass. Transactional leadership theory posits that people perform at their best when the chain of command is definite and clear. Transactional leadership examines leadership as an exchange between management and employees, and the impact of supervision on group and organizational performance.

Transformational leadership theory was strongly influenced by James McGregor Burns, who wrote a bestselling book about political leadership.[22] Burns said that "transforming leadership" appeals to the moral values of followers, energy, and resources to reform institutions. Burns's definition of transforming leadership emphasizes an active process in which both leaders and followers raise one another to higher levels of motivation and morality.

Servant leadership theory was coined by Robert K. Greenleaf. The servant-leader is a servant first, serving others and ensuring their needs are met. The servant-leader shares power and puts the needs of others before their own, helping people develop and perform as highly as possible.[23]

Charismatic leadership theory is grouped with transformational leadership theories. Charismatic leaders inspire excitement and commitment among followers. While charismatic leaders may enhance productivity, the negative side of this leadership style is overreliance on the leader, as well as charismatic leaders who become egocentric, narcissistic, autocratic, and invincible.[24]

1980s–Today

Participative leadership theory (also called shared leadership and democratic leadership) suggests that the ideal leadership style is one that includes participant input. Participative leaders share power and influence rather than centralizing it in the hands of a single individual who acts as a dominant superior.

Participative leaders invite contributions from group members. They help group members to feel relevant and committed to the decision-making process. This improves commitment and increases collaboration, leading to business success.[25] Shared leadership encourages transparency, a safe environment for discussing ideas, and supports autonomy and independent thinking and contributions.[26]

Shared leadership can falter in situations where speed or efficiency is essential. During a crisis, for instance, a team can waste valuable time gathering input, especially when team members lack knowledge or expertise to provide high quality input.[27]

Ethical leadership theory combines standards that reflect a comprehensive, universal set of values including justice, fairness, and equity. Ethical standards contribute to the overarching objective of a leader's duty to fulfill the public interest.[28] Ethical leadership includes a commitment to the mission and values of the organization, and knowing one's self as a leader.[29]

Authentic leadership theory begins with developing personal authenticity that in turn increases self-awareness and courage. Authenticity, by definition, involves being true to oneself—not trying to please others.[30]

Authentic leaders display a high degree of emotional intelligence, building from a deep knowledge of oneself that provides the capacity to nurture others. This nurturing helps others cope with change and the resulting sense of loss when change occurs.[31]

Authentic leaders exhibit confidence, hope, optimism, resiliency, and a dedication to developing leadership capabilities in others as they prepare for change. Authentic leaders set high moral and ethical standards for themselves and others. This leads to higher organizational performance, because authentic leadership helps people find meaning and connection in work through a more optimistic, ethical climate.

Adaptive leadership theory is defined as leadership that adapts and responds in complex environments where incomplete information, ever-changing networks, and tension exist.[32] Adaptive leaders address unpredictable and sometimes unexplainable external and internal dynamics with flexibility.[33]

The following theories are related to adaptable leadership.

Complexity leadership theory is a model of leadership grounded *not* in bureaucracy, but in complexity. Complexity leadership theory seeks to foster complex, adaptive system and informal network dynamics while at the same time enabling structure.[34]

Open systems learning is both a practice and a culture where organizations are open to learning from the external environment and adapting as needed.[35]

Chaos theory focuses on the chaos of nature and ecosystems woven together that purposefully create a new order of ecosystem or organizational structure.[36]

Learning theories focus on the ability to adapt to new situations by inspiring curiosity and new discovery.[37]

Strategic leadership theory emphasizes that leaders can create a sense of urgency by monitoring the external environment and by identifying threats and opportunities for the organization.[38] Strategic leadership is a practice in which executives develop a vision for their organization that enables it to adapt to or remain competitive during continual change.

This includes determining long-term objectives and priorities, assessing current strengths and weaknesses, identifying core competencies, evaluating the need for a major change in strategy, identifying promising strategies, evaluating the likely outcomes of a strategy, and involving other executives in selecting a strategy.[39]

The need for strategic leadership is greater when an organization faces an uncertain environment including times of crisis. A leader's ability to influence change depends on *time and circumstance*.[40] When strategic leadership encourages democratic governance, it fosters collaboration, group engagement, and idea sharing.[41]

Agile leadership is not a theory, but an operational style and leadership mindset.

Agility helps organizations to accomplish work in rapid cycles of thinking and doing, closely aligned to processes of creativity and accomplishment. Leaders encourage and facilitate a continual learning process.

A rapid iteration of thinking, doing, and learning supports the organization's ability to innovate and operate in an agile way, according to McKinsey & Company.[42]

For example, at the team level, agile organizations radically reinvent the working model, moving away from top-down, "waterfall," and "stage gate" project management approaches featuring bureaucratic decision-making. At the enterprise level, organizations deploy a rapid-cycle model to accelerate strategic thinking and execution. Rather than traditional annual planning, budgeting, and review, some organizations are moving to quarterly cycles, dynamic management systems such as objectives and key results (OKRs), and rolling twelve-month budgets.

Agile leadership abilities include the following:

- Leading and facilitating the creation of purpose and strategy for the organization
- Creating a network of empowered teams
- Leading and creating rapid decision and learning cycles

- Igniting passion in people and creating a cohesive community

- Enabling next-generation technology[43]

If modern technology has taught us anything, it's that the pace of change is increasing at lightning speed. Those stuck in their ways go the way of the dinosaur.

As the metaverse evolves, your leadership capacity will evolve. Now is the time to build three critical leadership skills you'll need in the metaverse.

METAVERSE LEADERSHIP SKILL 1: THE AGILE STRATEGIC LEADER

The agile strategic leader combines nimbleness with being strategic and strategy-driven. This brings clarity and purpose to organizations, connecting physical and digital worlds. Agile strategic leaders create clear direction and the ability to swiftly respond to market conditions.

Agile strategic leaders facilitate participative teamwork. They guide their organizations to continuously monitor the external and internal environments to seek opportunities and minimize risks. They create and effectively communicate a clear and compelling case for change, dialoguing with stakeholders. With frequent environmental scanning, agile strategic leaders and their organizations are nimble and prepared to adapt to change while keeping the vision in sight.

How You Can Become an Agile Strategic Leader

To become an agile strategic leader, you must be future-oriented—one eye on external trends, and the other on your organization's strategy—having the organization's big picture in clear view.

All this means is that you are perceptive to trends in the external environment, and that you understand the potential impact of those trends on your organization. (We'll discuss open, agile strategy in more depth in chapter 7.)

First, you must understand the dynamics of your external environment, including market competitors in both physical and digital worlds.

➡️ GROW THIS SKILL

Use my metaverse PESTLE worksheet and have your team describe the political, economic, socioeconomic, technological, legal, and environment trends that impact your world, your industry, and your organization.

PESTLE ANALYSIS Metaverse Worksheet

	Top Trends: physical & digital	Implications: physical & digital	Potential Strategies/ Actions: physical & digital
Political	• (list)	• (note implications)	• For each implication, describe potential strategies or actions
Economic	• (list)	• (note implications)	• For each implication, describe potential strategies or actions
Socioeconomic	• (list)	• (note implications)	• For each implication, describe potential strategies or actions
Technological	• (list)	• (note implications)	• For each implication, describe potential strategies or actions
Legal	• (list)	• (note implications)	• For each implication, describe potential strategies or actions
Environmental	• (list)	• (note implications)	• For each implication, describe potential strategies or actions

You must also be aware of your organization's *internal* capacities and shortfalls in both physical and digital worlds. You must be open-minded, seeking diverse input from all areas of the organization to understand your organization's strengths, weaknesses, opportunities, and threats (SWOT), and compare observations with your competition's physical–digital SWOT.

→ GROW THIS SKILL

Use my metaverse SWOT worksheet and ask your team to describe your organization's strengths, weaknesses, opportunities, and threats. Ask your team to keep in mind your organization's top competitors when completing this worksheet, doing their best to assess both physical and digital worlds.

Metaverse SWOT Analysis Worksheet

	Strengths		Weaknesses	
I N T E R N A L	**Physical world** ♦ List in bullets... succinct descriptions. ♦ ♦ ♦ ♦	**Digital world** ♦ List in bullets... succinct descriptions. ♦ ♦ ♦ ♦	**Physical world** ♦ List in bullets... succinct descriptions. ♦ ♦ ♦ ♦	**Digital world** ♦ List in bullets... succinct descriptions. ♦ ♦ ♦ ♦
	Opportunities		Threats	
E X T E R N A L	**Physical world** ♦ List in bullets... succinct descriptions. ♦ ♦ ♦ ♦	**Digital world** ♦ List in bullets... succinct descriptions. ♦ ♦ ♦ ♦	**Physical world** ♦ List in bullets... succinct descriptions. ♦ ♦ ♦ ♦	**Digital world** ♦ List in bullets... succinct descriptions. ♦ ♦ ♦ ♦

Equally important, if you are going to become an agile strategic leader, you must grow your ability to facilitate inclusion and welcome participation, openness, and vulnerability. You must be an excellent listener—which is easier said than done. These are important leadership skills you'll need to become agile and strategic.

➡ GROW THIS SKILL

Host strategy meetings with your team or core group of leaders. Have small teams present the findings of the PESTLE and SWOT worksheets. Discuss how the findings impact your physical–digital metaverse world. Develop and prioritize action steps to gain advantage over your competition.

Thankfully, there's no perfect strategy—just as there are no perfect leaders.

Agile strategic leaders know that no single individual person owns the strategy playbook for success. To be both agile and strategic takes a wide array of viewpoints from a broad stakeholder base, plus relevant data, to set the stage for shaping strategy.

Use clear, compelling, and consistent communication in both physical and digital hybrid worlds.

Synthesize and simplify to succinctly communicate your organization's strategic future. Clearly communicate the direction of the organization, including the competitive strategy, top priorities and goals, and the most important issues and ideas.

Agile strategic leaders distill, synthesize, and simplify complex information. They capture the attention of a highly distracted, distributed workplace. They provide focus and clarity, bringing many pieces of information from the physical and digital worlds together under one umbrella.

Clear, strategic communication ensures the entire organization is focused on the same direction. This shared understanding of the direction is sometimes called "creating one truth" for the organization.

Global search firm Heidrick & Struggles found that 67 percent of high-accelerating organizations had embraced simplicity in their strategy, operating model, and culture.[44] This is especially important for considering how the metaverse will create many worlds, and each of those worlds will be operating under their separate "one truth" for that one organization.

Strategies often fail because of a leader's failure to communicate the strategy in a way that is understandable, compelling, and actionable. Metaverse users will expect to be entertained, and therefore leaders must improve their ability to communicate using vital, visual, and visible techniques (see chapter 9).

→ GROW THIS SKILL

Take the one-minute strategy communication challenge. Review your organization's strategic plan or strategy for the future. Create a one-minute presentation. Sift out the most important information, including your purpose, mission, and top three initiatives or goals.

Practice your one-minute presentation. Keep polishing it until you are happy with the results. You are now prepared to give a succinct elevator speech when describing your company's future.

Be committed to making every conversation count. That means your metaverse meetings (physical and digital) are impeccably organized. Put your focus on the content and quality of discussion, not on the technology, whether speaking with one person, a small group, the entire organization, or a community. Create a simple agenda for each of your meetings—whether formal or informal meetings.

Improve your ability to transcend physical and digital worlds. Aim for consistency in messaging, meeting structure, and opportunities for human connection. The metaverse is new and requires lots of experimentation—so have fun as you get comfortable traversing worlds and discovering what works and what doesn't.

Take a participative approach. Participation, diverse input, and use of solid data will prepare you to lead with agile strategy.

Agile strategic leaders are decisive. They test new strategies in unchartered waters and quickly pivot as needed. This test-and-learn agile approach requires both agility and humility that is always looking forward, being both strategic and authentic, adaptive and collaborative at the same time.

Agile strategic leaders develop an organization culture of decision-making based on evidence and calculated hunches. This requires an ongoing process of environmental scanning and strategy assessment—processes that will be supported by metaverse immersive experiences and analytic technology.

Roselinde Torres, senior partner emeritus of Boston Consulting Group, was ahead of her time when she shared her TED Talk about taking courageous leaps. She could have been talking about the metaverse.

She says that "great leaders are those who are preparing themselves *not* for the comfortable predictability of yesterday, but for the realities of today, and also those unknown possibilities of tomorrow."

She goes on to say that key to developing agile strategy is including diversity of insight:

> Great leaders understand that having a more diverse network is a source of pattern identification at different levels, and also of solutions because you have people thinking differently than you are.
>
> What is your capacity to develop relationships with people very different from you? This could be biological, physical, functional, political, cultural, socio-economic . . . and yet, despite all these differences, people connect with you, and they trust you enough to cooperate with you and achieve a shared goal.[45]

→ GROW THIS SKILL

Create and lead an interdisciplinary strategy community of practice.
Cast a wide net for strategy participation. Actively recruit strategic
input.

This allows an organization and its leaders to be proactive, participative, and nimble in adjusting strategy when needed—timely choices
that differentiate an organization from competitors and achieve superior market results.

By creating a cross-departmental community, you'll create a powerful, multiperspective lens for strategy shaping and problem-solving.
Invite participants to engage their employees when possible, such as
finding solutions to address a major challenge. Diversity includes not
only demographics including age, race, gender, economic status, and
ethnic background, but also geographic location (such as global versus
national or local), community participation, industry sector, organizational type, professional skill, level of management seniority, and
constituent type (such as customer, or supplier).

Diverse input is critically important to reinventing strategy and
community building during times of uncertainty and constant change.
Agile strategic leaders actively seek wisdom from a wide variety of
front-line, boots-on-the-ground operational perspectives, knowing
that no one person or skill set has the playbook.

Agile strategic leaders incorporate diverse insights—the wisdom of
the crowd, which creates the effect of a gigantic think tank of experts
from different perspectives. They are inclusionary and interdisciplinary, seeking the viewpoints of customers, suppliers, employees,
donors, board members, and other stakeholders.

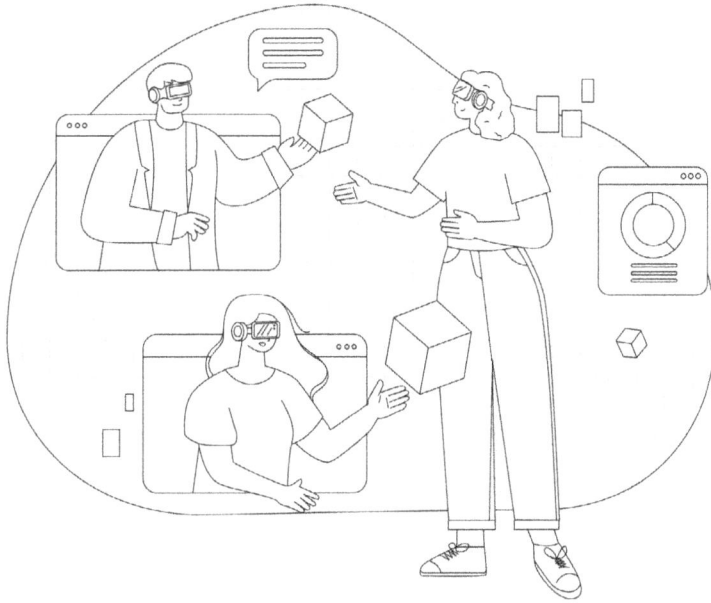

Agile strategic leaders are skilled at inviting contributions. Similar to an investigative news reporter, agile strategic leaders know how to get beyond petty chatter to ask important strategy questions followed by listening to a diverse array of input, ideas, and opinions. They have built skills in asking questions, listening, and summarizing the input so that participants know they are heard, and that their voice counts.

Include data analysis. Compile data and bring it to your strategy sessions when needed.

Often the financial analysts and data sources are noticeably missing from the strategy table. Data supports decisiveness. Use the metaverse (or available technology) to spotlight and discuss your organization's key data, such as performance metrics, in an immersive experience.

Include employees from across your organization who are data experts. For example, this could include department directors, operational experts, and those crunching operational data.

Convene the group on a periodic basis to discuss strategic issues, review goal dashboard performance, discuss data, and turn it into strategic insight. Ask data experts to help moderate the sharing sessions. Invite internal and external speakers to share trends, creating windows to the future.

Practice using metaverse technology to discuss the direction of your organization or community. Share "what-if" scenarios and play those situations as metaverse games.

Grow your metaverse convening and consensus-building skills, bringing together physical and digital discussions. As the field of strategy has developed, strategic leaders must also grow in the skills needed to bring together diverse stakeholder groups and combine input to solve complex problems.

➡️ GROW THIS SKILL

Ask your strategy participants to help moderate community-of-practice sharing sessions in the metaverse, as well as plan for internal and external speakers. This can build agile strategy and metaverse experience throughout an organization.

Develop a small strategy group to monitor metaverse and strategy best practices. This is a new frontier. Metaverse strategy exercises will grow over time.

Expand your capacity to build upbeat, exciting strategy meetings and events. Create new techniques to welcome individuals to your meetings, metaverse spaces, and events. Inspire your team with an information-packed opening message.

Always plan your meeting wrap-ups. Provide an inspirational ending for all of your metaverse meetings. Recap next steps. Thank people for their contributions.

Become an expert at leading hybrid meetings, using technology tools to help you gather data. The tools are constantly changing.

Experiment with hosting meetings in a more immersive technology environment if your organization is not already exploring the metaverse. For example, get familiar with webinar and digital whiteboard technology.

Do not be intimidated if you are a hybrid-meeting newcomer— seek training and find mentors. Many leaders *still* are not proficient at leading conversations and creating a strong sense of community in a hybrid world. Upscale your metaverse techniques as new technology becomes available.

METAVERSE LEADERSHIP SKILL 2: THE AUTHENTIC LEADER

Authentic leaders in the metaverse will create truth. They will foster trust and transparency—*not* lies. They are consistent and will do what they say.

While it may seem obvious that authenticity is key when it comes to being a good leader, creating an authentic digital presence isn't always easy. If you've ever recorded yourself and then watched it, you've probably noticed that oftentimes your voice or behavior changes.

While the subtle change of your voice is no big deal, you want to make sure you're not changing who you are just because you're interacting through a digital medium. Being an authentic leader means learning how to make your digital persona just as smart, empathetic, professional, and human as your in-person self.

Most importantly, authentic leaders don't hide behind metaverse avatars. In both physical and digital worlds, they don't misrepresent themselves, or try to trick others with a fake or misleading identity. Authentic leaders provide a respite from the constant bombardment of fakes, cyberattacks, polarized opinions, and rising extremism.

However, authentic leaders know that they are far from perfect. They admit their mistakes and learn to do better. They stay current with ethics training. They are on the alert to spot and prevent ethical dilemmas—either personally, or for their organizations.

Authentic leaders in the metaverse will provide a voice of reason and serve as a critical force against the five Ds. Leading theories of authentic leadership emphasize four dimensions.[46] These four leadership qualities will help us grapple with balancing physical–digital lives in the unchartered metaverse.

- **Self-awareness:** Understanding how you make meaning of the world and how that meaning-making process affects self-image over time; awareness of strengths, weaknesses, your multifaceted nature, and your impact on others.

- **Relational transparency:** Presenting your authentic self to others; promoting trust through disclosure, information sharing, and the expression of true thoughts and feelings.

- **Balanced processing:** Objective analysis of all relevant data before making decisions; a willingness to solicit and consider views that challenge your own.

- **Internalized moral perspective:** Self-regulation guided by internal moral standards and values rather than external standards; behaving and making decisions consistent with these internalized values.

How You Can Become an Authentic Leader

Research shows that leader trust is based on three essential qualities:

- Genuine concern for other human beings
- Personal integrity
- Personal abilities or competence[47]

Followers who trust a leader are willing to be vulnerable to the leader's actions because they are confident that their rights and interests will not be abused.[48] Related dimensions of trust include integrity, competence, consistency, loyalty, and openness.

In the metaverse, trusted leaders will seek truth and expose lies or disinformation. Their words (what they say) are consistent with their actions (what they do). Trusted leaders are not conspiracy theorists spinning webs of lies.

While they are optimists, authentic leaders also are realists. They don't gloss over the facts or put a false spin on information. This authenticity builds resiliency, helping team members have real conversations, deal with tough times, and problem-solve with grit and fortitude—not just metaverse fun and games.

Be authentic and empathic with yourself.

We cannot give what we don't have. Self-empathy and self-care are essential for building your capacity to live your best, most authentic self, supporting your process of getting to know yourself.

➜ GROW THIS SKILL

Practice self-care. Leaders must find the energy to genuinely care about humans—employees, constituents, volunteers, and colleagues. Healthy and happy leaders have a well of capacity from which to draw empathy and compassion for others.

Practice patting yourself on the back when you reach a goal or get something done, even if it's not perfect in your mind.

Show genuine concern for other human beings.

Authentic leaders build trusted human relationships in both the physical and digital worlds.

Get to know your team, whether in person or in digital contexts. Knowing people at an individual level is already challenging even in the physical world without adding social media and the metaverse. The metaverse will add complexity to knowing employees and team members.

In both the digital and physical worlds, take time to get to know others, and show them that you care about them. Start your meetings, when possible, with a few minutes of informal, authentic get-to-know-others dialogue. Plan to arrive to your meeting destination five or ten minutes early, to provide an opportunity for others to arrive early and engage in warm-up conversation with you. This allows you, the leader, to show genuine interest in their projects, and demonstrate that you care about their situations at a human level. Use this bit of informal chat to be curious about others, and their wellness.

Here are five questions developed by executive coaches John Baird and Edward Sullivan. These simple, open-ended questions have potential to foster meaningful leader conversations with each individual employee, and are very applicable to the metaverse:[49]

- What need isn't being met?
- What fear holds you back?
- What is really driving (motivating) you?
- What gift is going unexpressed?
- What is your real purpose?[50]

Demonstrate personal integrity. This builds trust.

Lead by example. Share your *own* personal stories about standing up for what is right and handling ethical moments of truth. Find ways to reward and spotlight ethical behavior in your metaverse community or organization.

➡ GROW THIS SKILL

Take the initiative to review your company's ethics policies. Conduct ongoing ethics discussions with your team.

Provide ethics training. Spotlight realistic ethics and "what-if" scenarios—these could be role-played in the metaverse—to reinforce ethics, standards, policies, and procedures.

Inspire confidence in your personal abilities and competence. Sometimes leaders downplay their skills, or they may be managing people who are unaware of their qualifications. Let others see the competence in you.

➡ GROW THIS SKILL

Join your team side by side to personally support the work. Share your valuable expertise and pull from personal experience to show you are a thought leader and have dealt with similar situations. This allows others to see your expertise in action. Don't hold back information; be generous in sharing your insights and wisdom.

Look for opportunities to build your technical skills. The metaverse is going to be an ever-changing medium, and it's important to continuously improve your technical skills, as well as the human skills needed for leading meetings and discussions both in person and virtually.

Share candid, authentic, and unvarnished two-way communication to create a clear, compelling direction. Effective communication must be truthful, timely, and relevant, to cut through clutter, eliminate confusion, and facilitate two-way dialogue, making sure voices are heard.

Demonstrate your competence in communication within the physical and hybrid worlds. Foster participation within a decentralized, distributed environment.

METAVERSE LEADERSHIP SKILL 3: SERVANT LEADER-COMMUNITY BUILDER

I find that interactions in the digital world often lack the normal warmth and consideration found in physical-world interactions. It's not something many of us are conscious of, but it is something of which every leader should be aware.

That's where the idea of the servant leader as a community builder comes into play. This type of leader cares deeply about human beings in the seamless context of both the physical and digital worlds. They are leaders who skillfully bond and bridge physical and digital worlds.

The servant leader-community builder leads by example.

They are champions of diversity, equity, and inclusion. The servant leader-community builder provides psychological safety for their group, team, department, entire organization. That is, the leader fosters a shared belief that their team is safe for interpersonal risk-taking. Team members feel accepted and respected.

In the metaverse, the servant leader-community builder plays a significant role in combatting the loneliness epidemic by demonstrating genuine human empathy, kindness, and compassion, and a servant's heart for community.

Important capacities include the following:

- Facilitation skills to foster interaction, conversation, action, and results.

- Listening skills to genuinely listen with patience and focus, creating a safe and welcoming environment for people to speak for themselves. This includes helping people feel their voices are heard, important, and appreciated.

- Being present with others and in the moment, despite distractions and a distracting world.

- Convening skills, coalescing around issues and encouraging participation of diverse stakeholders to gain understanding of the issues and perspectives examining different points of view.[51]

- Distilling input and translating input into action and results.

How You Can Become a Servant Leader-Community Builder

The servant leader-community builder transverses physical and digital worlds to strengthen human connections—from individuals, to groups, organizations, neighborhoods, communities, cities, and communities of purpose.

In the metaverse, servant leader-community builders put a keen focus on humans, not the technology tools. You can have the coolest, newest, most advanced technology in the world . . . but you need to be able to connect it to the human element.

Community-building leaders are relationship builders. They create social capital—important networks—by bonding, bridging, and linking in both the physical and digital worlds.

Encourage bonding in the metaverse by creating a cohesive internal community.

Servant leader-community builders create bonds within their own organization or group. They create a sense of belonging to a community of interest. They foster inclusion and welcome diversity and opinions of all types, such as background, age, and ethnicity. They help the community or group members get to know each other. Bonding is an internal community-building activity, similar to building relationships within a family.

→ GROW THIS SKILL

Bonding. Leaders should invite members to participate in creating a shared purpose that bonds the group. Ask the community to help your organization or group create a shared purpose, values, and a few goals for the year.

Create ways for community members to get to know each other, to form bonds within the group. Develop an online bonding repository where community members can add their profiles, opting in where their privacy is secure. This also applies to an organization's *intra*net metaverse for employee engagement.

Facilitate conversation that creates a sense of belonging, kindness, and compassion.

Develop a metaverse welcome plan—provide your vision, mission, or purpose and top initiatives for all community members to engage your community. Help them see themselves in your community.

Develop a persistent place where members can visit, learn, and meet each other. Create ways for people to get to know each other, including their skills and insights. Develop a schedule of predictable mixers and forums for gathering, whether digital, physical, or hybrid.

Survey your community (your group, team, department, membership, etc.) to fully understand their hopes, needs, and opportunities for your metaverse and hybrid community.

Break your work into deep-dive metaverse project teams or exploratory committees. Select capable committee chairs or project leads to complete the work.

As mentioned earlier, develop your listening skills. Help people know that they are heard, understood, that they matter, and that they belong—and are welcomed in your metaverse community.

Train and mentor the next generation of leaders in community-building and servant leadership skills.

Build bridges internally and externally in the metaverse.

In traditional community-building terms, bridging has referred to a leader's efforts to create bridges of outreach to connect their group with people, networks, and resources *outside* of an organization. For an example, when a nonprofit leader creates a relationship with a private foundation and cultivates an opportunity to apply for a foundation grant to support the nonprofit's work, this act of outreach and relationship-building is an example of bridging.

The metaverse will create a unique dynamic for organizations: There will be those who engage online, in the metaverse, and never meet other community members in the physical world. There will be some community members who meet up in person. And others will choose to participate in both the physical and digital worlds, as a hybrid option.

➜ GROW THIS SKILL

Bridging. Leaders will need to become proficient at two distinct types of bridging:

- Bridging community members within their organization, bridging together the in-person, digital, and hybrid members.

The idea of creating bridges between an organization's physical, digital, and hybrid communities is new—and is very different from the concept of internal bonding within an organization. Thousands or perhaps millions of community members or fans may connect online. Consider: How might a leader bridge the in-person group with the online group?

Create multiple ways for in-person and online community members to dialogue, learn together, and get to know each other on an asynchronous (when convenient) basis, as well as at live events.

- Bridging the community with external groups and resources, whether these are in person, digital, or hybrid.

Develop and prioritize other work groups and leaders outside of your department or unit with which to build relationships or bridges. Then develop a plan for reaching out to each of these groups and individuals, setting a goal for each relationship, and how it can enhance your group's purpose or scope of work.

Look for ways to connect and collaborate with other people, organizations, and resources that align with and advance the purpose of your organization. Take a strategic approach to reaching out to leaders of other organizations where collaboration is in alignment with building strong communities of purpose.

When metaverse leaders see valuable opportunities to connect and collaborate, they link groups together to introduce new resources. This creates new social capital—valuable networks leading to other forms of capital—among groups *not* previously in communication with each other.

The community-building act of linking creates new networks of trusting relationships between people who are interacting across explicit, formal, or institutionalized power or authority gradients in society.[52] These linked relationships are described as *vertical*. That is, linked relationships are purposeful, and are cultivated between individuals and groups in different social strata in a hierarchy of power, social status, and wealth. The key feature is the difference in social position or power.[53]

For example, a relationship between a community-based organization and a government, or a donor who provides funding, would create a linked power-and-authority connection. The organization complies with formal requirements subject to the relationship, which creates new resources while also featuring a power structure.

➜ GROW THIS SKILL

Linking: Develop and priority-rank a list of influential institutions, funding sources, government leaders, and individuals relevant to your organization's vision, mission, and goals. Research and determine a leader or point person within each of the prioritized organizations with whom you or others in your organization must meet.

Develop an outreach plan for each organization, including a desired outcome for each conversation. If your organization has developed a metaverse, invite your prospective community collaborators to visit your metaverse.

For servant leader-community builders, bridging, bonding, and linking requires an enormous amount of time, focus, and *balance*. This can be extremely challenging.

If a leader spends too much time in bridging and linking activities, internal bonding will suffer. But if the leader spends too much time in bonding activities, external relationships and new resources will fail to be cultivated.

Maintaining a reasonable bonding–bridging balance in the metaverse will be complex and challenging, but critical. Leaders in the metaverse must grow their skills in building both physical and virtual relationships—an evolution of experimenting and agile learning.

LEADERSHIP STYLES INCONGRUENT WITH THE METAVERSE

Authoritarian leaders make decisions independently with little or no input from the rest of the group. Autocratic leadership is an extreme form of transactional leadership, where leaders have complete power over staff. While this is not an effective leadership style for most organizations today, autocratic leadership is typical in military and crisis settings where decisions rely on a chain of command or must be made quickly without dissent.

Bureaucratic leaders follow rules rigorously. They ensure that their staff also follow procedures precisely. This leadership style is common in workplaces involving strict protocols and serious safety risks, such as in military operations, manufacturing, electrical generation and transmission, and situations where machinery, toxic materials, or danger is eminent, or where large sums of financial investment are involved. Bureaucratic leadership is useful in organizations where employees do routine tasks.[54]

REFLECTION QUESTIONS

1. Describe your leadership style. Which of the three needed leadership competencies are most aligned with your existing skills, and why?

2. What metaverse leadership skill would you like to develop? How will you pursue growing this capacity?

3. In your opinion, which is the most difficult community-building activity: bonding, bridging, or linking, and why? Which do you predict will be most challenging in the metaverse, and why?

CHAPTER 7

LENS 2: OPEN, AGILE STRATEGY IN THE METAVERSE

IN THE METAVERSE, STRATEGY-MAKING CANNOT BE slow. It must be agile, open to participation, and not secretive.

Imagine you could test a future world with your metaverse strategy team.

The team selects a scenario, such as a world climate disaster. You hope to stress test the disaster to see the impact of expanding your company into new global markets.

The team goes into the company's metaverse to explore a decision to move the corporate headquarters out of City X and move to either City Y or City Z.

The simulated relocation snowballs into a series of consequences.

The supply chain issues in City Y are catastrophic, according to the 3D graphs appearing as you and your team walk around the potential neighborhood. More visual data about the local labor market floats over the neighborhood, adding an alarming depth of reality. You and your team better understand the financial impact of paying higher salaries and other previously unseen risks.

You motion to the group of frustrated avatars: "Let's get out of here!"

The team pulls out of City Y, and journeys into the world of City Z.

City Z is located at the hub of massive distribution centers, anchored by three universities pumping out local graduates. Then your team moves deeper into the situation and experiments with all of the operational levers and decision factors. The immersive view into City Z provides the best path forward, resolving the crisis.

You emerge from the scene with great relief. Thankfully, this was a simulation. But now you and your team need to get to work, to determine options for how to respond should this situation become a reality.

The metaverse will create immersive problem-solving platforms for decision-making in our volatile, uncertain, complex, and ambiguous world known for its conveyor belt of crises.

As the metaverse evolves, VR and AR technology will support agile decisions, helping us connect operational data with decision-making on a real-time basis.

WHAT IS A STRATEGY?

A strategy is a set of choices designed to achieve a competitively advantaged market position that delivers added value. Strategies help organizations perform different activities that outperform those of rivals or perform similar activities but in different ways to gain a competitive advantage.[1]

A strategy represents high-level guidelines an organization adopts to provide value to its stakeholders and gain an advantage over competitors. Whether these guidelines are deliberately designed or emerge in time, they determine how the rest of the efforts of the organization will be deployed.[2]

The process of strategy shaping is never an exact science with one "right" strategy choice. However, the metaverse is likely to be an incredible tool for organizations to visualize and analyze data and improve the ability to pivot as needed.

The essence of strategy also is what you choose *not* to do. Effective strategy leads to superior economic performance at all levels of an enterprise. That is, strategy is used to guide enterprise, as well as functional and tactical direction.

For example—

- At the enterprise level, strategies guide the vision, customer value proposition, key drivers of success, goals, and objectives.

- At a department or functional level, strategy would guide direction, such as a marketing strategy.

- At the tactical level, strategy would guide an activity or product, such as website design and optimization.

For example, Tesla's enterprise-level purpose and mission is to accelerate the world's transition to sustainable energy. Tesla's aim by 2030 is to sell twenty million electric vehicles (EVs) per year, compared to 0.94 million in 2021, reducing global emissions.[3]

But Tesla's initial enterprise-level strategy didn't focus on mass consumers. Instead, Tesla's strategy aimed at a small, elite audience—the luxury car market. Tesla built the world's first luxury EV car, the Tesla Roadster, in 2008. This luxury EV strategy created intense media buzz and prestige for the brand.

Tesla then focused its strategy on assuring its future by controlling its supply chain at functional and tactical levels. Tesla built an international network of stores, service centers, and Supercharger stations, and developed the largest lithium-ion battery factory in the world. In 2021, Tesla delivered almost one million EVs, reaching scale in selling a mass-consumer EV in at a price range of approximately US $50,000.[4]

An immersive metaverse experience could be created not only for customers and potential car buyers, but also internally for its management team, to illustrate the impact of Tesla's strategy decisions.

WHAT IS OPEN STRATEGY?

Open strategy is a strategic management approach that acknowledges that a diversity of perspectives is essential for shaping a robust, timely, and competitive strategy. This principle states that when you empower employees to contribute to foresight and strategy at all levels of your organization, and invite external input such as customer insight, you increase your organization's ability to anticipate the future and create competitive advantage.

In open strategy, no single person, CEO, or strategy team can know it all. Open strategy has been shown to improve strategy implementation and ownership by employees.[5]

This approach syncs with the ethos of an open and inclusive metaverse.

It takes multiple perspectives and interdisciplinary thinking to address complex problems. Boundary spanning—the ability to develop productive working relationships, credibility, and trust with people *outside* of your immediate work group, department, business unit, or organization—is an essential leadership skill for open strategy formation.

Boundary spanners welcome people with diverse skill sets, perspectives, backgrounds, and experiences to solve big challenges and wicked problems.

A wicked problem is a problem, usually social or cultural, that is profoundly difficult to understand, and is impossible to solve. Not only do wicked problems feature incomplete, contradictory, and changing information, but these are problems that cannot be solved as well. Also, there is no single solution to the problem.

Wicked problems involve numerous stakeholders and varying opinions, and usually carry a tremendous economic burden. Wicked problems may directly impact other problems. For example, poverty is closely related to homelessness, nutrition, health, and education.[6]

Open strategy provides a nimble and comprehensive approach for addressing wicked problems, helping leaders overcome bureaucratic silos that prevent systems thinking.

WHAT IS AGILE STRATEGY?

Agile strategy focuses on short-cycle strategy development and execution. Agile strategy provides an organization with the ability to adapt rapidly and cost-efficiently in prompt response to changes in the business environment, where strategy formation and implementation is an interactive, iterative process.[7]

An agile approach does not equate to reactiveness.

Agile strategy represents a style of short-cycle execution that keeps the long-term vision in view, *balancing the dual need* for organizational stability and response. Organizational agility improves market awareness, responsiveness, speed, flexibility, preparedness, and adaptability in times of constant volatility.[8]

The concept of agile strategy is compatible with the mantra of "failing fast" and pivoting. For example, organizations may experiment with pilot programs to test the market, see what works and what doesn't, and make adjustments.

Metaverse technology could be instrumental in supporting agile strategy pivots. For example, Target rapidly emerged as one of the most successful and profitable retailers allowing customers to buy online and pick up at a local store, thanks to agile strategy prior to and during the COVID-19 pandemic.

Target piloted its Drive Up service in 2018 in the United States. The pilot was expanded to all fifty states by 2019. In 2020, when the pandemic hit, Target agilely scaled fresh, refrigerated, and frozen groceries into the drive-up mix, at more than 1,600 stores across the United States.

Target's Pick Up and Drive Up services, along with the addition of delivery service Shipt, together grew 193 percent during the final two months of 2020. This was prior to the existence of a COVID-19 vaccine. Drive Up grew the fastest, spiking 500 percent and adding nearly $700 million to Target's US sales growth.[9]

Target made improvements to the Drive Up program, introducing the option for customers to pick up products in numbered parking spaces. This accelerated delivery speed and reduced wait times in cars, eliminating the need for Target employees to scan the customer's phone during pick-up.

Think of the possibilities: a metaverse created for Target decision-makers could create the ability to assess retail store locations, store volume, hours of operation, and other variables to help the retailer understand revenue outcomes.

Target also could create a metaverse metaspace for employee customer service training. Appearing as avatars, trainees could practice serving virtual customers, learn policies and safety procedures, and experience a variety of real-life customer service scenarios and challenges.

HOW THE METAVERSE SUPPORTS OPEN, AGILE STRATEGY

Strategy management includes the continuous cycle of all strategy-related activities for an organization to succeed in the long term.

Similar to multiplayer online gaming, the metaverse may introduce an open, agile strategy tool—and a new way for leaders to gather great minds to discuss trends, review performance data, and make fluid decisions.

The combination of open and agile strategy-making offers the promise of helping organizations be nimble and pivot quickly to adapt to frequent changes in both internal and external environments.

The International Association for Strategy Professionals notes five key groups of strategy activities within an organization's entire strategic management process or strategy life cycle. An immersive metaverse experience could bring to life each phase.

The strategy activities include formulating the strategy, implementing or transforming the organization by developing a transformation plan detailing and sequencing the projects that will be required to align the operating model to the new strategy, executing the strategy, engaging employees, and governing the strategy.[10]

By better understanding the strategy framework, leaders can prepare to be agile and innovate metaverse techniques to continuously visit and update activities for the key steps as needed, nonsequentially, based on market conditions.

From Boring to Engaging

No matter how smart technology may seem, strategy shaping is a human decision-making experience. Sudden market changes require that organizations be ready and nimble to respond and engage employees and stakeholders.

The metaverse could bring to life and transform an organization's strategic management system. Imagine the opportunity for a strategic management metaspace within its metaverse. Each phase of the model could feature an immersive experience.

For example, imagine that for each phase of the strategy management process, an organization could feature "submetaspaces" where participants can jump in, discover trends, view issues, explore risks, observe competitors, envision multiple futures for the organization, and update strategy decisions.

Case Study: DXC Technology

IT consulting giant DXC Technology is a Fortune 500 global IT services company operating with more than 130,000 consultants in excess of seventy countries.

DXC Technology hosted its first metaverse sales strategy conference attended by members of its Europe, Middle East, and Africa (EMEA) sales teams.

Approximately 1,300 attendees gathered in a main stage area, followed by a variety of virtual breakout rooms for smaller presentations and discussions. The company created metaverse spaces for business strategy and social interaction, unlimited by physical hotel space and budget.

"Like in the real world, people don't want to be confined to their seats or locked in one space for hours on end. Mix things up and provide people with a variety of spaces and experiences for them to explore and have the chance to network," explains Louise Preedy, director of marketing and communications at DXC Technology EMEA.

She goes on: "We used outdoor spaces including a beach, as well as the expo hall and dance club, and hosted a treasure hunt. Give people the chance to experience those serendipitous moments of running into each other, something that a videoconference can't replicate."

The company learned the importance of setting guardrails for permissions to access conference areas. Someone's avatar mistakenly wandered across the main stage during a presentation.[11]

METAVERSE STRATEGY WORLDS

In the metaverse, strategic thinking could become embedded into an organization's culture and ongoing way of operating. For example, the strategic plan could be brought to life through 3D visuals, digital storytelling, and places where an avatar could jump in and explore the vision and wander through the organization's strategic goals. This immersive experience could create an emotional connection to the long-range accomplishments to be achieved in accordance with the organization's vision and mission.

"People could make decisions in a totally different way to determine a preferred future," notes Cathy Hackl, metaverse author and futurist.[12]

Within an organization's metaverse, leaders could create a dedicated metaspace to communicate the plan to employees and external audiences such as customers.

Cloud-base tracking tools could be incorporated into a strategic management metaverse, creating an exciting experience.[13]

Circling Back: Leadership Styles
Needed for Open, Agile Strategy

- **The agile strategic leader** is focused on the entire strategy cycle, while monitoring performance. The long-term vision and focus on the short-term execution cycle is perfectly matched for leading strategy at each stage of this model.

- **The authentic leader** knows that she or he doesn't know it all. Participation, diversity, and inclusion of insight is critical to the entire process of strategy.

- **The servant leader-community builder** will build internal and external communities of insight, serving the organization by ensuring a comprehensive understanding of trends, issues, and opportunities.

POWER TO THE PEOPLE: AGILITY THROUGH INCLUSION

Today, technology allows employees to have far more insight into what's going on in their companies than ever before. When leveraged effectively, this can allow you to lead with incredible agility.

Being agile requires teamwork, trust, and continuous dialogue at all levels of an organization. A good leader knows they don't have all the answers and tapping into those you manage will help you solve problems faster and with a more well-rounded set of input.

Because the metaverse is based on a foundational theme of decentralization, leaders should leverage the opportunity for inclusive participation, with the premise that no one person has the "right" solution for future success.

Decentralized strategic thinking can drive innovation and participation. This ambition is at the core of the Open Insulin Foundation.

Case Study: Open Insulin Foundation

The metaverse may provide an ideal way for the Open Insulin Foundation to share its vision and road map with stakeholders.

The Open Insulin Foundation is a nonprofit creating the means for communities in need to have local sources of safe, affordable, high quality insulin through decentralized participation. Open Insulin takes a community-based approach to strategy, pushing beyond the expert-only mindset. The vision is "to give people who depend on insulin ownership over their lives."[14]

The foundation's model of open-source (i.e., freely available) insulin production focuses on sustainable, small-scale manufacturing and open-source alternatives to production.

The company openly shares its strategy to democratize the production of insulin, where communities would own the manufacturing systems and insulin would be produced and distributed on a local level.[15]

The foundation notes that it "shares governance between people with diabetes and people working on the project. Our working groups collaborate to develop new tools for open drug production, from R&D to manufacturing for medical use. Our goal is that people living with diabetes and their communities can own and govern the organizations that produce the medicine they depend on to survive."[16]

A participative, decentralized strategy approach empowers an organization's employees and stakeholders to share insight, understand the strategy, and to be prepared for the future. This distributes the power from the center of an organization all the way to the periphery.

Case Study: IFF Community Hub

International Futures Forum (IFF) is a global nonprofit think tank of strategists, business leaders, and policymakers headquartered in Scotland. The twenty-year-old nonprofit organization practiced an agile strategy technique to create a new online learning community.

Community members were asked: What kind of a space do we want the Community Hub to be? How do we want the Community Hub to feel? What should the community provide and enable?

The process described on IFF's website notes that "this was a call for a community of *like-hearted* people. We don't all agree on everything. We want multiple perspectives, grit in the oyster. But we equally enjoy a culture of mutual support. Argument amongst friends."[17]

Community input was posted on a virtual whiteboard. Feedback was organized into major themes. This provided a transparent and real-time approach for community visioning.

Metaverse tools will provide immersive cocreation systems for thinking, visualizing, and developing an imagined future.

In the following figure, members of IFF, a community of futurists and strategists, were invited to share ideas for building an online IFF

IFF Community Hub - what do we hope to create together?

In a series of short orientation sessions on 14 and 15 January 2021 members of the community were asked to consider their hopes for the IFF Community Hub. What kind of a space do we want it to be? How do we want it to feel? What do we hope it might provide and enable? All the comments generated are gathered here, clustered under a number of themes.

A special quality of conversation

Growth and learning

IFF more accessible

Diversity of views and people

A welcoming human space

Embracing complexity

Open for serendipity

Like-hearted people

Talk can lead to action

Connection and support

Play, love, joy

A network of hope for this moment

BUILDING A NETWORK OF HOPE

Now is the time...

And...

I read this statement and thought "I have found my people". We look to our shared humanity as a source of hope and abundance of art and science, of vision and imagination, solidarity and magic. Also, as the source of art marred with the mundane — turning able to associate my work with the mindset others, not feeling alone etc. Some of it is more subtle...

Community Hub. Participants' ideas were grouped into themes and shared online. This example illustrates how community ideas can be gathered and shared using digital tools and used to form strategy.

DRIVING STRATEGY THROUGH PARTICIPATION

Open, agile strategy requires participation and a democratized, boots-on-the-ground approach that goes beyond departmental silos and strategy provided by the experts. Stakeholders such as customers and suppliers are invited to the strategy table. This undergirds a knowledge-based, widely distributed, and decentralized workforce and often uncovers an organization's blind spots. Many organizations, such as Sandia National Laboratories, are using premetaverse technology to equip teams with tools and resources to better anticipate, prepare for, and adapt to changing circumstances.

Case Study: Sandia National Laboratories

Sandia National Laboratories is a multimission laboratory managed and operated by National Technology and Engineering Solutions of Sandia, LLC, a wholly owned subsidiary of Honeywell International, for the US Department of Energy's National Nuclear Security Administration.[18]

For more than seventy years, Sandia has delivered science and technology innovation to address US security issues. Its vision is to be the nation's premier science and engineering laboratory for national security and technology innovation.

Sandia's website is immersive, filled with virtual self-guided tours packed with photography, video, 360-degree views, and infographics that spotlight Sandia's work (see Sandia.gov). While exploring, visitors can click on icons to view 3D imagery of the organization's work in biosciences, laser and nanotechnologies, combustion research, wind farm technology, and robotics.

Sandia also engages its national workforce in strategy using pre-metaverse technology. Staff members were empowered to take the initiative to design a virtual scenario skill-building training series open to the entire workforce.

The training is designed to develop and spark futuristic thinkers throughout the company. The program builds companywide foresight, strategy capacity, and skill, and it bolsters Sandia's institutional resilience.

Training is available in real time, supported by a strategy library available on a persistent basis. The digital library features a virtual bookshelf filled with strategy learning resources such as articles, videos, and an archive of recorded employee strategy forums.

In keeping with an open strategy approach, the program focuses on bringing together the widest possible group of employees who are interested in learning about strategy. By inviting all interested employees, Sandia is able to force multiply—it dramatically accelerates the effectiveness of group interaction and large-scale learning—by engaging a variety of perspectives, managerial levels, and fields of expertise throughout the organization.

Through this training program, Sandia continually creates new employee networks and builds awareness of internal expertise and contact points. The training helps Sandia create a common set of strategy language and skills.

The organization aims to strengthen two communities of practice: one focused on futures and foresight, and the other dedicated to shaping strategy. The training series includes a strategy peer mentorship and networking program.

An internal communication system provides a national forum for posting strategy updates and resources. Employees meet other employees across department boundaries. Employees are invited to meet external strategy experts outside of the organization who serve as workshop speakers.

New bonds of teamwork and connectivity are continually being built across the organization, spanning cities and work locations. Training organizers say that the network has created deeper appreciation of the company's cultural diversity. Sandia discovered that its metaverse-like strategy process has become a transformational experience within its national workforce.

This example illustrates the potential of using persistent metaverse technology as a tool to empower your workforce and build capacity throughout your organization.

GAME-CHANGING METAVERSE STRATEGY TOOLS AND TECHNIQUES

Many successful strategy techniques for envisioning the future and exploring external and internal trends are likely to be enhanced by a more experiential, immersive metaverse. Consider the following activities, and how you might engage metaverse creators to enliven your organization's strategy conversations.

Scenario Planning

Similar to strategy simulation, scenario planning is a structured process for making key strategic decisions in the face of uncertain futures. It usually involves sketching out three to four external scenarios, and then identifying the internal actions an organization will take to prepare for and respond to those scenarios. The scenarios are broadly defined and crafted more as planning guides than as exact future predictions. The scenarios focus on the organization's near future, in contrast to strategic foresight that examine longer-term time horizons of ten years or more.

Scenario planning is a process pioneered by the US military. The military conducts scenario planning to plan for twenty-year time horizons where research and development must be carefully planned.[19]

Strategy Simulation

Imagine the possibilities of traveling to the future—or going backward in time, to problem-solve a crisis using real data.

Strategy simulation helps strategists answer two questions: First, what will happen if a certain action is taken versus a different action? And second, which strategy should be selected?[20] Metaverse simulation will help companies explore multiple futures, potential dangers, and blind spots.

Strategy simulation supports learning organizations. Metaverse gaming techniques may allow many people from multiple functions and departments, such as marketing, HR, R&D, sales, finance, and operations for expertise, perspectives, and buy-in.

For example, metaverse gaming with a company's global MMORPG could allow a large number of employees embodied as avatars to participate in strategy simulation.

Visioning

Visioning is a participative method for determining a preferred future. After conducting an environmental scan, a strategy group would envision a number of probable futures and select the preferred future.

Forecasting and Strategic Foresight

While visioning helps leaders select a preferred future, strategic foresight includes an understanding of the future as a range of potential outcomes or variations that could occur as a future unfolds. Forecasting is a technique that uses historical data as inputs to make informed estimates that are predictive in determining the direction of future trends.

Horizon Scanning

Horizon scanning is a technique to detect and identify emerging developments, trends, and other signals of change through analysis of trusted source materials. It is used by businesses, organizations, and governments to identify risks and opportunities in the emerging environment.

Backcasting

Backcasting is a planning method that starts with defining a desirable future and then works backward to identify policies and programs that will connect that specified future to the present. Backcasting explores the question, "If we want to attain a certain goal, what actions must be taken to get there?"[21]

While forecasting involves predicting the future based on current trend analysis, backcasting approaches the challenge of discussing the future from the opposite direction; it is a method in which the future desired conditions are envisioned, and steps are then defined to attain those conditions.

Collective Intelligence

Collective intelligence is the combination of artificial intelligence (AI) and human intelligence (HI), providing breadth of knowledge, speed, and collaborative thinking. This intelligence feeds into strategy, planning, and policy formation.[22]

AI is the technology that mimics the problem-solving and decision-making capabilities of the human mind. HI is the process of collecting views, opinions, and knowledge from key stakeholders for the purpose of solving business and societal issues.

Competitive Intelligence

Competitive intelligence, sometimes referred to as corporate intelligence, refers to the ability to gather, analyze, and use information about competitors, customers, and other market factors that contribute to a business's competitive advantage.

Competitive intelligence activities can be grouped into two categories: tactical and strategic. Tactical intelligence is shorter-term and seeks to provide input into issues such as capturing market share or increasing revenues. Strategic intelligence focuses on longer-term issues, such as key risks and opportunities facing the enterprise.[23]

Business Wargaming

Computer-based simulation has the capacity to analyze multiple strategy options to create a variety of imagined futures.

In the metaverse, wargaming could include a variety of gamelike scenarios created to examine financial risks, such as the impacts of supply chain interruptions or customer behaviors. Wargaming can provide early warnings and improve response time for responding to crises and sudden market shifts.

Business war games involve human teams in role-playing situations. Teams interact with other teams and make decisions. War games typically take one or more days. Several scenarios or strategies are assessed by groups ranging from fifteen people to more than one hundred.[24]

In the future, with AR and VR in metaverse worlds, strategy teams may be able to step into simulated futures, play war games, and potentially walk through the impact of decisions.

Business wargaming is a game-like experiential group exercise where an organization can pressure test an existing strategy. Business war games create new plans and ideas by role-playing the competitors' strategy before making full-scale investments. Wargaming shakes things up, challenges norms, and takes a fresh look at the market through the lens of other key players.[25]

Teams usually include the company's home team, competitor teams, a marketing team, and a regulator or control team serving as the game facilitator.

For example, Arbor Biotechnologies, a life sciences company developing genetic medicines to treat genetic and acquired diseases, conducted a participative war game outdoors at a park. Although the low-tech approach was hosted in person, the activity could be digitized in the metaverse with avatars breaking into teams.

The firm hired an external facilitator. Scenarios were created for small group discussion and problem-solving. Each scenario was ranked according to likelihood and impact.[26]

Participants were cross-functional, from all company departments including manufacturing, R&D, and the voice of the customer. The combination of viewpoints built unity and agility across the entire company and resulted in updated action plans.

POWERED BY DATA

Data is the key to monitoring strategic progress, assessing outcomes, and refining targets. To be truly effective, the use of organizational data should be integrated into the organization's governance practices at all levels.

Open, agile strategy is driven by the use of data for continuous planning and execution.

US public sector leaders and managers were recently surveyed about strategy and implementation. Only 8 percent of the government leaders review and report their organization's progress on a monthly basis. This points to why strategy implementation efforts are not seen as priorities for many government organizations.[27]

The metaverse could provide a visual, interactive resource for sharing goals and progress updates. Agile strategy requires frequent, regular data monitoring and check-ins throughout an organization, to keep a pulse on whether the strategy is working or needs to shift.

"Progress on strategy could became part of an organization's weekly and monthly operational rhythms," notes strategist and technology expert Linda Parker Gates. "Through staggered meetings at multiple levels of the organization, operational and technical entities such as product development, service delivery, financial, and IT could align departmental outcomes with strategic intentions, make recommendations to leadership, and engage in two-way dialogue about key decisions and key performance measures."[28]

LEADERSHIP PRACTICES FOR BUILDING AN OPEN, AGILE CULTURE IN THE METAVERSE

Despite decades of shared knowledge about how to shape winning strategies and achieve results, a stunning 90 percent of businesses still fail to implement strategic goals.[29] One of the key reasons for this is ineffective communication throughout the entire strategic management process.

An average of 95 percent of employees don't understand their organization's strategic direction and what they need to do to make their strategy work. Furthermore, 85 percent of executive teams spend less than one hour per month discussing strategic goals, and more than half spend no time at all.[30]

As a result, employees don't understand their organization's strategy, and they lack the emotional commitment needed to achieve strategic goals.[31]

In the metaverse, the principles of Vital + Visual + Visible communication can enable organizations to foster employee engagement and create open, agile strategy, overcome long-standing strategic management challenges, and achieve results.[32] (3V communication is discussed further in chapter 9.)

As metaverse technology continues to be developed, now is the perfect time to get a jump start on considering how your strategic management process and your open, agile strategy-making could be enhanced.

➜ GROW THIS SKILL

Consider the following practices to help your organization build open, agile strategy in the metaverse.

- Seek collaborative involvement from your organization's stakeholders—both internal and external. Break old boundaries of exclusionary thinking to create new ways to meet up in topic forums, trend webinars, and strategy sessions.

- Build your personal understanding about metaverse technology. As managing director of Accenture Marcus Fromm says, it's time for leaders to grow their technology intelligence, mastering the implications of technology on their industries and moving from IQ to EQ (emotional intelligence), to TQ.[33]

- Understand the purpose for your metaverse with respect to how it could support open, agile strategy throughout your organization. Consider hiring a metaverse creative consultant if your budget permits.

- Teach leaders how to use strategy and decision analysis tools and techniques currently available on the market, such as digital white-boarding and digital brainstorming tools. Seek ideas and participation from younger, next-generation emerging leaders.

- Help your strategists get familiar with metaverse gaming, creator, collaborator, and business tools that exist today. Pilot a metaverse world for sharing your strategy and strategic direction.

- Develop strategy skills within your organization. Conduct a virtual strategy how-to conference within your organization for leaders, strategists, and potentially all employees as a leadership development opportunity.

- Discuss your organization's strategic plan and other relevant strategy topics. Introduce metaverse resources as these become available. Make strategy personal for each department, work unit, and individual.

REFLECTION QUESTIONS

1. Imagine your organization's metaverse. How could immersive experiences enhance your organization's ability to develop open, agile strategy?

2. How could the metaverse create more strategy participation throughout your organization?

3. What are the barriers for developing a metaverse as a strategy tool within your organization, and how might you overcome those barriers?

CHAPTER 8

LENS 3: COMMUNITY BUILDING IN THE METAVERSE

THE METAVERSE—WEB3—IS ALSO CALLED WEBME.[1]

WebMe is about "putting the me in metaverse"—designing our virtual lives to get what we *expect* and what we *want*.[2]

All of us will spend time interacting, learning, working, and relaxing in the metaverse according to the UK-based Meta-Verse research group. They note that some people may opt to spend nearly all of their waking hours there, considering the actual world to be tedious, limiting, and inefficient. They emphasize that the metaverse is not about putting in more time online but making the time you put in more worthwhile.[3]

They go on to say that status symbols such as the digital house you own, the digital dress and jewelry you put on, and the digital cosmetics you use will become just as essential as physical-world purchases and assets as we spend more time in the metaverse. Indeed, the amount of time spent in the metaverse as opposed to the physical world might be considered a status symbol in itself. Brands will take advantage of this desire by developing an ever-expanding range of virtual goods at real-world pricing.[4]

The metaverse may accelerate an individual mindset in societies of the future, driven by these immersive new consumer experiences. WebMe will be continuously "on" and running in the foreground and background of our lives: seamless, interoperable, physical, and virtual components of our lives. It will be intensely nagging—a resource that persistently gives us *what* we want, *when* we want it.

We will live in a multiplexity of online communities. We'll jump from one virtual world to the next as we please. We cannot imagine the toll this metaverse lifestyle will take not only on human mental health, but also the energy it takes to plug into community life on planet Earth. Much of our lives already are spent staring into a screen instead of interacting with one another.

WebMe will be intertwined with physical life, a seamless back-and-forth from physical to digital worlds, as quickly as our brains snap the orders. We are rapidly headed toward the metaverse. Will it create a vast, self-absorbed society, a world of isolated people cocooned in WebMe-Me-Me?

MOVING FROM WEBME TO WEBWE

Leaders have the opportunity to use the metaverse for good—to build and connect participative, inclusive communities that strengthen our planet Earth and fight social isolation.

Throughout the ages people have gathered together to celebrate, communicate, and take collective action based on common interests, purposes, and goals. Community building is the *act of* individuals coming together to form "we," a unified body of individuals.[5]

The metaverse will blend together physical and virtual communities in a way we cannot fully imagine. Yet the metaverse could become a powerful new tool for building social capital.

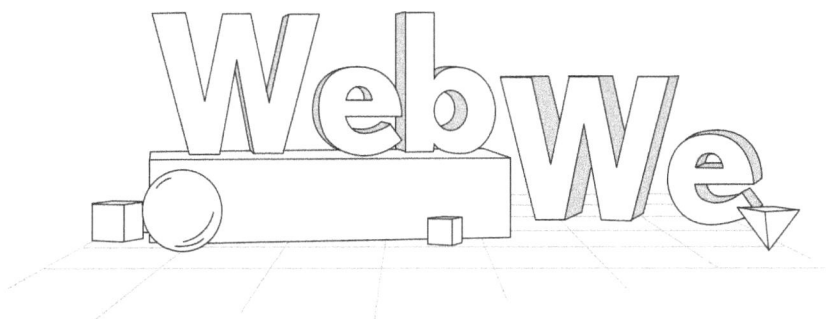

ALL COMMUNITIES NEED SOCIAL CAPITAL

Social capital is the valuable asset of human networks. Social capital can be summed up in two words: relationships matter. People's social networks are valuable assets.[6]

Social capital is a concept only recently incorporated into the social sciences during the past few decades, although it was first mentioned in the context of education, to explain the importance of community involvement for strengthening public schools.[7]

In 1916, rural school administrator L. J. Hanifan believed that the individual is helpless socially if left to himself. Hanifan posited that if a person comes into contact with his neighbor, there will be an accumulation of social capital that may immediately satisfy social needs and improve living conditions for the whole community.[8]

Social capital includes accessible resources embedded in one's network or associations.[9]

Social capital is one of seven tangible assets needed for building resilient and productive communities. Can leaders use the metaverse to help people grow social capital—valuable networks—so they can improve life on our *physical* planet Earth?

It can be argued that social capital leads to all other forms of community capital, including financial, human, cultural, political, physical (buildings and infrastructure), and environmental (the beauty of nature including climate and natural surroundings such as trees, mountains, and beaches).

Social capital requires social structures and networks needed for sustaining collective action—action that might not otherwise have taken place. As a result, social capital can be inclusionary, as well as exclusionary.

Social capital is not a homogeneous good. It varies from individual to individual.[10] The three most valuable elements of social capital are as follows:[11]

1. The number of persons within one's social network who can be mobilized and are prepared or obliged to help when called upon

2. The strength of the relationship indicating readiness to help

3. The resources of these persons

The structural definition of social capital primarily is derived from the work of Pierre Bourdieu and James Coleman,[12] both of whom defined social capital as access to resources available to individuals, thanks to their participation in social networks and forming social relationships. Both Bourdieu and Coleman emphasize the benefit of social capital for the *individual*.

Robert Putnam focused on the benefit of social capital for *collective society*. He suggested that social capital consists of certain individual values, such as civic virtue, that benefit the whole community and lead to generalized trust and civil society.[13] Putnam's research examined how individual community involvement aggregates to benefit an entire community, such as a neighborhood, city, or nation.[14]

Putnam used the metaphor of bowling to draw attention to US

decline in civic groups, such as bowling leagues—thanks to television and other cultural forces—and as a result, people are becoming more isolated and are choosing to "bowl alone."[15] Putnam's examination of the decline in US civic engagement provided a wake-up call for the continued decline in memberships for in-person community groups.

With so much time and attention spent toggling between virtual and physical worlds, will we be satisfied to bowl alone in the metaverse?

THE BATTLE TO WIN COMMUNITY ENGAGEMENT

When the world came to a full stop due to the pandemic in 2020, our lives became dramatically hybrid. Since then, we've become choosy about how we spend our time and how we decide to show up.

Many people are choosing *not* to return to the office. Many companies have eliminated offices or have opted for leasing shared work and conference room spaces, where employees can drop in and hybrid meetings can take place.

Today, leaders have a duty to create vibrant meeting content and meaningful employee conversations. This is not an option. We face relentless pressure and expectation to find new ways to engage and retain employees, customers, and stakeholders. The audience bar is set high.

The new question for community participants is this: Where and how to show up?

Those of us in hybrid work environments ask these questions on a moment-to-moment basis:

- Do I want to appear physically on camera? What should I wear?

- Should I show up with just a photo?

- Should I show up as some type of virtual avatar?

- What avatar outfit is appropriate for the meeting or occasion?

- For the audio, should I use my voice or a simulated voice?

It's no wonder that how to show up has become a more complicated decision these days, which is why many are choosing to not show up at all. Since 2020, more people are apt to ghost events, even after RSVPing, changing their minds without letting the host know.

Wedding planners have long known that 5 to 10 percent of those who RSVP will not show up at the wedding for people they know well—friends, family members, and coworkers. This type of no-show is costly and frustrating.

No-shows are escalating for expensive, big-ticket events. Prior to 2020, celebrity concert no-show rates were calculated at 1 to 3 percent of ticket sales.[16] By late 2021, the no-show rate escalated to 20 percent. No-shows result in a decline of social capital when people stay at home and become more isolated.

GRABBING FOR TIME AND ATTENTION

The pandemic gave people a good excuse to weed out low-priority time and money drainers. This included the opportunity to pare back community activities that either drained productivity from the workday, or where little appreciation had been shown to the volunteers, donors, and people who consistently showed up but were not thanked enough.

Today, dwindling community involvement is exacerbated by inflation and economic downturns, providing less incentive to attend in-person meetings and events unless there is a return on time investment.

Entrepreneurs know that for every minute not spent working on revenue-generating projects, an opportunity cost exists—that of time, money, and accomplishments. Even meeting for coffee or lunch is becoming price restrictive. As of this writing, it's nearly impossible to go out to lunch in the United States for under $30 per person. Those who choose to meet for lunch have high expectations for value in exchange for the time and costs invested.

Younger generations have been well trained in setting personal boundaries. They reject needless activities that encroach on personal wellness, recreation, and family time.

In this new hybrid world filled with rigorous expectations, we will see a new level of time and technology haves and have-nots. There will be those who have access to technology and work flexibility, and those who do not. For example, hands-on service providers such as workers in healthcare, classroom-based education, public safety, construction, retail, restaurant, and hospitality don't have flexibility to work from home.

The Great Resignation began in 2020 during the shutdown, when millions of people switched or quit jobs to start a business. Many organizations experienced an abrupt talent loss. On a positive note, the Great Resignation was the great weeding out, and it opened doors for younger generations to step up and to be promoted.

The Great Retirement of workers aged fifty-five and older was led by female baby boomers sixty-five and older, whether forced or by choice.[17] Community organizations will feel the impact of these retiring workers as they resign from nonprofit boards and service commitments. In the United States, there were 3.3 million or 7 percent *more* retirees in October 2021 than in January 2020.

The Great *Unreturn* has continued since 2021, when many organizations struggled with getting workers back into the office, either full- or part-time.

Our world of work, and our lives since the pandemic, have changed forever. Leaders who can build, bond, and bridge communities in our new culture of hybrid worlds will be the leaders who can effectively lead change resulting in real impact on planet Earth.

AS ONLINE COMMUNITIES GROW, SOCIAL CAPITAL DECLINES

Since 2020, personal community networks shrunk by nearly 16 percent—by more than two hundred people per person, due to isolation during the pandemic. Many people have not returned to prior levels of community engagement.

While social distancing and officing at home, many people shifted attention to strengthening relationships with family, friends, and closest colleagues. They stayed within their bubble. This is called "turtling up"—the effect of retreating into a shell. This trend negatively impacted community organizations as people sheltered at home, as well as impacted people's sense of belonging. The pandemic isolation also created disinterested workers, impacting job searches and employee turnover.[18]

In contrast, time spent online skyrocketed. If we're now spending two hours and twenty-seven minutes on social media each day, that equates to nearly sixteen hours per week, 826 hours—or *more than thirty-four days, each year*. The average adult will spend *six years and eight months* of their life on social media.[19]

Age demographics are swiftly changing, as ten thousand boomers are expected to retire *each day* until the year 2030, according to Pew Research Center.[20] Organizations must figure out how to engage and serve the next generation, at a deeper level, to move from WebMe to WebWe.

Time spent online in the metaverse will be the biggest competition to community groups relying only on in-person, human connectivity. Now is the time for community leaders to be thinking about the competition for time and focus and consider how the metaverse could complement in-person engagement.

New insights and skills are required to create community in distracted, hybrid worlds. Community building in the metaverse will require future leaders who are strategic, agile, authentic, and are human-centered servant leaders.

The metaverse will forever change our traditional definition of community. It will require us to rethink and innovate the way we build and strengthen communities, as well as develop the required leadership and strategy discussed earlier.

For example, the potential to build a global audience is immense; however, online audience churn is rapid. Virtual communities shorten time spans. A one-year duration in some communities is considered long-term in the gaming world.

METAVERSE COMMUNITIES: THE CONTRAST BETWEEN BIG C AND LITTLE C

To compete for stiff competition for time and attention, leaders must prepare for community building in a new dimension. We are no longer bound by place, time, or physical reality. Humans must transcend the physical and digital components of their lives, combining new and traditional definitions of community.

As defined by metaverse pioneers, community is much different from traditional paradigms. Community could mean collective funding, for example, or creators sharing work, or gaming communities, or fan-based communities. Table 2 contrasts common metaverse community definitions with traditional definitions of community.

THE NEW TWIST FOR METAVERSE COMMUNITY BUILDING

Traditional communities are very leader-centric and top-down. Community heads set the agenda, enforce the rules, and make all choices regarding the community's future. If there is ever any community member interaction, it's informal and used as decision-making guidance only.

Web3 communities flip this method on its head. Decentralized autonomous organizations in particular are building technological solutions to circumvent the need for central decision-makers. They distribute voting power through the issuance of tokens, representing fractional ownership of the project and its community. That way, the internal governance of each project gets democratized on a level that most tech communities have never seen before.

Table 2: Comparison:
Metaverse Communities vs. Traditional Communities

Metaverse Communities	Traditional In-Person Communities
• Users as a community • Communities that are decentralized with shared governance • Open systems of connectivity • Communities of collective charities, as well as creative funders, investors • Distributed, decentralized, autonomous, transparent • Shared creative work eliminating the middleman • Gamers and game creators • Diverse and inclusive • Communities of self-expression	• Place-based communities including neighborhoods, towns, regions • Communities of practice or profession • Employee communities • Learning communities • Support communities • Faith-based communities • Discussion communities • Action communities • Interest communities

Some projects have established smart contracts on the blockchain to make the vote and its results immutable and public. Every vote can be tracked and traced, increasing transparency, and allowing for honest discourse around the topic.[21]

In addition to crypto-based voting, which is often focused on long-term strategies and technical details, many communities use per-issue voting in their Discord communities. Automated systems track emoji-based responses to questions and polls, totaling results and keeping a record of all votes and polls in a community.

Community members feel more represented because they literally are; there are no intermediaries. All community decisions are majority votes. And because there are so many, most members will be on the winning side of one or another, further cementing their acceptance and support of the voting mechanism. This creates a strong sense of inclusion and belonging.[22]

My research revealed two distinctly different communities: Little c and Big C. Both are important to the metaverse ecosystem. But there is one, very significant difference.

LITTLE C COMMUNITIES

Little c metaverse communities—and there are millions of them out there—are communities of interest. Communities of interest are rallied around an activity, theme, cause, or topic of interest, such as a hobby, recreation, entertainment, games, and consumer products. While the topic or cause may be of mutual interest, the individual members may not know each other. Participation in Little c communities often is individualistic, such as attending a music concert online, as a solo patron.

Little c communities include members—or users—who might come and go. They may engage once or twice, or for a limited short-term duration. Or, they could be connected to the community for twelve months or longer (which, in metaverse terms, is considered to be long-term). Examples of Little c communities are featured at the end of this chapter.

BIG C COMMUNITIES

Big C communities are transformational communities of interest, action, and impact.

Big C communities inspire community members to take individual and collective action to create a positive impact for our life on physical, biological planet Earth.

Big C communities require significant human investments of time and depth of dialogue, debate, deliberation, and, potentially, the friction of civil discourse leading to decision-making, which usually includes problem-solving.

Big C problem-solving leads to action for the greater good for people and communities on our planet Earth. Let's dive deeper.

As you know, community building requires—

- **Bonding** within your group—key for creating a cohesive team

- **Bridging** to outside collaborating groups—pivotal for bringing in fresh ideas, financial resources, and collaboration critical to advancing the purpose and creating impact

- **A new form of hybrid bridging**—bringing together your community's physical and digital worlds to prevent relationship and communication gaps that may divide your physical–digital community

Community building in the metaverse will require lots of experimentation and novel thinking for effective hybrid community building, where people (as avatars) are participating in a persistent world, even when you are not there.

Clinical psychologist Sherry Turkle is skeptical. "In the metaverse you just walk away, you don't learn to negotiate. You don't learn to have the complex life and the complex love that are the things we really need to live a better life," she notes.[23] "Now more than ever before, we need to learn how to talk to people we don't agree with. In the metaverse we can just silo ourselves. We've siloed ourselves in places where we don't have to really develop these habits of dealing with community and dealing with friction."[24]

But there are opportunities for consciously developing Big C communities in the metaverse, such as when diverse community members join together with a topic of common interest.

For example, people who join together to protect the world's environment might take advantage of developing a Big C community. The virtual community has unprecedented potential to create global neighbors around common themes, creating new forms of collaboration leading to action and impact that transforms both physical and virtual worlds.

WHAT LITTLE C AND BIG C METAVERSE COMMUNITIES HAVE IN COMMON

All metaverse communities feature a basic foundation of Little c communities, which provide all of the attributes of a community, such as a welcoming gathering place and a sense of belonging and purpose, including—

- **Shared experience.** For example, gaming worlds offer a shared experience or chat with a virtual community, in a virtual world with a group online. A significant time investment is required.

- **Community membership.** Membership may be formal or informal. Dues or a subscription may or may not be required. Some memberships may offer novel types of rewards and recognition, such as the opportunity to earn NFTs and be recognized for creative work.

- **A general sense of belonging.** Community membership traditionally provides a sense of belonging in a place of emotional safety and boundaries, with personal investments and common identity symbolizing the community, such as a neighborhood, or organizational logo.

- **Two-way (bi-directional) influence and engagement.** A group cohesiveness is created, as well as individual empowerment. Community input is invited, may be shared on a chat feed, and may or may not result in something being acted upon within the community.

- **Integration and fulfillment of members' needs and a shared emotional connection.** This includes community members who share common values, find the information and community benefits needed, and may share history of being in the same community and working together, which cultivates trust.

BENEFITS OF BUILDING A BIG C METAVERSE COMMUNITY

Assuming that you've developed a purpose and strategy for your metaverse, here are just a few benefits to be gained from creating an impact-driven, Big C metaverse.

- **Creating immersive possibilities for community visioning.** Imagining the future and experiences of your programs, services, and products through virtual tours, 3D holograms, and more.

- **Reaching a global audience with impact and efficiency.** Bringing visitors up close with your organization with a new, experiential dimension.

- **Increasing customer efficiency.** Persistent worlds offer deeper experiences that complement your traditional in-person offerings.

- **Being seen as a leader in your space.** Through immersive audience connections and sharing valuable information, you can expand your sphere of influence by growing your network and audiences.

- **Promoting agile market input and response to market shifts.** You can use the metaverse to provide an interactive platform for maintaining dialogue and touchpoints with your community on a persistent, 24/7 basis. Rapid learning and diverse input allow you to make market pivots as needed. Community input can be turned into market insight, helping you anticipate your community's future needs.

- **Increasing revenue.** Your metaverse community can help foster more engaged followers, increasing retention and sales.

- **Creating a learning community.** Your metaverse participants can learn from each other, ask questions, and gain insight from a variety of contributors.

- **Convening a supportive network.** Metaverse communities can create a new hybrid supportive network where people not only belong online, but they can also give back and make a difference on planet Earth. People are craving a sense of community and belonging.

- **Bringing immersive experiences into nearly every aspect of life.** The metaverse will provide unprecedented opportunities for connecting people and bringing experiences to people anywhere in the world. This includes everything from hosting meetups to entertainment and the arts, buying, selling, virtual travel, visiting places such as museums, and many forms of learning and education.

BUILDING, BONDING, AND BRIDGING BIG C COMMUNITIES IN THE METAVERSE

Big C communities connect digital and physical worlds, include dialogue and potentially debate, and mobilize human action to make a difference in improving life on planet Earth.

Here are leadership practices for building Big C communities.

1. **Build your personal leadership skills to become an effective metaverse community builder.**

Develop the three metaverse leadership capacities discussed in chapter 6. Become an agile strategic leader. Become an authentic leader. Become a servant leader-community builder.

2. **Build the purpose and strategy for your organization's metaverse community (if it doesn't already exist). Then, develop business objectives for your metaverse, as well as the call to action.**

Believe it or not, many community groups are operating without a defined purpose. Over time, this creates distraction and confusion. I've observed how people are able to align with a clearly communicated community purpose, including vision, mission, core values, goals, and a compelling call to action.

Be clear about the desired WebWe impact this metaverse community will make in our physical world. The purpose is your community's "why." The why helps members seek and find the community. Along with the purpose, invite your community to create core values to guide the moral standards for how your metaverse community will operate.

Then, clearly define the purpose for your metaverse. For example, do you want to engage like-minded community members? Sell products? Create a movement leading to improved life on planet Earth? What are your experimental business goals for your metaverse? (Remember—the metaverse is new. Beta or experimental business objectives can help you test your metaverse markets. This provides an aspirational yet agile road map.)

Answer these questions: Is your plan to launch a metaverse clearly defined by a business strategy? To what extent does my audience want to have an immersive internet experience, including VR and 3D technology? Am I clear on the long- and short-term goals for this metaverse?

What problem(s) is your metaverse community trying to solve? Or, what positive impact will your community create? Keep in mind that the metaverse is all about creating an experience for your community. It's not about your brand, according to advertising experts.[25]

Determine three to five specific, measurable, and agile community goals for your metaverse community to accomplish during the next two years. Invite your community to share ideas and cocreate goals.

Determine how your metaverse will translate experiences, activities, and interactions with real-world outcomes. Develop and test strategies for connecting your metaspace with physical-world impact.

Refine these as needed to build upon what works and edit out what doesn't.

Create a clear set of community values to guide the experience of your metaverse community. Clearly define what authenticity and truth look like in your metaverse community. This sets the standards for your community.

3. **Focus on bonding your community (internally).** Create human kindness, empathy, and connection among your members. Remember, avatars are human beings. You, the leader, must serve as a caring example of how community members should treat each other, helping your members move from self-interested WebMe to community-interested WebWe.

- Describe the relationships you're trying to build within your community. What does a kind, caring, and compassionate community look like in your organization, and the organization's metaverse?

4. **Build a collaborative and creative metaverse management team— whether it is staffed by paid or volunteer members.** Define roles and responsibilities for the metaverse team. This team will administer, update, and facilitate your metaverse community. Along with your brilliant creative experts, your metaverse team should include members from senior leadership, as well as communication, marketing, and customer service experts.

5. **Create a personalized metaverse community experience that builds your brand, welcomes all participants, and bonds community members together with shared purpose, setting the standard for your metaverse world.** Determine how your metaverse dialogue and chat will be moderated and facilitated.

6. **Create significant opportunities for committee or small-group work.** Charge each committee leader and the committee to develop a work plan, with goals and activities leading to action and impact in our physical world.

- Create community guidelines. This includes rules and norms for behavior and interaction in your metaverse community. Plan to visibly post these in your community space. Be prepared to be agile, to adjust the content and programs as needs and opportunities evolve, based on ongoing community feedback.

7. **Bridge your metaverse community with other communities that align with and support yours.**

Create a priority list of other strategic collaborators that align with your organization's purpose and goals. Meet with leaders of those priority organizations. Cocreate ways to provide mutual support, maximize resources, and partner programs, products, and services. Regularly update this plan so that you are continually bridging your organization (and metaverse) with other relevant communities of mutual interests and purpose.

- Consider offering incentives to share with partnering organizations, such as NFTs, tickets, product samples, and other perks. Create metaverse brand ambassadors within your organization and reward them for their referrals. For example, ask your community members to invite their friends to visit your metaverse community. If relevant, create opportunities for monetizing your metaverse by selling products, services, and resources for your community.

More Steps for Defining Your Metaverse Community

Define your organization's target audiences—your community. Assess which audiences will participate online, in person, and in a hybrid combination.

Consider broadening your audience definition to include periphery audiences, to be as inclusive as possible. This builds bigger communities. The Open Garden approach developed by Amith Nagarajan provides fresh thinking for expanding memberships. This model expands two conventional audiences—members versus nonmembers—into four potential stakeholder groups as follows:[26]

- Members who pay dues

- Volunteers who are deeply committed to your organization

- Interested people who support your efforts

- The general public, who are occasionally interested in what you do, depending on the news cycle

In broadening your audiences beyond membership, you may discover people who want to join your community who visit your website, attend your events, read your newsletter, download your resources, and promote your organization to their networks.[27]

Study Your Community

Regularly study your target audiences to learn about your community's evolving wants and needs. Aim to provide quality of content and resources. Quality is better than quantity, to prevent information overload.

Your research could include formal surveys, focus groups, quick online polls, and keeping up with competitor news. Determine what types of quality content—articles, programs, resources in the metaverse—meet your audiences' needs.

Plan Your Content

Plan your metaverse content. Determine areas for persistent, interactive offerings—places where avatars will visit and explore—as well as scheduled online events and meetups. Along with content, determine the activities needed to achieve your community's purpose. For example—

- Host immersive team meetings in a persistent online space.
- Produce engaging educational forums, dialogues, and learning workshops.
- Host online events.
- Showcase products and places in 3D.
- Feature digital twins of real-world locations.
- Present an interactive, powerful alternative to a traditional website.

Select and Test Your Platform

Your metaverse platform should align with your metaverse goals. Choose the platforms your audience is already using, and which ones may be a good fit for your industry. Seek technical support as needed to develop and test your metaverse community space.

There are a number of existing platforms, some with bigger audiences than others. For example, Roblox has approximately sixty million users each day, where other platforms reach smaller audiences. Metaverse platforms will change as the market matures. Do your research and seek technical and creative advice before you make a platform decision.

If you lack creator skills, there are builders who can help you create your organization's metaverse, including the infrastructure, standards and protocols, scenes, content, activities, interaction, and interoperability.

Set Standards for How Leaders Show Up

Seek creative expertise to help you and your leadership team develop one or more avatars that represent each leader's style, as well as the purpose of your organization. Develop guidelines to set standards for what is and is not appropriate regarding how to show up as an avatar. Avatars should authentically represent leaders and their community leadership roles. The aim is not to quell creativity, but to establish basic community standards. This is an important step.

A SUMMARY OF COMPETENCIES FOR BIG C, WEBWE LEADERS

If you've suddenly found yourself leading a virtual community—congratulations! Don't be intimidated by the fact that leadership will be complex in the metaverse. We all are new leaders in the metaverse. We all have a lot to learn.

Keep in mind that communities need continual investment *and reinvestment* as people come and go. You need to be an active participant in your metaverse community, making sure it doesn't die on the vine.

Building community agreement is more difficult than ever, due to our polarized society fueled by social media and a constant intake of opinions and false information. But the other major challenge is declining memberships in community-based organizations, as people are less motivated to get involved and are spending more of their time online. It's not easy to retain members these days.

According to Vanessa Mason, research director at the Institute for the Future and author of her Future of Belonging website, belonging happens by design, not by accident. "You have to keep reinvesting in the communities you're in, and continuously re-evaluate your role," she says.[28]

As the metaverse evolves, leaders with the following WebWe community-building competencies will be in high demand.

Human empathy, or "heart competence." Fostering human compassion, conversation, listening, empathy, and connection to bridge humans across a decentralized, distributed environment.

Hybrid technical competence. While leaders must focus on human beings first, they must be able to manage multiple forms of technology. Gone are the days of fumbling around during live, online metaverse meetings. Fumblers and bumblers will lose community members. The ability to multitask, operating with multiple inputs, tools, and networks, is still a new phenomenon.

Community engagement competence, focused on connecting humans in physical and digital worlds, and bridging a variety of collaborating communities. To build a thriving metaverse community, leaders must create connection, value, and inspiration. This includes creating a culture of hospitality in meetings. Leaders who demonstrate excellent hosting and facilitating skills create engagement and meaningful conversations among participants.

Communication and dialogue competence. Purposeful, participative conversations require skillful preparation. Effective metaverse leaders will hone their communication skills. They will be on point, succinct, and make conversations interactive and interesting. See chapter 9 for 3V communication techniques.

Truth-telling competence. In our polarized world, disinformation is rampant on social media and other platforms. In a decentralized, distributed environment, knowing who and what to trust will be challenging. Effective leaders will foster truthful, timely, and relevant information, creating safeguards to combat harmful lies perpetuated by anonymous groups, fake communities and news, dark money, extremism, and deepfakes. The world needs leaders who can build communities of truth and trust. Truth means accurate, true information. Trust includes responsiveness, accessibility, transparency, responsibility, and ethics.

Door-opening competence for creating access to the metaverse. Leaders in all walks of life must address the world's digital divide and economic disparities. Solutions to this enormous issue go well beyond the scope of this book. However, as a leader, you can consider how you can create technology access for people and communities in need of technology resources.

Diversity, equity, inclusion competence. Metaverse communities are global communities. Your metaverse community may have the unprecedented opportunity to develop a richness of multiple cultures, ages, countries, and thought leadership.

Being open to continually grow your own leadership competence as a community builder. Effective community builders are leaders—many who rise quickly in an online community—who take a front seat in growing their own leadership and community-building skills. This includes the journey of building resiliency through self-care.

Leadership is a journey no matter what the position or situation. As you grow your leadership skills, you will become a driving force for positivity, inspiration, and possibility in the lives of others in the community.

EXAMPLES OF LITTLE C COMMUNITY BUILDING

There are endless Little c communities creating resources for communities of interest. Here are a few examples of well-known Little c communities bringing people together for fun and learning.

NIKELAND

In 2021, Nike introduced its metaverse NIKELAND, a fun, free metaverse to promote a healthy lifestyle. Nike created the metaverse to connect its community of interest—its fans—to create, share experiences, and compete, with the goal of turning sport and play into a lifestyle.[29]

While NIKELAND offers free fun for visitors who set up a free account on Roblox, this brilliant brand strategy is building the next generation of loyal customers while promoting a healthy, active lifestyle.

Buildings and fields inside NIKELAND are inspired by Nike's real-life headquarters and hold detailed arenas for the Roblox community to test their skills competing in various mini games. At launch, visitors can participate in games with friends. Using the NIKELAND tool kit, creators can easily design their own mini games from interactive sports materials.

The NIKELAND metaverse features the tagline "Dream it. Make it. Play it."

Players are rewarded with ribbons and medals for competing in and building their yards, exploring, and finding Easter eggs. This unlocks virtual rewards and products for avatars. A digital showroom allows users to outfit your NIKELAND avatar with Nike products.

Visitors can get more active by using their mobile devices to transfer offline movement to online play such as long jumps or speed runs.

NIKELAND is a Little c community. The community provides a sense of pure come-and-go fun while creating an inclusive Nike family. Although it creates a positive ethos of health and sports competition, this is not a metaverse for dialogue, debate, and problem-solving resulting in action that impacts the physical world.

Instant Pot

Instant Pot has three million Facebook members—its social media community. This is a brand of multicookers manufactured by Instant Brands. The multicookers are electronically controlled, combined pressure cookers and slow cookers. The original cookers are marketed as six-in-one or more appliances designed to consolidate the cooking and preparing of food to one device.

This popular brand hosts a Facebook page to create a Little c community or product users. Instant Pot users can ask questions, post unique recipes, and share the joy of cooking. Whether this company moves into the metaverse or not, it has cultivated a large virtual Little c community.

Peloton

Founded in 2012 and headquartered in New York City, Peloton supports seven million platform users, with a half-million accounts connected on Facebook.

Peloton is an interactive fitness platform with a community of more than 6.6 million members based on fitness equipment. The company pioneered connected, technology-enabled fitness and the streaming of immersive, instructor-led classes available virtually and asynchronously.

In addition to connecting its members through community resources on its website, the official Peloton member page is a private Facebook group featuring nearly a half-million Peloton members interested in Peloton.

As a community of interest, this Little c community consists of customers and users who come together to discuss Peloton products. It also serves a hub where those customers and users can learn about Peloton's latest announcements, feature rollouts, and product updates. Regarding information sharing, the community members share exercise plans, techniques, schedules, and training methods with one another.[30]

Rec Room

Rec Room is a Little c community focused on shared activities. It's a gaming and cocreator website inviting people to build and play games together. Rec Room is free, and cross-plays on multiple devices, from phones to VR headsets.

Visitors are greeted on the Rec Room's welcome page:

> Join the best community—Rec Room is a fun and welcoming place for people from all walks of life! Let us help you find people you'll LOVE to hang out with. Party up with friends from all around the world to chat, hang out, explore MILLIONS of player-created rooms, or build something new and amazing to share with us all.
>
> Customize and dress up your cute Rec Room avatar to express your style. Discover challenging, fun or straight up weird games made by creators just like you. Try your skill with the Maker Pen, the tool used by Rec Room creators to build everything from puppies to helicopters to entire worlds![31]

Dapper Labs

Dapper Labs and the National Basketball Association (NBA) joined together to create a community of NFT collectors—those who buy blockchain-based experiences and digital collectibles. Dapper Labs is the company behind NBA Top Shot and the Flow blockchain.

Dapper Labs says that it "uses blockchain technology to bring new forms of digital engagement to fans around the world by bringing fans closer to the brands they love, giving people a real stake in the communities they contribute to, and creating new ways for consumers to become creators themselves."[32]

The company is simplifying the purchase of NFTs and creating unique fan experiences, as well as unique marketing and partnership benefits.

Its more than one million users, reached in 2021, have transacted over one billion dollars in marketplace transaction for digital video sports "cards"—epic NBA video clips. The website provides a 24/7 peer-to-peer marketplace, nightly games, and challenges for prizes.

In 2022, the NBA and Dapper Labs announced the launch of the NBA All-Star VIP Pass NFT Auction and Giveaway. This is a sophisticated, novel way to reach fans.

- Hosted on NBA Top Shot, the auction included thirty unique NFTs, one-of-one digital collectibles representing every NBA team that grant each owner a VIP pass for the ultimate fan experience at the next five NBA All-Star Games. The company announced that "one lucky NBA fan will win an additional All-Star VIP Pass NFT, representing the NBA, through a giveaway that tips off today."[33]

- The giveaway included fan engagement with an exclusive QR code during the broadcast. When scanned, viewers gain entry into the giveaway. NFT owners receive additional perks including All-Star virtual panels, NBA receptions, tours, events, a merchandise bag, an NBA All-Star jersey, and a photo of the NBA All-Star Game court.

Dapper Labs' studio partners include the NBA and NBPA, and Warner Music Group. Notable investors in Dapper Labs include Google Ventures, Samsung, and the founders of DreamWorks, Reddit, Coinbase, Zynga, and AngelList.[34]

BIG C COMMUNITY BUILDING IN GOVERNMENT

Transparency in government refers to the openness of information. Research has shown that trust in government is enhanced by use of online systems (referred to as electronic or "e-government" systems). E-government positively influences the public's sense of government responsiveness.[35]

Government agencies are leading the way in developing metaverse technology, expanding the use of VR and AR for online community building. In fact, virtual public involvement is rapidly growing as an innovative method for governments seeking to improve community trust, engagement, and stakeholder input.

Public trust is built when e-government works efficiently and assures that confidential information is protected. In government settings, trust features multiple aspects,[36] as summarized in Table 3. Communication in government may be enhanced by the metaverse.

The following stories illustrate global government efforts to experiment with the metaverse, or premetaverse techniques, to create physical-world impact: these use cases include the city of Seoul, Korea; York Regional Police in Greater Toronto; and two US state departments in Iowa and Idaho.

Table 3: The Metaverse as a Tool

Government and Public Trust	Government and Communication
• **Responsiveness:** Speed and efficiency in responding to citizen needs. • **Accessibility:** Government systems can be accessed at any time, in any language, and in a manner that matches user needs. • **Transparency:** An institution-based trust factor based on the degree to which governments provide complete and open information. • **Responsibility:** How an institution handles privacy, equity, and ethical use of information about citizens and their interactions with government.	• **Efficiency and low cost:** Virtual tools and platforms can be made accessible to communities efficiently, many at a lower cost than traditional public engagement methods. • **Accelerated project delivery:** Robust public engagement helps identify issues early in the project planning process, which reduces the need to revisit decisions. • **Communication and collaboration:** Virtual public involvement can aid in establishing a common vision for transportation, ensuring the opinions and needs of the public are understood and considered during transportation planning and project development. • **Expanded engagement:** Virtual tools include stakeholders who do not participate in traditional approaches to public involvement. Greater engagement can improve project quality.

City of Seoul, South Korea

The city of Seoul pledged $33.1 million to a five-year metaverse implementation plan called Metaverse Seoul for community building. Seoul officials will debut its metaverse platform by 2022, and its Metaverse 120 Center civil service office will open its doors across the capital's economy, tourism, and education sectors in 2023.

BIG C IMPACT

- Seoul officials say their five-year plan will transform the city's public services by allowing employees to communicate to members of the public via an official metaverse platform using 3D avatars and immersive environments.[37]

- City officials have also confirmed the metaverse platform will host a future mayor's office, as well as a Fintech Lab and commerce office named Invest Seoul, resulting in economic development for the physical city.

- The city of Seoul notes that the metaverse will be a new solution and tool for boosting the well-being of socially disadvantaged individuals.

York Regional Police, Ontario, Canada

Located in Aurora, a few miles north of Toronto, York Regional Police was formed in 1971 when fourteen municipal police departments and the York County Security Police joined together to serve a growing urban region. More than 1,600 sworn officers and 600 civilians serve the area's 1.2 million citizens.

York Regional Police has made itself metaverse-ready by creating communities with extensive, innovative digital outreach practices.

In its strategic plan, the law enforcement agency focuses on two pillars: its employees (internal bonding) and its community (external bridging).[38] Virtual community building is used in addition to in-person initiatives to positively impact the safety and quality of life for Greater Toronto.

BIG C IMPACT

For more than a decade, York Regional Police has built its social media following and invites two-way communication through an active social media program.

- To create its three-year business plan, York Regional Police conducted extensive stakeholder outreach and research. This included emailed surveys, focus groups, and virtual public town halls, gathering input to understand community needs and wants.

- Attended by thousands of residents, town halls are hosted by the police chief on Twitter, accompanied by live chat and polling questions. Input has led to new community initiatives, such as the Positive Ticket Program that rewards young people who are caught in the act of demonstrating positive behavior and decision-making skills.

- Facebook is used to share live events and topics of community interest, such as traffic and safety information.

- Public comments posted on Facebook are reviewed to understand key themes and community issues. For example, word analysis is used to improve services and understand community needs and trends.

- The agency builds community engagement through its video series *Behind the Badge*, posted on YouTube. Viewers receive an inside look at specialty units and skills needed to keep the public safe. The community is helping to create the police force it needs and wants for the future.

Iowa Department of Transportation (DOT)

The metaverse will provide immersive experiences to help government leaders share visionary plans with stakeholders while expanding community input.

VR already is being used to help the public visualize government transportation projects such as freeways and bridges and offer input leading to better project design, outcomes, and stakeholder support.

In the United States, the Iowa Department of Transportation (DOT) collaborated with Iowa State University to develop a VR demonstration leading to public support for the Interstate 74 Mississippi River Bridge. The bridge project consisted of reconstructing 5.5 miles of I-74, including new river bridges over the Mississippi River to replace the old suspension bridges.

Residents were invited to use VR goggles to drive or fly over the bridge. They walked along its pedestrian path. They observed the view from a scenic deck. Users also could take a virtual dive into the river to learn about the fish and underwater species, guided by a US Fish and Wildlife Service biologist.[39]

BIG C IMPACT

The investment in VR resulted in project approval. VR expedited the public's understanding about why the new bridge was needed, resulting in public input and engagement.[40]

The VR project cost less than $50,000 to produce—very reasonable for securing approval for the $1 billion construction project. The 3D model of the bridge was developed by a consultant, while other 3D content for the simulation was designed by Iowa DOT and Iowa State University.

Boise's Downtown 11th Street Bikeway

In Boise, Idaho, 3D VR images were created for the Downtown 11th Street Bikeway study to show the public visual images of proposed street and bike lane improvements for city intersections. Using an online mapping tool called ArcGIS StoryMaps, citizens were able to attend a Downtown 11th Street Bikeway Virtual Open House.

BIG C IMPACT

The VR images were used in conjunction with an online survey to help Boise's partnering government entities plan the new bikeway.[41]

BIG C COMMUNITY BUILDING IN NONPROFIT ORGANIZATIONS

The metaverse may provide creative and efficient ways for nonprofit organizations to create Big C communities. For example, a nonprofit arts organization could collaborate with a technology trade association to explore opportunities to enhance the quality of life for high-tech workers. The arts organization could create a metaverse performance that inspires physical-world ticket sales, leveraging a strategic partnership along with a hybrid approach to connect with new audiences. During the pandemic, a nonprofit research hospital used virtual reality to grow its donor base.

St. Jude Children's Research Hospital

Based in Memphis, Tennessee, St. Jude Children's Research Hospital is one of the world's premier pediatric cancer research centers. Its mission is to find cures for children with cancer and other catastrophic diseases through research and treatment.

During the pandemic when many nonprofits suffered, St. Jude

grew its community of donors and cultivated new audiences who are now aware of its mission. The hospital created a compelling VR self-guided tour of its campus. Visitors can choose to hear stories, see specific facilities, and tour at their own pace.

The online tour features storytelling segments told by St. Jude patients. The virtual campus tour debuted on Twitch to kick off St. Jude's annual fundraising season.

The tour features narration and personal stories told by those who are alive today because of the medical treatment and nurturing support provided to patients and entire families.

BIG C IMPACT

The research hospital received record fundraising because online visitors could emotionally connect with the people and the facilities. More than 100,000 visitors have experienced St. Jude's compassion and breakthrough medical care through the self-guided VR tour.

The project created new and influential collaborative relationships—an example of effective bridging. St. Jude's fundraising arm, ALSAC (the American Lebanese Syrian Associated Charities), partnered with Google to create a 360-degree video called "An Inside Look: A St. Jude Immersive Experience."

BIG C COMMUNITY BUILDING IN BUSINESS ORGANIZATIONS

The line between Little c and Big C communities can be blurry.

The telltale sign is this: Big C communities require an *investment* of participation, which could include dialogue and debate, leading to a commitment to take action that makes some type of positive impact for physical life on planet Earth.

While metaverse hoppers may visit many Little c communities,

Big C metaverse communities require a depth of member investment leading to action and human impact.

Gemie and Metaverse Polling

Gemie is a unique use case. Because of its fan-based digital polling platform and impact on physical-world entertainment, it is featured as a metaverse Big C example. Gemie is an Asian entertainment-focused metaverse platform, an NFT marketplace geared toward allowing top Asian celebrities to customize planets and collectibles to interact with fans.

Gemie's vision is to bring Asia's entertainment industry to the metaverse and help artists achieve their full potential by providing them with the tools, resources, and opportunities they need to reach their goals and interact with fans from all over the world without limitations.

As a DAO, Gemie is focused on entertainment. Fans vote for favorite celebrities. Digital polling and voting make collecting group opinions speedy and efficient.

BIG C IMPACT

- The voting allows fans to participate in the democratization of entertainment decision-making, determining the fate of who and what gets supported.

- Gemie offers membership to its DAO, allowing users to make proposals and secure rights to vote on certain decisions on behalf of their favorite celebrities. The virtual rooms in the Gemie metaverse are private spaces where users can choose to customize and decorate with digital collectibles. There, they can hang out with their friends and other users who share similar passions and preferences with them.

- Gemie aims to disrupt the entertainment industry in Asia with its platform, providing various perks for users who participate by delivering an immersive metaverse and exclusive utility-driven NFTs.[42]

- Gemie provides users with an online store and marketplace where they can buy and sell their custom NFTs, including digital collectibles, wearables, and other items.

- Gemie users gain access to virtual concerts of their favorite artists, movie premieres, after-parties, and exclusive meet-and-greet events with A-list celebrities via the Gemie concert halls.

Circling Back: Leadership Styles Needed for Big C in the Metaverse

- **The agile strategic leader** ensures a purposeful Big C community, bridging digital and physical worlds, and bridging collaborative relationships with other community groups for creating positive impact on planet Earth.

- **The authentic leader** knows that participation, diversity, and inclusion of insight is critical to the entire process of Big C community building.

- **The servant leader-community builder** is an expert at internal community building, creating meaningful and action-oriented bonds within the Big C community.

REFLECTION QUESTIONS

1. What bonding steps (internally) can you take to strengthen your Big C metaverse community?

2. What leadership skills do you need to develop so that you can be proficient in bridging digital and physical worlds, creating a strong metaverse organization?

3. For external bridging, list five priority community partners or collaborators. For each mentioned, develop one or two action steps you can take to reach out, and bridge your organization with those priority groups.

CHAPTER 9

3V COMMUNICATION
IN THE METAVERSE

WHILE THE METAVERSE WILL BRING INNOVATION and the opportunity to immerse in WebMe, the world needs leaders who can create WebWe.

Even today, only 21 percent of employees worldwide are *engaged*—emotionally invested—in their jobs, committing time, talent, and energy in adding value to their team and advancing the organization's initiatives.[1]

The highly entertaining metaverse will create pressure and high expectations for leaders to communicate effectively in both digital and physical worlds, as hybrid communicators. The metaverse will be an exciting tool for leaders to communicate in a relatable, powerful, and attention-grabbing way.

How can metaverse leaders engage their community, build human bonds, and bridge to other communities in a metaverse world challenged by the five Ds?

Cut through the clutter. To bring your organization's purpose and key messages to life, use this 3V communication strategy to provide a helpful framework for your leadership and your metaverse.

3V Communication =

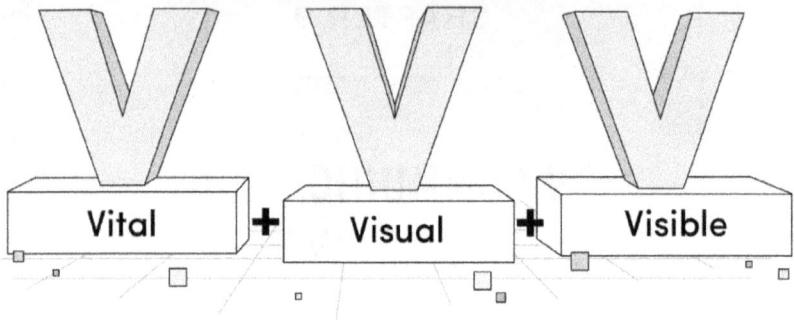

Vital **+** Visual **+** Visible

PRINCIPLES FOR 3V COMMUNICATION

The principles of Vital + Visual + Visible communication provide a helpful framework to share open, agile strategy and lead authentically, while serving others. With a 3V communication strategy, you can more effectively work with creatives who have the skills to help you develop your organization's metaverse.

3V communication borrows from communication theory focused on exploring the ongoing, interactive process of omnidirectional discussion and construction of meaning in both internal and external communication arenas so that messages are understood.[2]

To Be Vital

Communication about the direction of an organization and the purpose, strategy, and plans for the organization must be *essential and meaningful* throughout the organization. The CEO and leadership team create "vital" for the entire organization. They engage employees in creating the organization's future. Employees see themselves as vital to their organization's purpose and strategies.

When an organization's strategic management process is valued and indispensable to the organization's future, all interconnected and continuously executed groups of strategic management activities are viewed as vital. For example, the strategic plan is highly regarded as a life-giving road map to the future—a plan worthy of implementation—not a shelf ornament.[3]

To Be Visual

In the metaverse, strategy communication must *include an immersive experience* with relevant illustrations and picture elements. Visual, in the context of communicating an organization's strategy, aims to bring to life the entire strategic management process through immersive infographics, animated diagrams, charts, photography, and newer techniques such as AR and VR.

Visuals help to create at-a-glance meaning. This helps to clarify complex information. Visuals help employees grasp key messages and discover how their respective roles contribute to the organization's envisioned future success. Visuals also enhance communication with external stakeholders—customers, investors, donors, elected officials, and community leaders.

To Be Visible

Communication about your organization's purpose and direction has to *be easily seen* in a conspicuous, continuous spotlight—not hidden. Your metaverse will be a more immersive internet and the prime tool for reaching your internal and external audiences. When strategies are visible, organizations are well positioned to create stakeholder engagement.[4]

PRACTICES FOR 3V COMMUNICATION IN THE METAVERSE

As discussed earlier, strategic management is a continuous process that draws together an entire enterprise to provide vision, open and agile strategy, and build communities. Here are a few Vital + Visual + Visible communication practices or how-to's for engaging employees and building human communities in the metaverse.

Vital Communication Practices

The CEO and leadership team must take responsibility for creating "vital," as the chief communicators and strategy ambassadors. CEOs are expected to be the face for the company, communicating directly with employees, the public, and investors about financial and strategic issues.

An organization's metaverse space should feature its CEO and leadership team as human beings first—not avatars. This creates leadership accountability, gravitas, authenticity, and urgency for an all-hands-on-deck tone for the community, priming the pump for purposeful strategy conversations.

An organization's strategy communication team should include the chief communication officer (CCO), along with a diverse group of creatives and marketing experts, serving alongside the CEO and senior staff. This is a game-changing concept. Many organizations do not routinely include CCOs, communication staff, and creatives in the strategic management process.[5]

These stakeholders play a key role as internal strategists. Communication, marketing, and creative professionals are experts at developing communication plans, strategy tool kits, and creative digital and social media communication to bond and bridge audiences.

All leaders (from executives to project teams) should have access to a strategy tool kit and strategy training support. For example, your metaverse could provide secure access to your organization's strategic plan, goal dashboard, and training for how to link departments and work groups to the organization's plan.

Leader and employee access to your company's strategy tool kit creates a definite sense of "vital."

Consider creating an interactive metaspace within your organization's metaverse featuring a strategy tool kit and online training modules to equip managers, supervisors, and team leaders to connect unit goals, activities, and performance incentives to enterprise-level goals. The tool kit should prompt interactive strategy discussions for departments and work groups and support one-on-one employee–supervisor meetings throughout the organization.

CASE STUDY: MERCEDES-BENZ GROUP AG

A metaverse-ready global company demonstrating vital strategy communication practices is the Mercedes-Benz Group AG.

Chief executive officer and chairman of the board of management Ola Källenius takes the leading role in communicating the organization's all-electric vehicle strategy "Electromobility by 2030."

To spotlight the EV strategy, Källenius and his executive team host live, global online strategy forums to update employees and external stakeholders, including investors. Forums are recorded and posted on the company's website for later viewing, to support asynchronous learning.

The Mercedes-Benz Group AG communication department also plays a prominent role in supporting the strategy by developing communication tools including strategy videos, animated illustrations, and an exceptional employee website.

In 2022, Mercedes-Benz announced its entry into the NFT space with the launch of an NFT collection honoring the company's G-Class line. This experiment may lead to a fully immersive metaverse.[6]

Visual Communication Practices

As mentioned earlier, the human brain processes visual images 60,000 times faster than text. An astounding 90 percent of information transmitted to the brain is visual illustrations and pictures.[7]

Creative professionals can help your organization develop meaningful visuals including infographics, 3D, VR, and AR techniques to bring your communication to life in the metaverse.

Create visual, animated infographics to simplify, engage, summarize, and inform your audiences. For example, the Winnipeg Public Library in Canada, with the help of creative Sam Bradd, owner of Drawing Change, created an infographic to connect the library's four strategic priorities to eleven strategic goals. The infographic was produced as a poster for use in both the physical and digital worlds.

Transform a lengthy (and boring) written strategic plan into an exciting digital magazine and metaverse experience. Include places for avatar exploration. Feature infographics, videos, photography, and animation. Even organizations with limited budgets can hire a designer to produce an abbreviated, innovative, magazine-style digital story. For example, the North Carolina Museum of Natural Sciences prominently showcased its strategic plan on the museum's website, creating visual impact with big, bold photography paired with carefully selected, poignant data points.[8]

Consider how novel visual communication tools, such as AR and VR, could visually inspire a shared view of the future. This groundbreaking technology could be used to create immersive visual experiences that simulate future scenarios, transcend time and distance, and engage stakeholders in imagining the future.

Visible Communication Practices

Along with being vital and visual, strategic management must be visible—easily seen. The following communication practices support large-scale visibility for ongoing strategy management, using the metaverse as an immersive new tool.

Host frequent, interactive, all-employee strategy forums presented by the CEO and executive team. Live forums can be recorded for rebroadcast—whether held virtually in the metaverse, in person, or in a hybrid format. Metaverse forums can build audiences while cultivating community trust, especially when the audience can participate and engage in dialogue. Strategy forums in the metaverse could include goal celebration, Q&A with the executive team, and employee breakout discussions where people get to know each other.

Maximize your metaverse as a visible, expansive strategy communication platform. An organization's immersive website is the most powerful, cost-effective global marketing and communication tool available, working 24/7 as a visible strategy communication channel. As of today, few global Fortune 500 companies use corporate websites to share strategic initiatives such as excerpts from the strategic plan,

CEO and leader op-ed columns, strategy white papers, podcasts, and videos.[9] This is a missed opportunity.

Walmart uses its website brilliantly to share strategic priorities such as sustainability, diversity, equity, and inclusion on its external corporate website. Videos and photos spotlight employee success stories to show how employees are helping the company achieve strategic priorities. Walmart uses its internal intranet to build a Big C employee community.

Walmart appears to be experimenting with early metaverse technology, including a collection of NFTs, and will be creating its own cryptocurrency. In December of 2021, Walmart filed new trademark applications with the US Patent and Trademark office indicating that the retailer intends to make and sell virtual electronics, appliances, furniture, musical instruments, home decorations, toys, sporting goods, personal care products, and more.[10]

Use social media to create visible, wide-reaching strategy communication to complement your organization's metaverse. By a more than two-to-one ratio, employees said they would prefer to work for a CEO who uses digital and social media. A majority of employees believe the CEO's social media presence has a positive impact on a company's reputation.[11] However, less than half of S&P 500 and Financial Times Stock Exchange (FTSE) 350 CEOs boast a presence on social media.

Hence, organizations should use social media to complement metaverse strategies, to elevate reputation through the CEO, as well as the voices of employees and customers.

Starbucks encourages its baristas to become visible influencers on social media. The company established "Starbucks Partners" on Instagram and Facebook where baristas can share their Starbucks customer service and product stories.

The principles of Vital + Visual + Visible communication provide a framework to build Big C metaverse communities. While these principles and practices may *seem* standard, most are rarely deployed.[12]

As the metaverse evolves, 3V communication provides a mindful methodology to help you forge employee engagement and enhance external stakeholder value.

TACTICS FOR DESIGNING 3V METAVERSE COMMUNICATION

The metaverse may seem like an overwhelming feat for small companies, nonprofits, and organizations with limited staff resources and budgets. Metaverse development resources are growing for those of you who are nontechs, including nonprofit leaders, teachers, and business owners, to help you learn how to develop and scale a metaverse appropriate for your companies, projects, and classrooms.

Creatives across the globe are developing their metaverse skills even as you read this book. They are and will become the talented resources to help you with developing your metaverse.

1. Determine the purpose for your metaverse. Research your audience to assess if there is interest or need for experimenting with a metaverse environment.

2. Partner with one or more creatives who can help you design an engaging metaverse experience based on your goals and research. Include metaverse strategies for bonding and bridging. Create a call to action to ensure your audiences contribute to the desired physical-world impact.

3. Create a persistent welcome station. This is your organization's virtual arrival area for people who visit your metaverse. Provide a warm greeting and sense of belonging from the get-go.

4. In your metaverse welcome area, offer prominent links to allow your visitors to dig deeper into your organization's vision, mission or purpose, priorities, and future destination.

5. Allow visitors to explore your organization in a virtual, creative, and immersive way. For Big C communities, it's important to clearly communicate the purpose of your organization so that the welcoming space is more than just a "cool place." Infuse your organization's purpose. Allow visitors to take a journey into the future. Spotlight goals and key aspirations.

6. Develop an event or program stage to promote and host upcoming live and prerecorded programs. When programs are in progress, the space provides the live show. When not in use, the space becomes a digital billboard to promote your upcoming events.

7. Create a metaspace to share the impact your community members make to advance your organization's purpose. Your community includes employees, volunteers, donors, suppliers, contractors, and beneficiaries of your organization's work.

8. Create clear action steps—your call to action—for supporting your organization's purpose in physical life on planet Earth.

9. Offer fun, free resources in your metaverse space to nurture and build your Big C community. This reinforces your organization's value and commitment to bringing together your community.

10. Update your metaverse resources on a frequent basis. Provide timely, relevant content and places for people to interact. For service and learning organizations, this encourages long-term engagement with your organization.

REFLECTION QUESTIONS

1. What is (or will be/should be) the communication purpose for your organization's metaverse?

2. To prepare for the metaverse—or at the least for more immersive, engaging communication—what specific steps should you be taking to improve your existing hybrid communication?

    o For **vital:** How can your CEO or top executive serve as the leading communication ambassador?

   o For **visual:** How can you create an exciting visual experience for your metaverse community?

   o For **visible:** How will you promote your organization and its metaverse so that it gains visible recognition?

3. How can an immersive metaverse experience support your organization's strategy and community building?

   o How will the metaverse help you enhance internal bonding?

   o How will the metaverse help you bridge hybrid worlds internally?

   o How will the metaverse help you bridge to external collaborating groups?

CLOSING THOUGHTS: AN EVOLVING, CONTINUING CONVERSATION

FOR THOSE WHO AIM TO BUILD Big C communities in our rapidly evolving metaverse world, this is a beginning conversation.

As our society gravitates toward highly individualized hybrid worlds, as well as digitized, automated systems to stay competitive, I'm concerned about the human impact. Will the quest for a more immersive internet lead to an individualistic and even more fractured society? Will our efforts to enhance speed, streamline repetitive processes, improve efficiency, and reduce costs of service delivery defeat the purpose of meeting customer expectations, and subtract simple acts of human kindness from the customer service process? Will human hearts become hardened, where employees prefer to *not* speak with customers, or each other? These are scary thoughts, because connection, kindness, and the sense of acceptance and belonging are basic human needs.

In our hybrid environment where digital and physical worlds are becoming seamless, I believe competitive advantage will favor organizations led by effective leaders—those who are authentic, agile, and strategic. Those who are dedicated to being servant leaders, who are prepared to build, bond, and bridge communities—not just in the traditional physical world, but also in digital metaverse worlds.

As we rapidly move toward the metaverse, our world needs kind, compassionate, and wise leaders. Effective leaders in the metaverse will create meaningful, truthful conversations—fostering civil discourse and human belonging to create productive, Big C impact in organizations, communities, cities, countries—and in the hearts and lives of human beings.

The desire for humans to connect with each other is a profoundly deep, emotional need. The leadership, strategy, and community-building chapters each could have been written as a separate book. However, it was my intent to bring together these critical subjects to be significantly impacted by Web3, knowing that the metaverse is in a nascent stage.

Future generations will not know a world prior to the metaverse. As we prepare for the metaverse sea change to come, now is the time to cultivate the needed skills and help future generations strengthen their personal leadership resiliency and capacity to be human-focused.

Leadership, strategy, and community building in hybrid contexts are still a novel topic, with unchartered waters ahead. I look forward to frequently updating this book, bringing fresh insight for effective leadership, strategy, and Big C community building in the metaverse.

You'll find additional case studies, video interviews, tools, and timely articles on my website (https://carolpoore.com). I invite you to reach out to me if you would like to share a metaverse case study to contribute to the body of knowledge of leadership in the metaverse—including principles, practices, and insights.

I look forward to learning together with you in the metaverse. As you grow your leadership, strategy, and community-building skills, you will make a Big C difference in people's lives on planet Earth.

ACKNOWLEDGMENTS

I THANK EVERY METAVERSE PIONEER, INDUSTRY executive, and creative professional contributing thought leadership and cited in my book. I was thrilled to learn about the metaverse from you.

I'm grateful for my editorial team, Anne Sanow, Diana Coe, and Sally Garland. I thank the entire team at Fast Company Press and Greenleaf Book Group for their belief in this book's contributions to the future of leadership, strategy, and community building in our evolving, unprecedented metaverse world.

I always will cherish the fascinating conversation with my sons, Nathan Poore and Justin Poore, in late 2021 as we took a holiday walk on the beach. We had a remarkable—seemingly eccentric—conversation about the metaverse. I was shocked to consider future implications for human relationships, including principles for leadership, strategy formation, and community building. That discussion sparked my intent to write this book.

I thank Justin Poore for creating brilliant illustrations, bringing to life my key themes. I thank each case study organization for providing a compelling example, demonstrating great commitment to serving customers, constituents, and communities.

A METAVERSE GLOSSARY

THIS GLOSSARY PROVIDES AN OVERVIEW OF innovation leading up to the metaverse. Here's a roundup of terms and concepts relevant now and as the metaverse continues to develop.

3D movies, drawings, or experiences feature depth beyond the two dimensions of width and height, adding realism. 3D eyewear usually is required.

3D-plus will provide a more immersive, multidimensional internet experience within the metaverse. These dimensions go beyond 3D to offer deeper levels of immersive experiences.[1]

4D is based on a 3D experience but adds a new element to the mix: motion. For example, it incorporates a dynamic seat system that moves with the flow of the movie and further enhances the immersive experience.

5D is based on 4D and includes an additional element: sensation. For example, the user will feel wind, mist, snow, and so forth throughout the experience. Aromas also could be classified in a 5D immersive experience.

7D is based on a 5D experience, but it includes some interactivity. For instance, a user can point an artificial gun at a target and guide the movie's plot in a new direction. The audience participates in the film's storyline and further immerses themselves in the overall experience.

9D includes virtual reality (VR). This means the user can wear a VR headset and block out the physical world around them. The audience is fully immersed in a virtual experience.

10D represents the ongoing evolution of 3D, 4D, 5D, 7D, and 9D and offers a superior immersive experience with enhanced visual and interactive effects. It signifies the constant improvement of the user's immersive experience.

5G networks are critical to metaverse speed in transmitting large media files. 5G is the fifth-generation telecommunications technology standard for broadband cellular networks, giving people the ability to enjoy faster connections from almost anywhere in the world. 5G networks are predicted to have more than 1.7 billion subscribers worldwide by 2025, according to the GSM Association.[2] Similar to its predecessors, 5G networks are cellular networks in which the service area is divided into small geographical areas called cells. All 5G wireless devices in a cell are connected to the internet and telephone network by radio waves through a local antenna in the cell. 5G networks feature greater bandwidth providing higher download speeds, and thus improve the quality of internet services in crowded areas. (Note: 6G networks are already in development stages.)

Ambient technology refers to a future beyond computer screens and goggles, when our interaction with the digital world takes place through intuitive technology that anticipates our needs. This emerging technology supports metaverse development.

Artificial general intelligence (AGI). The intention of an AGI system is to perform any task a human would have the capacity to perform. If perfected, the capacities of AGI would exceed human capacities because of its ability to access and process huge data sets at incredible speeds. Today, no true AGI systems exist. AGI systems share in common with humans the ability to reason, apply abstract thinking, and use background knowledge and common sense. AGI processes visual, auditory, and other input to adapt to environments in a wide variety of settings.

Artificial intelligence (AI) is intelligence demonstrated by machines, as opposed to the natural intelligence displayed by humans. Each of today's AI systems can perform only one narrowly defined task.[3] AI is designed for complex, nonrepetitive tasks, to analyze and react to environmental data. AI evolves and learns based on prior and current data. It helps organizations analyze data and can identify patterns.[4] Examples of newer AI technology include Grammarly, an online service for rewriting whole sentences, and a sales support system called Liveperson, featuring conversational bots that answer customer queries.

Augmented reality (AR) combines virtual images on top of the real world, augmenting your senses to create new experiences. For example, you might point your smartphone to a piece of art in a museum, and information about the artist appears as you view the art. AR often is combined with virtual reality (VR).

Autonomous (self-driving) cars are vehicles capable of sensing their environment and operating without human involvement. A human passenger is not required to take control of the vehicle at any time, nor is a human passenger required to be present in the vehicle at all. The Society of Automotive Engineers currently defines six levels of driving automation, ranging from Level 0 (fully manual) to Level 5 (fully autonomous). These levels have been adopted by the US Department of Transportation.

Avatar. An avatar is a visual, graphical representation of a computer user or the user's character or persona. Avatars can be two-dimensional icons, or they can take the form of three-dimensional characters, as used in online worlds and video games.[5]

Blockchain technology is a shared, immutable ledger that facilitates the process of recording transactions and tracking assets in a business network. An asset can be tangible (a house, car, cash, land) or intangible (intellectual property, patents, copyrights, branding). Virtually anything of value can be tracked and traded on a blockchain network, reducing risk and cutting costs for all involved.[6] Blockchain provides immediate, shared, and completely transparent information stored on an immutable ledger that can be accessed only by permissioned network members. A blockchain network can track orders, payments, accounts, production, and all details of a transaction end to end, sharing a single view or "truth" for the transaction. Key elements of blockchain include distributed ledger technology, immutable records, and smart contracts.

Bored Apes Yacht Club is a collection of 10,000 unique Bored Ape NFTs. These are unique digital collectibles living on the Ethereum blockchain. Each Bored Ape doubles as a Yacht Club membership card and grants access to members-only benefits, the first of which is access to The Bathroom, a collaborative graffiti board. Future areas and perks can be unlocked by the community through road map activation. (Visit www.BoredApeYachtClub.com for details.)

Cryptocurrency, sometimes referred to as "crypto" or "coin," is a digital currency designed to work as a medium of exchange through a computer network that is not reliant on any central authority, such as a government or bank, to uphold or maintain it.[7] Cryptocurrency is a tradable digital asset or digital form of money, built on blockchain technology that only exists online. Cryptocurrencies use encryption to authenticate and protect transactions. There are more than a thousand different cryptocurrencies in the world. Bitcoin, Ethereum, and Tether top the list of dozens of cryptocurrency companies that have emerged since Bitcoin's launch in 2009. Individual coin ownership records are stored in a digital ledger, a computerized database using strong cryptography to secure transaction records, control the creation of additional coins, and verify the transfer of coin ownership. Cryptocurrencies are not considered to be currencies in the traditional sense. While varying treatments have been applied, including classification as commodities, securities, as well as currencies, cryptocurrencies are generally viewed as a distinct asset class.

Decentralized, autonomous organizations (DAOs). Sometimes called a decentralized autonomous corporation (DAC), a DAO is an organization constructed by rules encoded as a computer program that is often transparent, controlled by the organization's members and not influenced by a central government. These are member-owned communities without centralized leadership. A DAO's financial transaction records and program rules are maintained on a blockchain. This approach eliminates the need to involve a mutually acceptable, trusted third party in any decentralized digital interaction or cryptocurrency transaction.[8]

Decentralized finance (DeFi) offers financial instruments without relying on intermediaries such as brokerages, exchanges, or banks by using smart contracts on a blockchain. DeFi platforms allow people to lend or borrow funds from others, speculate on price movements on assets using derivatives, trade cryptocurrencies, insure against risks, and earn interest in savings-like accounts.[9]

Deepfake is media, either video or audio, in which a person in an existing image or video or audio track is replaced with someone else's likeness. While the act of creating fake content is not new, deepfakes leverage powerful techniques from machine learning and artificial intelligence to manipulate or generate visual and audio content that can more easily deceive audiences. Deepfakes have garnered widespread attention for their uses in creating child sexual abuse material, celebrity pornographic videos, revenge porn, fake news, hoaxes, bullying, and financial fraud. This has elicited responses from both industry and government to detect and limit their use.[10]

Digital assets are anything that is stored digitally, are uniquely identifiable, and that people or organizations can use to realize value. Digital assets include photos, logos, digital art, and digital information resulting in business transactions.

Digital twins are digital replicas of a physical process or assets (such as a car engine, or a city's street infrastructure) that can be measured for performance through the internet, equipped to monitor the real-life system or process. For example, a digital twin could replicate a city's system of roads, electrical transmission, and sewer and water lines, as well as other data to help monitor real-time traffic, energy use, and interaction.

Distributed ledger technology is a distributed ledger and its immutable record of transactions made available to all network participants. With this shared ledger, transactions are recorded only once, eliminating the duplication of effort that is typical of traditional business networks.

Exchange-traded funds (ETFs) are a type of investment fund and exchange-traded product traded on stock exchanges. By August 2021, $9 trillion was invested in ETFs globally, including $6.6 trillion invested in the United States. ETFs are similar in many ways to mutual funds, except that ETFs are bought and sold from other owners throughout the day on stock exchanges, whereas mutual funds are bought and sold from the issuer based on their price at day's end. An ETF divides ownership of itself into shares held by shareholders.[11]

Exponential intelligence goes beyond the traditional AI realm. While AI-fueled organizations have used machine intelligence to make decisions that augment or automate human thinking, the next-generation intelligence—from analyst to predictor to actor—will increasingly access human behavioral data at scale. Exponential intelligence will better understand and emulate human emotion and intent—an emotional AI. For example, a smile, a thoughtful pause, or a choice of words could be data-aggregated and used to help an organization develop a more holistic understanding of customers, employees, citizens, and students.[12]

Extended reality (XR) is a term referring to physical (real) and virtual combined environments and human–machine interactions generated by computer technology and wearables. XR includes AR, mixed reality (MR), and VR. XR is a superset that includes the entire spectrum from "the complete real" to "the complete virtual" in the concept of reality.[13]

GIS mapping is a geographic information system (GIS) that creates, manages, analyzes, and maps all types of data. GIS connects data to a map, integrating location data with descriptive information. This provides a foundation for mapping and analysis that is used in science and industry. For example, a mapping tool is contributing to research and sustainability of coral reef health by allowing Allen Coral Atlas researchers and policymakers to use satellite data to track and analyze coral reef health around the world. Prior to the Allen Coral Atlas, this data had not been available at this scale.[14]

Haptic technology or haptics, also known as kinesthetic communication and 3D touch, refers to any technology that can create an experience of touch by applying forces, vibrations, or motions to the user. These technologies can be used to create virtual objects in a computer simulation, to control virtual objects, and to enhance remote control of machines and devices (telerobotics).[15]

Holograms are physical structures that diffract light into an image. The term can refer to both the encoded material and the resulting image. A viewer's eyes perceive virtual images as if they were real objects. The recording of light wave interference patterns can be played back to create a high-resolution image in full color and three dimensions.[16]

Immutable records mean that no participant can change or tamper with a transaction after it's been recorded to the shared ledger. If a transaction record includes an error, a new transaction must be added to reverse the error, and both transactions are then visible.

Intranet is a private platform for employees that companies use for internal communication, document management, and knowledge sharing. It may be an on-site solution accessible only from the office, or a cloud-based intranet platform that employees can access remotely.[17]

Massively multiplayer online role-playing game (MMORPG) is a video game that combines aspects of a role-playing video game and a massively multiplayer online game. As in role-playing games, the player assumes the role of a character and takes control over the character's actions. MMORPGs commonly feature persistent game environment, some form of level progression, social interaction within the game, in-game culture, system architecture, membership in a group, and character customization. The virtual world in which the game takes place is never static; even when a player is logged off, events are occurring across the world that may impact the player when they log in again.

Mixed reality (MR) is the merging of real and virtual worlds to produce new environments and visualizations, where physical and digital objects coexist and interact in real time. Mixed reality does not exclusively take place in either the physical world or virtual world but is a hybrid of augmented reality and virtual reality. While augmented reality takes place in the physical world, with information or objects added virtually like an overlay, virtual reality immerses you in a fully virtual world without the intervention of the physical world.[18]

Movies about the metaverse such as Ernest Kline's *Ready Player One*. This science fiction novel was published in 2011 and was produced into a movie directed by Steven Spielberg in 2018. The story plot presents a metaverse (the OASIS) that was escapist and nostalgic. The story, set in a 2045 dystopia, follows protagonist Wade Watts on his search for an Easter egg in a worldwide virtual reality game, the discovery of which would lead him to inherit the game creator's fortune. *The Matrix* movie series, the first of which debuted in 1999, also features a multiworld, metaverse theme.

Nonfungible token (NFT) is a noninterchangeable unit of data stored on a blockchain, a form of digital ledger, that can be sold and traded. For example, NFT data units could include digital files such as photos, videos, audio files, and digital art. With today's growing investor interest in the NFT space, a new study predicts that the existing $3 billion market will reach $13.6 billion by the end of 2027.[19] Driving forces include celebrity influencers, gamers and the gaming community, and the growing demand for digital artwork, retail, and fashion.

Online gambling is the act of placing wagers on risk-based games for the chance of winning money. Sports matches, casino games, and popular card games such as poker are common forms of online gambling. Online gambling is a massive business worldwide. In the United States alone, the current size of the gambling industry is $46 billion and is expected to more than double in size, to more than $94 billion by 2024.[20] After sports betting was legalized in the United States by the Supreme Court in 2018, online gambling companies are now able to grow their sports betting sectors, thereby further supporting the market's growth.

Online gaming from companies such as Roblox and Epic Games are bringing huge depth to virtual worlds. Roblox says its mission is to build a "human co-experience platform" that enables shared experiences among billions of users in their creator community. As of this publication date, the number of daily active users on Roblox was 52.2 million average daily users, up 21 percent year over year.[21]

OpenSea. Founders Devin Finzer and Alex Atallah launched OpenSea in December 2017, the first and largest open digital marketplace for crypto collectibles and NFTs, enabling users to buy, sell, and discover exclusive digital items when the Ethereum blockchain was born. OpenSea raised $100 million at a $1.5 billion valuation, as trading volumes—gross merchandise volume—was reported to top $3.4 billion by August of 2021.[22] Today, OpenSea is the largest general marketplace for user-owned digital items, supporting multiple blockchains, with the broadest set of categories. OpenSea aspires to be the most accessible marketplace for buyers, sellers, and creators.

Quantum technologies exploit the quirky properties of subatomic particles to allow us to solve seemingly intractable problems using physics instead of mathematics. Quantum represents as big a leap over digital as digital was over analog. For example, quantum computing can solve complex computational problems by processing enormous data sets in new ways. Quantum computers have demonstrated they can complete specialized tasks in five minutes that would take classical supercomputers thousands of years. Quantum communication is hardware-based technology that can vastly improve cybersecurity by creating theoretically tamper-proof networks that can detect attempts at interception and eavesdropping. This secure communication will use emerging techniques such as quantum key distribution, which is a way to more safely exchange encryption keys to transmit data across optical networks. Quantum sensing devices are more responsive and accurate than conventional sensors. These are being tested in energy, transportation, and healthcare fields. Quantum sensors may be lighter, more portable, more energy efficient, and less expensive than their predecessors.

Rec Room is a gaming and cocreator website inviting people to build and play games together. Rec Room is free and cross-plays on a variety of tech tools, from smartphones to VR headsets.

Robotics is an interdisciplinary branch of computer science and engineering. Robotics involves design, engineering, construction, operation, and use of robots. The goal of robotics is to design machines that can help and assist humans, as well as substitute for humans and replicate human actions.[23] Robots can take on a variety of forms. Some are made to resemble humans in appearance. Robots can be used for many purposes, such as in dangerous environments including inspection of radioactive materials, bomb detection and deactivation, and manufacturing processes, or where humans cannot survive, such as in high temperatures and underwater.

The Sandbox is an online community-driven platform where creators can monetize voxel assets and gaming experiences on the blockchain. The Sandbox is a multiplayer virtual world backed by a real cash economy. The players are creators who can build 3D games for free, with no coding required. The Sandbox metaverse is made up of LANDS that are parts of the world, owned by players to create and monetize experiences. Only a quantity of 166,464 LANDS are available, which can be used to host games, build multiplayer experiences, create housing, or offer social experiences to the community. Ownership of LAND allows users to sell their assets and events, such as concerts, as well as vote on governance decisions. SAND is the utility token used throughout The Sandbox ecosystem as the basis for transactions and interactions. It is an ERC-20 utility token built on the Ethereum blockchain. There is a finite supply of 3,000,000,000 Sand.

Smart contracts used to speed transactions are a set of rules stored on the blockchain and executed automatically. A smart contract can define conditions for corporate bond transfers, include terms for travel insurance to be paid, and much more.

Smart homes. A smart home refers to a convenient home setup where appliances and devices can be automatically controlled remotely by the homeowner anywhere with an internet connection, using mobile or other networked devices. Devices in a smart home are interconnected through the internet, allowing the user to control functions such as security access to the home, temperature, lighting, and home theaters.

Social media is a computer-based technology that facilitates the sharing of ideas, thoughts, and information through the building of virtual networks and communities. As of this publication date, there are more than 4.7 billion social media users around the world (out of a total world population of 7.98 billion).[24] Social media typically features user-generated content and personalized profiles. The largest social media networks include Facebook (now Meta), Instagram, Twitter, YouTube, and TikTok.

Space tourism, also known as "NewSpace" and privatized space travel, encompasses international and multinational efforts to privatize spaceflight as a commercial industry. Private spaceflight is space travel or the development of spaceflight technology conducted and paid for by an entity other than a government agency. Space tourism is human space travel for recreational purposes. There are several different types of space tourism, including orbital, suborbital, and lunar space tourism. In late March of 2022, Blue Origin performed its fourth crewed suborbital spaceflight with six passengers on board the *New Shepard*. In early April 2022, SpaceX's *Crew Dragon* space capsule was launched by a Falcon 9 rocket for the first American space tourist mission to the International Space Station. The crew on board the Axiom Space–operated mission included one professional astronaut (space vehicle commander) and three tourists. Known as Axiom Mission 1, the mission lasted more than seventeen days and was the first wholly commercially operated crewed mission to the International Space Station.[25]

Virtual reality (VR) immerses users in an entirely fictitious world designed for VR headsets and goggles, allowing users to explore new worlds and experiences designed exclusively for VR devices. The newest headsets projecting digital imagery are sleek, similar to putting on a pair of glasses.

Voting and polling through digital means enables organizations to gather information about how people feel about any given topic, and is available through Zoom, Mailchimp, and other apps. Users are given voting rights, and in some cases the ability to decide the fate of a product or project, or share suggestions. For example, Reddit is home to communities that are invited to vote and post conversations based on topics of interest. The Reddit website says, "Whether you're into breaking news, sports, TV fan theories, or a never-ending stream of the internet's cutest animals, there's a community on Reddit for you."[26]

Wearable technology—also called wearables, fashion technology, smartwear, tech togs, streetwear tech, skin electronics, or fashion electronics—are smart electronic devices (electronic device with micro-controllers) worn close to or on the surface of skin. Wearables detect, analyze, and transmit body signals such as vital signs or ambient data to allow biofeedback to be transmitted. Wearable devices such as activity trackers represent the "things" of the internet. Things include electronics, software, sensors, and connectivity, enabling objects to exchange data, including data quality through the internet, with a manufacturer, operator, or other connected device without requiring human intervention. Wearable technology has a variety of applications that grow as the field itself expands. It appears prominently in consumer electronics with the popularization of the smartwatch and activity tracker. Wearable technology is being incorporated into navigation systems, advanced textiles, and healthcare.

METAVERSE PIONEERS DESCRIBE COMMUNITY

THE METAVERSE HAS BEEN DESCRIBED AS the new Wild, Wild West. The following conversations explore the new paradigm of community building in the metaverse in the eyes of metaverse thought leaders.

COMMUNITY AS USERS (USERS VERSUS MEMBERS)

Because the metaverse is being created by large tech companies, most of which are involved in online gaming, it's helpful to investigate the definition of community through the lens of gamers who are loyal members of certain communities.

Digital Native blogger Rex Woodbury considers the idea of community as the world's citizens, as one, digitally connected species.

"Around 60 percent of the human race, or 4.5 billion people, are online," Woodbury notes. "What's fascinating is that today's communities are both the deepest and the broadest in human history. On the one hand, maybe only one in a thousand people like the same things as you—but with four billion people online, that's four million people who share your interests. On the internet, no niche is too niche . . . the internet's scale unlocks breadth . . . this scale has never been seen before."[1]

He notes that 142 million Netflix accounts watched *Squid Game* in its first month—67 percent of all accounts around the world.

While this might represent a community for Netflix, the community may have a shorter lifespan based on the popularity of the game, or the show—connected to the cultural phenomenon or trend.

To extend the duration of an online community, some companies are creating loyalty "friction" to incentivize community members to stay loyal and feel as if they are part of an elite group.

For example, Chinese streaming site Bilibili makes users pass a hundred-question test before they're authorized to join the community—that is, before they are permitted to upload videos or post comments. This community retained 80 percent of its users after twelve months, signaling that the friction produced by the test ensured a super–fan base of loyal gamers.

COMMUNITY AS SHARED GOVERNANCE

A core Web3 community principle is shared governance. This includes the removal of the middleman of large tech companies to enable peer-to-peer social and transactional relationships. Community members are rewarded based on their actual contributions, both financially and through social recognition.

For example, Braintrust is a decentralized talent network bringing together freelance creatives and clients without taking a portion of the freelancer's pay or charging fees to the freelancer. Freelancers and clients are combined stakeholders who form community ownership and participate in governance, contributing to discussions and voting on community decisions.

Braintrust's website says that it is the world's first decentralized talent network—owned and controlled by its users rather than a central corporation. Its network is built on cryptocurrency, enabling decentralization at a large scale. According to Braintrust, the blockchain is "immutable":

> It provides a record that cannot be altered over time, making the user's record of ownership and control over the network incorruptible. This form of blockchain is a permissionless system because it can be accessed by anyone around the world with an internet connection, no prior authorization is required.
>
> Everyone is an owner, owning not just a portion of the benefits from the value they produce, but also their work histories, reputations, and data. This is in stark contrast to extractive models, which often monetize that critical information at their own users' expense.[2]

VitaDAO is a DAO collective for community-governed and decentralized drug development. The company offers a new approach to drug development. Members can earn tokens through contributing funds, work, or valuable research data or IP assets; in return, they're given governance and decision-making power, and the tokens act as equity in the project.

Its core mission is "the acceleration of research and development in the longevity space and the extension of human life and healthspan. VitaDAO collectively funds and digitizes research in the form of intellectual property (IP) NFTs."[3]

COMMUNITY AS OPEN SYSTEMS OF CONNECTIVITY

In Web3 terms, the definition of "community" equates to open chambers or open systems of connectivity and interoperability across all metaverse platforms.

For example, Adobe defines the metaverse community as a place open and accessible to all:

> Where the creative technology is simple to use. And where everyone can create, shop, and connect . . . The metaverse is a rich, persistent, interactive experience featuring co-creation and fully functioning shared economies. As one type of shared immersive experience, the metaverse is an always-on digital environment where visitors can shop, socialize, train for their jobs, play games, take classes, attend meetings, have cultural experiences, and more.[4]

COMMUNITY COLLECTIVE FUNDERS FOR CREATIVE PROJECTS

Many companies are emphasizing communities of funding. This includes nonprofit communities of funding, as well as for-profit investment, into business ventures and ideas.

Reddit is a social news aggregation, content rating, and discussion website. Its crowdfunding is focused on supporting creative projects nominated by its community. Note that this is entrepreneurial giving, rather than philanthropic giving.

Registered users submit content to the site such as links, text posts, images, and videos, which are then voted upon by other members. Reddit defines their community as "home to endless human creativity, connection, and collaboration. People come together to do surprising, incredible, and inspiring things."[5]

Reddit is experimenting with creating a community fund for creative projects nominated by its community. Projects have included a comics tournament, a community-designed musical artist billboard in New York City's Times Square, and a digital conference for history buffs. Reddit notes that "community funds align with our mission of bringing community and belonging to everyone in the world. We believe that empowering moderation teams and their communities to do more by awarding funds to support their best ideas is one way we can accomplish this."[6]

COMMUNITY AS DECENTRALIZED, AUTONOMOUS, AND TRANSPARENT

The community as decentralized, autonomous, and transparent is highly connected to blockchain technology and shared governance. Decentralization means there are no centralized bodies or gatekeepers required for users. Similar to laissez-faire leadership, power is in the hands of people, not a single entity.

Decentralized platforms include DAOs and DeFi platforms. DAOs function through smart contracts, creating transparency and authentication deployed on blockchain networks. Members with stake in the particular DAO possess certain voting rights on governance plans.[7]

Transparency in decentralized platforms is critical for members in the community to—

- Trust in the idea of the community.
- Actively take part in discussions.
- Pitch in suggestions.
- Be a part of governance proposals.
- Help onboard new members.
- Promote the community.
- Maintain a relevant environment.[8]

COMMUNITY AS CREATORS SHARING WORK

Creativity and the recognition of individual contributors is driving community engagement on common ground in virtual groups. For example, Rove is a user-owned and user-created metaverse for people creating their own metaverse spaces. Rove's website says that "everything in Rove is permissionless by design. Anyone can create their website and operate it freely outside the jurisdiction of centralized institutions and corporations."[9]

Assets in Rove are owned by "Rovers"—the users, not Rove. Rovers hold their private keys and have sole control over what they create, represented by cryptographic NFTs. Unstoppable smart contracts are used to program relationships between these assets.

Rove discusses communities as "metaverse developments." These are virtual places where creators inspire the development of new projects, as follows:

- **Give back to your community.** The community is the centerpiece of a project's success. Engage your community with additional utilities such as exclusive personal homes for members, content sharing and interactive games, all within the Rove-powered metaverse.

- **A virtual community space where everyone can live.** Build a place where your members belong, where people can celebrate their identities, share ideas with others, and bring life to their NFTs.

- **Create a thriving digital economy** and **valuable NFT assets for your members.** Explore new ways to generate revenues for your project and community's ongoing development.[10]

COMMUNITY AS GAMERS AND GAME CREATORS

Gaming websites build communities from the moment a gamer arrives. For example, *Minecraft,* a Microsoft Xbox game, welcomes gamers to their website by describing their community as follows: "Our Minecraft community never stops amazing us with their creativity. On this page, we gather some of their best work—videos, builds, and more."[11]

> The Minecraft website features community news and a community town hall. An online store reinforces gamers' sense of identity by selling branded apparel and products. Gamers can send a message to #FeatureMeMinecraft to explore an opportunity to be featured on the website.

COMMUNITY AS OPEN, DIVERSE, AND INCLUSIVE

Developing open, diverse, equitable, and inclusive communities is a top priority for organizations to thrive. Big C community builders may find helpful insight by examining Meta's five principles and initiatives for building metaverse communities of diversity and inclusion. Meta notes its early efforts to build a diverse and inclusive metaverse include the following principles.

Asking the right questions: To work toward an inclusive metaverse, we need to ask the right questions about what inclusivity must look like in immersive experiences. We're doing that through a two-year, $50 million investment in partnerships, exploring issues related to the metaverse from different perspectives. Through a partnership with Howard University, researchers will explore historical barriers to information technology and offer recommendations on how we can remove those barriers.

Building networks of diverse talent: Diverse people shouldn't just participate in the metaverse as consumers; they should be its architects and builders as well. To make that happen, we need to increase the diversity of people working in the tech industry, particularly in areas like AI, gaming, VR, and AR. We're partnering with institutions across the

United States—historically Black colleges and universities, Hispanic-serving institutions, and Asian American and Native American Pacific Islander—serving institutions—to attract more students to deep learning courses and increase diversity and equity in the field of AI.

Breaking down language barriers: People will feel more connected to others if they can communicate, work, or produce art in their chosen languages. They'll also have the potential to immediately reach billions of others across the world regardless of their preferred language. Can you imagine how that would change our lives? Possibilities like these drive our long-term efforts to build new translation tools that will give creators and consumers the ability to participate equally in the metaverse in more languages and reach people in the farthest corners of the globe.

Broadening access to the metaverse for users and creators: Participation in the metaverse will not depend on having access to a headset. There will be many entry points through which people can participate using any device, including mobile phones. Enabling access for creators from diverse backgrounds is equally important . . . our Spark AR platform is being used by creators in 190 countries to build immersive experiences across Meta's apps and devices.

Creating myriad options for self-expression: Representations in the metaverse should reflect the diversity of the real world. Recently, we announced improvements to our Meta avatars, including new facial shapes and assistive devices such as cochlear implants, over-the-ear hearing aids, and wheelchairs for people with disabilities. When you create your avatar, you can choose the facial features, body type, clothing styles, and more that are right for you. We offered more than one quintillion different combinations when we launched our updated avatars last year, and we're continuing to add more options to give people even more ways to express themselves.[12]

NOTES

PREFACE

1. Bosworth, Andrew, and Nick Clegg (2021). "Building the Metaverse Responsibly," Meta, September 27, 2021, https://about.fb.com/news/2021/09/building-the-metaverse-responsibly/.
2. Kotter, John P. (1996). *Leading Change* (Boston: Harvard Business School Press, 1996).
3. Proulx, Mike (2021). "Consumers Aren't Ready for the Metaverse Yet," Forrester, September 21, 2021, https://www.forrester.com/blogs/consumers-arent-ready-for-the-metaverse-yet/.

CHAPTER 1

1. Newton, Casey (2021). "Mark Zuckerberg in the Metaverse," The Verge, July 22, 2021, https://www.theverge.com/22588022/mark-zuckerberg-facebook-ceo-metaverse-interview.
2. Stephenson, Neal (1992). *Snow Crash* (New York: Penguin Random House, 1992).
3. Villar, Toin (2022). "What Is Second Life? A Brief History of the Metaverse," MUO, April 11, 2022, https://www.makeuseof.com/what-is-second-life-history-metaverse/.
4. Wong, Jeff (2021). "The Metaverse: An Innovation Worth Leadership Attention," *Fast Company*, December 10, 2021, https://www.fastcompany.com/90705119/the-metaverse-an-innovation-worth-leadership-attention.
5. Denton, Jack (2022). "Metaverse May Be Worth $13 Trillion, Citi Says. What's Behind the Bullish Take on Web3," *Barron's*, March 31, 2022, https://www.barrons.com/articles/metaverse-web3-internet-virtual-reality-gaming-nvidia-51648744930.
6. Marr, Bernard (2022). "The Effects of the Metaverse on Society," *Forbes*, April 4, 2022, https://www.forbes.com/sites/bernardmarr/2022/04/04/the-effects-of-the-metaverse-on-society/?sh=6addb7d3765b.

7. Major, Jordan (2021). "Roblox CEO Says We're 'in the Middle of the Metaverse Right Now.'" Review of Bloomberg Technology's Marketcap interview by Emily Chang, Finbold.com Technology News, November 17, 2021, https://finbold.com/roblox-ceo-says-were-in-the-middle-of-the-metaverse-right-now/#:~:text=%E2%80%9CWe%20shared%20a%20vision%20today,amazing%20brands%2C%E2%80%9D%20Baszucki%20said.

8. Gelles, David (2021). "What Bosses Really Think about the Future of the Office," *New York Times*, November 12, 2021, https://www.nytimes.com/2021/11/12/business/corner-office-return.html.

9. Kropp, Brian and Emily Rose McRae (2022). "11 Trends that Will Shape Work in 2022 and Beyond," *Harvard Business Review*, January 13, 2022, https://hbr.org/2022/01/11-trends-that-will-shape-work-in-2022-and-beyond.

10. Parker, Kim, Juliana Menasce Horowitz, and Rachel Minkin (2022). "COVID-19 Pandemic Continues to Reshape Work in America," Pew Research Center, February 16, 2022, https://www.pewresearch.org/social-trends/2022/02/16/covid-19-pandemic-continues-to-reshape-work-in-america/.

11. CNET Highlights, "Watch Mark Zuckerberg's Vision for Socializing in the Metaverse," October 28, 2021, https://www.youtube.com/watch?v=b9vWShsmE20.

12. Liao, Shannon (2021). "Roblox, the Game Company Made Wildly Popular by Kids, Goes Public with $41 Billion Valuation," *Washington Post*, March 10, 2021, https://www.washingtonpost.com/video-games/2021/03/11/roblox-ipo/.

13. Ureneck, Elise Italiano (2022). "The Metaverse Is Coming. Can It Be Saved?" Angelus, April 4, 2022, https://angelusnews.com/arts-culture/here-comes-the-metaverse-are-we-ready/.

14. Bloomberg Intelligence, "Metaverse May Be $800 Billion Market, Next Tech Platform," Bloomberg Intelligence, December 1, 2021, https://www.bloomberg.com/professional/blog/metaverse-may-be-800-billion-market-next-tech-platform/.

15. Ball, Matthew. Metaverse author and venture capitalist and also cofounder of Ball Metaverse Research Partners, which maintains the Roundhill Ball Metaverse ETF.

16. Desjardins, Jeff (2018). "How Long Does It Take to Hit 50 Million Users?" Visual Capitalist, June 8, 2018, https://www.visualcapitalist.com/how-long-does-it-take-to-hit-50-million-users/.

17. Hackl, Cathy, Dirk Leuth, and Tommaso Di Bartolo (2022). *Navigating the Metaverse: A Guide to Limitless Possibilities in a Web 3.0 World* (Hoboken, NJ: Wiley, 2022).

18. Stackpole, Thomas (2022). "Exploring the Metaverse." *Harvard Business Review*, July–August 2022, https://hbr.org/2022/07/exploring-the-metaverse.

19. Ravenscraft, Eric (2022). "What Is the Metaverse, Exactly? Everything You Never Wanted to Know about the Future of Talking about the Future," *WIRED*, April 25, 2022, https://www.wired.com/story/what-is-the-metaverse/.

20. Raz-Fridman, Yonatan, Matthew Kanterman, and Rebecca Sin(2022). "The Metaverse ETF Boom Is No Virtual Reality," *Into the Metaverse* (podcast), February 23, 2022, https://podcasts.apple.com/us/podcast/the-metaverse-etf-boom-is-no-virtual-reality/id1593908027?i=1000552018640.

21. Zuckerberg, Mark (2021). "The Metaverse and How We'll Build It Together," Connect 2021, Meta, YouTube, October 28, 2021, https://www.youtube.com/watch?v=Uvufun6xer8.

22. Newton, Casey (2021). "Facebook's CEO on Why the Social Network Is Becoming 'a Metaverse Company,'" The Verge, July 22, 2021, https://www.theverge.com/22588022/mark-zuckerberg-facebook-ceo-metaverse-interview.

23. Wilser, Jeff (2022). "Matthew Ball: Metaverse Man," CoinDesk, April 18, 2022 and updated May 23, 2022, https://www.coindesk.com/business/2022/04/18/matthew-ball-metaverse-man/.

24. Ball, Matthew (2022). *The Metaverse: And How It Will Revolutionize Everything* (New York: Liveright, 2022).

25. Ball, *The Metaverse*.

26. Ball, The Metaverse.

27. Ball, Matthew. *The Metaverse Primer*, MatthewBall.vc, June 29, 2021, https://www.matthewball.vc/the-metaverse-primer. One of the world's top metaverse thought leaders, Matthew Ball generously shared his definition of the metaverse on his website in the public domain.

28. Hackl, Cathy (2021). "Defining the Metaverse Today," *Forbes*, March 2, 2021, https://www.forbes.com/sites/cathyhackl/2021/05/02/defining-the-metaverse-today/?sh=58e405886448.

29. Jeff Wilser, "Cathy Hackl: The 'Godmother of the Metaverse,'" CoinDesk, May 23, 2022, https://www.coindesk.com/business/2022/04/12/cathy-hackl-the-godmother-of-the-metaverse.

30. Scott Stein, "The Metaverse Isn't a Destination. It's a Metaphor," CNET, March 21, 2022, https://www.cnet.com/tech/computing/features/the-metaverse-isnt-a-destination-its-a-metaphor/.

31. Major, "Roblox CEO Says We're 'in the Middle of the Metaverse Right Now.'"

32. Harkavy, Liz, Eddy Lazzarin, and Arianna Simpson (2022). "7 Essential Ingredients of a Metaverse," Future, May 6, 2022, https://future.a16z.com/7-essential-ingredients-of-a-metaverse/.

33. Harkavy, Lazzarin, and Simpson (2022). "7 Essential Ingredients of a Metaverse."

34. Harkavy, Lazzarin, and Simpson (2022). "7 Essential Ingredients of a Metaverse."

35. Kim, Sohee (2021). "Metaverse Is a Multitrillion-Dollar Opportunity, Epic CEO Says," Bloomberg, November 16, 2021, https://www.bloomberg.com/news/articles/2021-11-17/metaverse-is-a-multitrillion-dollar-opportunity-epic-ceo-says.

36. Sullivan, Mark (2022). "Epic Games CEO Tim Sweeney Talks the Metaverse, Crypto, and Antitrust," *Fast Company*, April 25, 2022, https://www.fastcompany.com/90741893/epic-games-ceo-tim-sweeney-talks-the-metaverse-crypto-and-antitrust.

37. Kim, "Metaverse Is a Multitrillion-Dollar Opportunity."

38. CoreAxis, "Metaverse: The Next Step in Immersive Learning," white paper, January 2022, https://coreaxis.com/wp-content/uploads/2022/01/CoreAxis-Metaverse-White-Paper-v1.pdf.

39. Sullivan, Mark (2021). "What the Metaverse Will (and Won't) Be, According to 28 Experts," *Fast Company*, October 26, 2021, https://www.fastcompany.com/90678442/what-is-the-metaverse.

40. Winters, Terry (2021). *The Metaverse: Prepare Now For the Next Big Thing!* (independently published, 2021).

41. Stein, "The Metaverse Isn't a Destination. It's a Metaphor."

42. Sullivan, "What the Metaverse Will (and Won't) Be."

43. Bloomberg Intelligence, "Blockchain-Enabled Virtual Worlds With Ubisoft's Nicolas Pouard," *Into the Metaverse* (podcast), January 20, 2022, https://podcasts.apple.com/us/podcast/blockchain-enabled-virtual-worlds-with-ubisofts/id1593908027?i=1000548468934.

CHAPTER 2

1. Jewiss, Connor (2022). "What Is the Metaverse? Next-Gen Virtual Worlds Explained," Stuff, February 10, 2022, https://www.stuff.tv/features/what-is-the-metaverse/.

2. Ravenscraft, Eric (2022). "What Is the Metaverse, Exactly?" *WIRED*, April 25, 2022, https://www.wired.com/story/what-is-the-metaverse/.

3. Moran, Jocelyn (2022). "Saratoga-Based Mojo Vision Nears Rollout of Smart Contact Lens That Provides Augmented Reality View," CBS San Francisco March 30, 2022, https://www.cbsnews.com/sanfrancisco/news/mojo-vision-smart-contact-lens-augmented-reality-view/.

4. Sullivan, Mark (2021). "What the Metaverse Will (and Won't) Be, According to 28 Experts," *Fast Company*, October 26, 2021, https://www.fastcompany.com/90678442/what-is-the-metaverse.

5. Mosseri, Instagram, February 22, 2022, https://www.instagram.com/p/CZe7TfGgyFU/.

6. Harkavy, Liz, Eddy Lazzarin, and Arianna Simpson (2022). "7 Essential Ingredients of a Metaverse," Future, May 6, 2022, https://future.a16z.com/7-essential-ingredients-of-a-metaverse/.

7. Zuckerberg, Mark (2021). "The Metaverse and How We'll Build It Together," Connect 2021, Meta, YouTube, October 28, 2021, https://www.youtube.com/watch?v=Uvufun6xer8.

8. Collins, Jayden (2022). "Nike Sells Virtual Sneaker for $186,000 in the Metaverse and Users Can't Even Wear Them," LADBible, April 28, 2022, https://www.ladbible.com/news/latest-nike-sells-virtual-sneakers-for-186000-in-the-metaverse-20220428.

9. Zuckerberg, "The Metaverse and How We'll Build It Together."

10. Raz-Fridman, Yonatan, Matthew Kanterman, and Rebecca Sin (2022). "The Metaverse ETF Boom Is No Virtual Reality." *Into the Metaverse* (podcast), February 23, 2022, https://podcasts.apple.com/us/podcast/the-metaverse-etf-boom-is-no-virtual-reality/id1593908027?i=1000552018640.

11. Sharma, Upanishad (2022). "What Is an Avatar in the Metaverse?" Beebom Media, February 5, 2022, https://beebom.com/metaverse-avatars-explained/.

12. Asare, Kwasi Amaing (2022). "In the Metaverse, Community Transcends Technology, Time and 'Myspace.'" *Fast Company*, April 8, 2022, https://www.fastcompany.com/90738406/in-the-metaverse-community-transcends-technology-time-and-myspace.

13. Sharma, "What Is an Avatar in the Metaverse?"

14. Metamandrill.com (2022). "Metaverse Avatar Guide; Embody Yourself in the Metaverse," https://metamandrill.com/metaverse-avatar/.

15. Jones, Tony (2021). "We Need Better Avatars for the Metaverse: Who Controls the Avatars," *Ultra Reality* (blog), August 12, 2021, https://medium.com/the-ultra-reality/we-need-better-avatars-for-the-metaverse-fa91d1c3ea4d.

16. Sullivan, "What the Metaverse Will (and Won't) Be."

17. Habitat for Humanity Central Arizona (2022). "You're Invited! Habitat for Humanity Central Arizona Metaverse Fundraiser," YouTube, March 24, 2022, https://www.youtube.com/watch?v=2_o1R8GWuC0.

18. Accenture (2022). "Metaverse Continuum," https://www.accenture.com/us-en/services/metaverse-index.

19. Jankelow, Andrea (2022). "Motley Fool Issues Rare 'NFT' Stock Alert," The Motley Fool, June 13, 2022, https://www.fool.com/ext-content/motley-fool-issues-rare-nft-stock-alert/?utm_source=google&utm_medium=contentmarketing&utm_campaign=nfts-stockalert&aid=10621&pa id=10621&waid=10621&source=erbgglwdg0500026&psource=erbgglwdg05 00026&wsource=erbgglwdg0500026&gclid=Cj0KCQjwwJuVBhCAARIsAO PwGARJfaStln2FDKlSI-0o5nnY4mtNjIWQNbW2FuLevokIdQfa4xFm5hw aAs-PEALw_wcB&testId=a-rb-nfts&cellId=0&campaign=rb-nfts.

20. This Week in Metaverse (2021). "How Metaverse and NFTs Work: Explained in Simple Terms," November 20, 2021 https://mirror.xyz/0x22fA828b332da19e7Da8e6ffD446a1D1Ba923A69/xRBTwzQe7IQcQaBw7OzxhjTRnPaO-fxQiUU68sYaQCM.

21. This Week in Metaverse, "How Metaverse and NFTs Work."

22. This Week in Metaverse, "How Metaverse and NFTs Work."

23. Sullivan, Mark (2022). "Epic Games CEO Tim Sweeney Talks the Metaverse, Crypto, and Antitrust," *Fast Company*, April 25, 2022, https://www.fastcompany.com/90741893/epic-games-ceo-tim-sweeney-talks-the-metaverse-crypto-and-antitrust.

24. Patairya, Dilip Kumar (2022). "Life-Changing Money: The 10 Most Expensive NFTs Sold to Date," *Cointelegraph*, May 16, 2022, https://cointelegraph.com/news/life-changing-money-the-10-most-expensive-nfts-sold-to-date.

25. Block, Fang (2021). "PAK's NFT Artwork 'The Merge' Sells for $91.8 Million," Barron's Penta, December 7, 2021, https://www.barrons.com/articles/paks-nft-artwork-the-merge-sells-for-91-8-million-01638918205.

26. "How to Create an NFT: A Guide to Creating a Nonfungible Token," *Cointelegraph,* July 6, 2022; https://cointelegraph.com/nonfungible-tokens-for-beginners/how-to-create-an-nft.

27. See this article: Whittaker, Matt (2022). "What Are NFTs? A Guide for Investors," *U.S. News and World Report*, August 16, 2022, https://money.usnews.com/investing/cryptocurrency/articles/what-are-nfts-a-guide-for-investors.

28. Sullivan, "What the Metaverse Will (and Won't) Be."

29. Today Headline (2020). "How a 24-year-old Roblox Game Developer Made $1 Million," September 26, 2020, https://todayheadline.co/presenting-how-a-24-year-old-roblox-game-developer-made-1-million/.

30. Metamandrill (2022). "Metaverse Virtual Worlds; the Best Way to Experience the Metaverse," https://metamandrill.com/metaverse-virtual-worlds/.

31. WebWise. (2022). "Explained: What Is Fortnite Battle Royale?" https://www.webwise.ie/parents/explainers/explained-what-is-fortnite/.

32. Khillar, Sagar (2022)."Difference Between Roblox and Fortnite," DifferenceBetween.net, 2022, http://www.differencebetween.net/technology/difference-between-roblox-and-fortnite/.

33. Cryptopedia Staff (2021). "Somnium Space (CUBE): A VR World for the Decentralized Age," December 23, 2021, https://www.gemini.com/cryptopedia/somnium-space-what-is-an-nft-marketplace.

34. The Sandbox (2022). https://www.sandbox.game/en/.

35. HyperVerse (2022). https://thehyperverse.net/.

36. Matrix World Whitepaper (2021). "Matrix World—A Programmable 3D Multichain Metaverse," November 8, 2021, https://d2yoccx42eml7e.cloudfront.net/website/whitepaper.pdf?date=1658174460114.

37. NFT Worlds (2022). https://www.nftworlds.com/.

38. ZK (2022). https://www.zkrollups.xyz/Worldwide-Webb.

CHAPTER 3

1. See the Meta Festival website and recorded presentations here: https://www.meta-festival.com/.

2. Combs, Veronica (2021). "The Metaverse: What Is It?" TechRepublic, October 29, 2021, https://www.techrepublic.com/article/metaverse-what-is-it/.

3. Organic Robotics Corporation (2022). organicroboticscorp.com.

4. Wikipedia (2022). "Wearable Technology," https://en.wikipedia.org/wiki/Wearable_technology.

5. eXp Life (2020). "eXp Realty's World-Class Tools and Technology Platform Was Created for the Future of Work," April 29, 2020, https://life.exprealty.com/exp-realty-tools-technology/#:~:text=Everyone%20has%20an%20avatar%2C%20which,a%20room%20with%20a%20colleague.

6. Interview and visit to eXp World with Matt Battiata on June 27, 2022.

7. eXp Life (2020). "eXp Realty's World-Class Tools and Technology Platform."

8. The Daily Charge (2022). "Figuring Out What the Metaverse Really Is," interview with Scott Stein on March 21, 2022, https://harkaudio.com/p/the-daily-charge-cnet/figuring-out-what-the-metaverse-really-is-the-daily-charge-3212022-cnet.

9. Makransky, G., R.E. Mayer (2022). "Benefits of Taking a Virtual Field Trip in Immersive Virtual Reality: Evidence for the Immersion Principle in Multimedia Learning," *Educational Psychology Review*, April 22, 2022, https://doi.org/10.1007/s10648-022-09675-4.

10. Poore, Carol A. (2022). Field research: Discussion with college students about the pros and cons of VR and avatars in the classroom.

11. Brogan, Tallula (2021). "Sandwell College Training Students with Virtual Reality in Global Study," Education Technology, December 15, 2021. https://edtechnology.co.uk/e-learning/sandwell-college-training-students-with-virtual-reality-in-global-study/.

12. Author's interview with Lisa Flesher, ASU Dreamscape Learn, on May 25, 2022.

13. Niedan, Christian (2022). "The IRL Reality of Virtual Reality Biology Class," The Elective, April 26, 2022, https://elective.collegeboard.org/dreamscape-learn-arizona-state-virtual-reality-metaverse-classroom.

14. Magic Leap. "About," 2022, https://www.magicleap.com/about.

15. Magic Leap. "About," 2022, https://www.magicleap.com/about.

16. Level Ex. https://www.levelex.com/.

17. "Visible Body Virtual 3D Human Heart Anatomy Walkthrough," https://www.youtube.com/watch?v=9I-XcW0XXzg and other life science videos. https://www.visiblebody.com/.

18. "Turn Any Room into an Anatomy Lab!" Visible Body, 2022, https://www.visiblebody.com/ar.

19. Ureneck, Elise Italiano (2022). "The Metaverse Is Coming. Can It Be Saved?" Angelus, April 4, 2022, https://angelusnews.com/arts-culture/here-comes-the-metaverse-are-we-ready/.

20. Langer, Daniel (2022). "What Luxury Brands Need to Know to Success in the New Metaverse," Jing Daily, January 17, 2022; https://jingdaily.com/luxury-brands-metaverse-customer-centricity/.

21. Combs, "The Metaverse: What Is It?"

22. Kidwai, Aman (2022). "Procter & Gamble Is Placing a Big Bet on the Metaverse to Support Its Suite of Brands," *Fortune*, May 25, 2022, https://fortune.com/2022/05/25/procter-gamble-metaverse-gaming-virtual-worlds-design/.

23. Cision PR Newswire (2021). "McDonald's® USA Unveils First-Ever NFT to Celebrate 40th Anniversary of the McRib," October 28, 2021, https://www.prnewswire.com/news-releases/mcdonalds-usa-unveils-first-ever-nft-to-celebrate-40th-anniversary-of-the-mcrib-301410515.html.

24. Bissada, Mason (2022). "McDonald's Files Trademark for Metaverse-Based 'Virtual Restaurant,'" *Forbes*, February 9, 2022, https://www.forbes.com/sites/masonbissada/2022/02/09/mcdonalds-files-trademark-for-metaverse-based-virtual-restaurant/?sh=58698c0e6678.

25. Chipotle (2022). "Chipotle Announces Fourth Quarter and Full Year 2021 Results," https://newsroom.chipotle.com/2022-02-08-CHIPOTLE-ANNOUNCES-FOURTH-QUARTER-AND-FULL-YEAR-2021-RESULTS.

26. Hultgren, Kaylee (2022). "Brands on Fire: Chipotle," Chief Marketer, March 18, 2022, https://chiefmarketer.com/brands-on-fire-chipotle/.

27. Chipotle (2022). "Fans Can Roll Burritos at Chipotle in the Metaverse to Earn Burritos in Real Life," April 5, 2022, https://newsroom.chipotle.com/2022-04-05-FANS-CAN-ROLL-BURRITOS-AT-CHIPOTLE-IN-THE-METAVERSE-TO-EARN-BURRITOS-IN-REAL-LIFE#:~:text=On%20April%207%2C%20the%20first,com%2C%20or%20Chipotle.ca.

28. Microsoft (2022). "Introducing Microsoft Mesh," https://www.microsoft.com/en-us/mesh.

29. Hoffman, Claire (2022). "Is the Metaverse the Future of Events? We Weighed the Pros and Cons," BizBash, January 21, 2022, https://www.bizbash.com/event-tech-virtual/hybrid-virtual-event-production/article/22005694/is-the-metaverse-the-future-of-events.

30. Morand, Tatiana (2020). "Should Organizations Worry about a Decline in Membership? 3 Experts Weigh In," *Personify/WildApricot* (blog), December 11, 2020, https://www.wildapricot.com/blog/decline-in-membership#amanda-kaiser.

31. de la Peña, Nonny, Peggy Weil, Joan Llobera, Elias Giannopoulos, et al. (2010). "Immersive Journalism: Immersive Virtual Reality for the First Person Experience of News," *Presence: Teleoperators and Virtual Environments* 19, No. 4, 291—301.

32. Mauk, Ben (2021). "Inside Xinjiang's Prison State," *New Yorker*, February 26, 2021, https://www.newyorker.com/news/a-reporter-at-large/china-xinjiang-prison-state-uighur-detention-camps-prisoner-testimony.

33. The USSF was established December 20, 2019 with enactment of the Fiscal Year 2020 National Defense Authorization Act.

34. Erwin, Sandra (2022). "Space Force Eyes Its Own Version of the Metaverse," *Space News*, February 10, 2022, https://spacenews.com/space-force-eyes-its-own-version-of-the-metaverse/.

35. Erwin, Sandra (2022). "Space Force Chief Technologist Hints at Future Plans to Build a Digital Infrastructure," *Space News*, January 13, 2022, https://spacenews.com/space-force-chief-technologist-hints-at-future-plans-to-build-a-digital-infrastructure/.

36. Combs, "The Metaverse: What Is It?"

37. Scheiderer, Juliana (2021). "What's the Difference Between Asynchronous and Synchronous Learning?" Ohio State University, March 24, 2021, https://online.osu.edu/resources/learn/whats-difference-between-asynchronous-and-synchronous-learning.

38. Rupareliya, Kamal (2022). "How Does the Digital Twin and Metaverse Technologies Relate?" *Business of Apps*, March 24, 2022, https://www.businessofapps.com/insights/how-does-the-digital-twin-and-metaverse-technologies-relate/.

39. Digital Twin Consortium. (2022). "The Definition of a Digital Twin," https://www.digitaltwinconsortium.org/initiatives/the-definition-of-a-digital-twin/.

40. Lukesh, Todd, Eric Ottinger, Nipun Bajaj, et al. (2021). "Digital Twin: The Age of Aquarius in Construction and Real Estate," EY report, file:///C:/Users/Carol/Documents/Metaverse%20book/Metaverse%20topic%20research/Digital%20twin%20-%20Ernst%20&%20Young%20EY%20research%20paper%20emission%20reduction.pdf.

41. Lukesh, Ottinger, Bajaj, "Digital Twin."

42. Bianzino, Nicola Morini (2022). "Metaverse: Could Creating a Virtual World Build a More Sustainable One?" EY, April 7, 2022, https://www.ey.com/en_se/digital/metaverse-could-creating-a-virtual-world-build-a-more-sustainable-one.

CHAPTER 4

1. Kepios (2022). "Digital 2022 Global Snapshot Report," https://datareportal.com/reports/digital-2022-april-global-statshot.

2. Pew Research Center (2021). "Social Media Fact Sheet," April 7, 2021, https://www.pewresearch.org/internet/fact-sheet/social-media/.

3. Leonhard, Gerd (2022). "The Metaverse—or the Metaperverse?" Gerd, https://www.futuristgerd.com/topics/core-topics/#metaverse.

4. Levin, Yuval (2021). "The Changing Face of Social Breakdown," The Dispatch, November 16, 2021, https://thedispatch.com/p/the-changing-face-of-social-breakdown.

5. Claridge, Tristan (2017). "The Empathy Challenged Employee: A Growing Problem?" Institute for Social Capital, September 28, 2017, https://www.socialcapitalresearch.com/empathy-challenged-employee-growing-problem/.

6. Numerous studies about reading habits, including a 2021 study conducted by the Pew Research Center: https://www.pewresearch.org/fact-tank/2021/09/21/who-doesnt-read-books-in-america/.

7. Mark, Gloria, Daniela Gudith, and Ulrich Klocke (2008). "The Cost of Interrupted Work: More Speed and Stress," *CHI* 2008.

8. Anderson, Janna and Lee Rainie (2018). "Stories from Experts about the Impact of Digital Life," Pew Research Center, July 3, 2018, https://www.pewresearch.org/internet/2018/07/03/the-negatives-of-digital-life/.

9. Rosenberg, Louis (2021). "Metaverse: Augmented Reality Pioneer Warns It Could Be Far Worse than Social Media," Big Think, November 6, 2021, https://bigthink.com/the-future/metaverse-augmented-reality-danger/.

10. Pew Research Center (2021). "Social Media Fact Sheet," April 7, 2021, https://www.pewresearch.org/internet/fact-sheet/social-media/.

11. Pew Research Center (2021). "The State of Online Harassment," January 13, 2021, https://www.pewresearch.org/internet/2021/01/13/the-state-of-online-harassment/.

12. VanFossen, Lorelle (2022). "Educators in VR Cyberbullying Team State of the Metaverse," Educators in VR, March 5, 2022, https://educatorsinvr.com/2022/03/05/educators-in-vr-cyberbullying-team-state-of-the-metaverse/.

13. Wikipedia (2022). "Fake News," https://en.wikipedia.org/wiki/Fake_news.

14. Jardine, Eric (2022). "Beware Fake News," Centre for International Governance Innovation, https://www.cigionline.org/articles/beware-fake-news/?utm_source=google_ads&utm_medium=grant&gclid=EAIaIQobChMIi4DVrZSO-AIVrBTUAR2WkgVyEAAYAiAAEgIVr_D_BwE.

15. Jardine, "Beware Fake News."

16. Vosoughi, Soroush, Deb Roy, and Sinan Aral (2018). "The Spread of True and False News Online," *SCIENCE* 359, No. 6380 (March 9, 2018): pp. 1146–1151, https://www.science.org/doi/full/10.1126/science.aap9559#con2.

17. To understand how false news spreads, the MIT scholars used a data set of rumor cascades on Twitter from 2006 to 2017. They found that about 126,000 rumors were spread by approximately three million people more than 4.5 million times.

18. Sample, Ian (2020). "What Are Deepfakes—and How Can You Spot Them?" *Guardian*, January 13, 2020, https://www.theguardian.com/technology/2020/jan/13/what-are-deepfakes-and-how-can-you-spot-them.

19. Wikipedia (2022). "Conspiracy Theory," https://en.wikipedia.org/wiki/Conspiracy_theory.

20. Rosenberg, "Metaverse."

21. G., Deyan (2022). "How Much Time Does the Average American Spend on Their Phone in 2022?" *Techjury*, June 3, 2022, https://techjury.net/blog/how-much-time-does-the-average-american-spend-on-their-phone/#gref.

22. Asurion (2019). "Americans Check Their Phones 96 Times a Day," CISION PR Newswire, November 21, 2019, https://www.prnewswire.com/news-releases/americans-check-their-phones-96-times-a-day-300962643.html. *The Brussels Times* (2022). "People Touch Their Smartphone over 2,600 Times a Day, Research Shows," June 3, 2022, https://www.brusselstimes.com/232851/people-touch-their-smartphone-over-2600-times-a-day-research-shows.

23. Putnam, Robert (2000). *Bowling Alone: The Collapse and Revival of American Community* (New York: Simon & Schuster).

24. Anderson and Rainie, "Stories from Experts."

25. Mason, Vanessa (2021). "Blog #44: Belonging and Civics," Future of Belonging, January 21, 2021, https://belonging.substack.com/p/issue-43-belonging-and-civics?s=r.

26. Beres, Damon (2021). "Questionable Decisions in the Metaverse," Unfinished, November 5, 2021, https://unfinished.com/news/editors-letter-questionable-decisions-in-the-metaverse/.

27. Rosenberg, Lizzy (2022) "Even though It's Virtual, the Metaverse Does Actually Impact the Environment," World Economic Forum, February 16, 2022, https://www.weforum.org/agenda/2022/02/how-metaverse-actually-impacts-the-environment.

CHAPTER 5

1. Cigna 2018 and 2020 Loneliness Indexes. In partnership with Ipsos, Cigna fielded a national online survey of 20,000 US adults to explore the impact of loneliness in the United States. The survey revealed that most Americans are considered lonely, as measured by a score of 43 or higher on the UCLA Loneliness Scale, a twenty-item questionnaire developed to assess subjective feelings of loneliness, as well as social isolation: https://www.cigna.com/assets/docs/newsroom/loneliness-survey-2018-fact-sheet.pdf.

2. Kaiser Family Foundation study partnered with *The Economist*. DiJulio, Bianca, Liz Hamel, Cailey Munana, and Mollyann Brodie (2018). "Loneliness and Social Isolation in the United States, the United Kingdom, and Japan: An International Survey," Kaiser Family Foundation, August 30, 2018, https://www.kff.org/report-section/loneliness-and-social-isolation-in-the-united-states-the-united-kingdom-and-japan-an-international-survey-introduction/.

3. According to a 2019 study by "1N5: Kids at Risk" conducted by Child Mind Institute.

4. Hawkley LC and JT Cacioppo (2010). "Loneliness Matters: A Theoretical and Empirical Review of Consequences and Mechanisms," *Annals of Behavioral Medicine* 40, No. 2 (October 2010): pp. 218–27, https://academic.oup.com/abm/article/40/2/218/4569527.

5. Perlman, Daniel, and L. Anne Peplau (1981). "Toward a Social Psychology of Loneliness," in Duck, N. and R. Gilmour, (eds.). *Personal Relationships in Disorder* (London Academic Press, 1981), pp. 31–56.

6. Hawkley and Cacioppo, "Loneliness Matters."

7. Ross, Ashley (2018). "The War against the Loneliness Epidemic," *Daily Beast*, June 30, 2018, https://www.thedailybeast.com/the-war-against-the-loneliness-epidemic.

8. Murthy, Vivek (2020). *Together: The Healing Power of Human Connection in a Sometimes Lonely World* (New York: HarperCollins, 2020).

9. Kunal, Bhattacharya, Asim Ghosh, Daniel Monsivais, Dunbar, Robin I. M., Kimmo Kaski (2016). "Sex Differences in Social Focus across the Life Cycle in Humans," *R Soc Open Sci.* 3, No. 4 (2016): 160097, doi: 10.1098/rsos.160097, https://www.ncbi.nlm.nih.gov/pmc/articles/PMC4852646/citedby/.

10. Holt-Lunstad J, and TB Smith (2016). "Loneliness and Social Isolation as Risk Factors for CVD: Implications for Evidence-Based Patient Care and Scientific Inquiry," *Heart*, (April 18, 2016) 102: 987–989.

11. Holt-Lunstad and Smith, "Loneliness and Social Isolation."

12. Holt-Lunstad and Smith, "Loneliness and Social Isolation."

13. DiJulio, Hamel, et al., "Loneliness and Social Isolation in the United States."

14. Anderson, Oscar G. and Colette Thayer (2018). "Loneliness and Social Connections: A National Survey of Adults 45 and Older," AARP Research, September, 2018, https://www.aarp.org/research/topics/life/info-2018/loneliness-social-connections.html.

15. Cigna 2018 and 2020 Loneliness Indexes. In partnership with Ipsos, Cigna fielded a national online survey of 20,000 US adults to explore the impact of loneliness in the United States. The survey revealed that most Americans are considered lonely, as measured by a score of 43 or higher on the UCLA Loneliness Scale, a twenty-item questionnaire developed to assess subjective feelings of loneliness, as well as social isolation: https://www.cigna.com/assets/docs/newsroom/loneliness-survey-2018-fact-sheet.pdf.

16. Scheimer, Dorey, and Meghna Chakrabarti, (2020). "Former Surgeon General Vivek Murthy: Loneliness Is a Public Health Crisis," March 23, 2020, https://www.wbur.org/onpoint/2020/03/23/vivek-murthy-loneliness.

17. Murthy, Vivek H., and Alice T. Chen (2020). "The Coronavirus Could Cause a Social Recession," *Atlantic*, March 22, 2020, https://www.theatlantic.com/ideas/archive/2020/03/america-faces-social-recession/608548/.

18. Will, George F. (2018). "We Have an Epidemic of Loneliness. How Can We Fix It?" *Washington Post*, October 12, 2018, https://www.washingtonpost.com/opinions/we-have-an-epidemic-of-loneliness-how-can-we-fix-it/2018/10/12/e8378a38-cd92-11e8-920f-dd52e1ae4570_story.html.

19. Case, Anne, and Angus Deaton (2020). *Deaths of Despair and the Future of Capitalism* (Princeton, NJ: Princeton University Press, 2020).

20. National Safety Council analysis (2019). https://www.nsc.org/in-the-newsroom/for-the-first-time-were-more-likely-to-die-from-accidental-opioid-overdose-than-motor-vehicle-crash.

21. Clement, J. (2021). "Weekly Hours Spent Playing Video Games Worldwide 2021, by Country," Statistica, April 23, 2021, https://www.statista.com/statistics/273829/average-game-hours-per-day-of-video-gamers-in-selected-countries/.

22. Vuorre Matti, Johannes Niklas, Kristoffer Magnusson, and Andrew K. Przybylski (2022). "Time Spent Playing Video Games Is Unlikely to Impact Well-Being," *The Royal Society Publishing*, July 27, 2022, https://royalsocietypublishing.org/doi/10.1098/rsos.220411.

23. Stevens, Matt, Diana Dorstyn, Paul H. Delfabbro, Daniel L. King, (2021). "Global Prevalence of Gaming Disorder: A Systematic Review and Meta-Analysis," *The Australian and New Zealand Journal of Psychiatry*, National Institutes of Health, NIH National Library of Medicine, PubMed.gov, https://pubmed.ncbi.nlm.nih.gov/33028074/. (Note: Gaming disorder was defined in the 11th Revision of the ICD-11. A gaming addiction meta-analysis extracted data from fifty-three studies conducted between 2009 and 2019, and included 226,247 participants across seventeen countries.)

24. Adair, Cam (2022). "Video Game Addiction Statistics 2022—How Many Addicted Gamers Are There," Game Quitters, https://gamequitters.com/video-game-addiction-statistics/.

25. Statistica (2021). "Distribution of Video Gamers in the United States in 2021, by Age Group," https://www.statista.com/statistics/189582/age-of-us-video-game-players/.

26. Game Quitters notes that it is the world's largest support community for video game addiction, serving 75,000 members in ninety-five countries.

27. Adair, "Video Game Addiction Statistics 2022."

28. Luker, Edward (2022). "Are Video Games, Screens Another Addiction?" Speaking of Health, Mayo Clinic Health System, July 1, 2022, https://www.mayoclinichealthsystem.org/hometown-health/speaking-of-health/are-video-games-and-screens-another-addiction.

29. American Psychiatric Association (2022). "Internet Gaming," https://www.psychiatry.org/patients-families/internet-gaming.

30. Luker, "Are Video Games, Screens Another Addiction?"

31. US Federal Bureau of Investigation (2022). "FBI: Active Shooter Incidents in

the United States in 2021," https://www.fbi.gov/file-repository/active-shooter-incidents-in-the-us-2021-052422.pdf/view.

32. US Federal Bureau of Investigation "FBI: Active Shooter Incidents in the United States in 2021."

33. Bonn, Scott A. (2014). "Serial Killers and the Essential Role of Fantasy," *Psychology Today*, October 13, 2014, https://www.psychologytoday.com/us/blog/wicked-deeds/201410/serial-killers-and-the-essential-role-fantasy.

34. Turkle, Sherry (2011). *Alone Together: Why We Expect More from Technology and Less from Each Other* (New York: Basic Books, 2011).

35. American Psychological Association (2022). "Is Technology Killing Empathy?" with Sherry Turkle, *Speaking of Psychology* (podcast), episode 189, May, 2022, interviewed by Kim Mills, https://www.apa.org/news/podcasts/speaking-of-psychology/anti-empathy-machine.

36. Nextdoor (2020). "Global Study Finds Knowing as Few as 6 Neighbors Reduces the Likelihood of Loneliness," December 2, 2020, https://about.nextdoor.com/press-releases/global-study-finds-knowing-as-few-as-6-neighbors-reduces-the-likelihood-of-loneliness/. Nextdoor partnered with Brigham Young University in the United States, University of Manchester in the United Kingdom, and Swinburne University of Technology in Australia.

37. Cox Communications (2021). "How Wearable Tech Is Transforming Lives for the Better," July 15, 2021, https://www.cox.com/residential/articles/how-wearable-tech-is-transforming-lives-better.html.

CHAPTER 6

1. Thermopylae Sciences + Technology (2014). "Humans Process Visual Data Better," September 15, 2014, https://www.t-sciences.com/news/humans-process-visual-data-better.

2. Burns, James McGregor (1978). *Leadership* (New York: Harper and Row, 1978).

3. Bennis, Warren G., and B. Nanus, (1985). *Leaders: The Strategies for Taking Charge* (New York: Harper and Row, 1985).

4. Almenta International (2018). "Effective Leadership: Leading Self, Leading Others, Leading Community," June 24, 2018, https://almentainternational.com/effective-leadership-leading-self-leading-others-leading-community/.

5. Gardner, John W. (1965). "Annual Report of the Carnegie Corporation of New York."

6. King, Albert S. (1990). "Evolution of Leadership Theory," Vikalpa, 15, No. 2 (April 1, 1990): p. 14.

7. Kotter, John P. (1995). "Why Transformation Efforts Fail," *Harvard Business Review*, March–April, p. 61. Kotter, John P. (1996). *Leading Change* (Boston: Harvard Business School Press, 1996).

8. Lewin, Kurt (1951). *Field Theory in Social Science: Selected Theoretical Papers* (New York: Harper & Row).

9. Carlyle, T. (1907; original 1841). *Heroes and Hero Worship* (Boston: Adams, 1907). Galton, F. (1869). *Hereditary Genius* (New York: Appleton, 1869).

10. Mumford, E. (1909). *The Origins of Leadership* (Chicago: The University of Chicago Press, 1909).

11. Bernard, L.L. (1926). *An Introduction to Social Psychology* (New York: Holt, 1926). Bingham, W.V. (1927). *Leadership*, in H.C. Metcalf, *The Psychological Foundations of Management* (New York: Shaw). Bird, C. (1940). *Social Psychology* (New York: Appleton-Century, 1940). Kilbourne, C. E. (1935). "The Elements of Leadership," *Journal of Coast Artillery* 78 (1935): pp. 437–439. Tead, O. (1929). *Human Nature and Management: The Applications of Psychology to Executive Leadership* (New York: McGraw-Hill, 1929).

12. Aaronovich, G.D. and B.I. Khotin (1929). "The Problem of Imitation in Monkeys," *Novoye v Refleksologii I Fiziologii Nervnoy Systemi* 3, pp. 378–90. Mawhinney, T.C., and J.D. Ford (1977). "The Path Goal Theory of Leader Effectiveness: An Operant Interpretation," *Academic Management Review* 2, pp. 398-411. Scott, W.A. (1967). *Organizational Theory: A Behavioral Analysis for Management* (Homewood, Illinois: Irwin, 1967). Sims, H.P (1977). "The Leader as a Manager of Reinforcement Contingencies: An Empirical Example and a Model," in J.G. Hunt and L.L. Larson (eds.) *Leadership: The Cutting Edge* (Carbondale: Southern Illinois University Press). Davis, T.R., and F. Luthans (1979). "Leadership Reexamined: A Behavioral Approach," *Academic Management Review* 4, pp. 237–248.

13. Freud, S. (1922). *Group Psychology and the Analysis of Ego* (London: International Psychoanalytical Press, 1922). Fromm, E. (1941). *Escape from Freedom* (New York: Farrar and Rinehart, 1941), Erikson, E. (1964). *Insight and Responsibility* (New York: Norton, 1964). Levinson, H. (1970). *Executive Stress* (New York: Harper and Row, 1970).

14. Case, C. M. (1933). "Leadership and Conjecture," *Sociology and Social Research* 17, pp. 510–13.

15. STU Online (2018). "What Is Laissez-Faire Leadership? How Autonomy Can Drive Success," https://online.stu.edu/articles/education/what-is-laissezfaire-leadership.aspx#:~:text=Kurt%20Lewin%20is%20often%20credited,group%20dynamics%20and%20organizational%20psychology.

16. Homans, G.C. (1958). "Social Behavior as an Exchange," *American Journal of Sociology* 63, pp. 597–606. March, J.G., and H.A. Simon (1958). *Organizations*

(New York: Wiley, 1958). Thibaut, J.W., and H.H. Kelley (1959). *The Social Psychology of Groups* (New York: Wiley, 1959). Blau, P. M. (1964). *Exchange and Power in Social Life* (New York: Wiley, 1964). Jacobs, T.O. (1970). *Leadership and Exchange in Formal Organizations* (Alexandria, Virginia: Human Resources Research Organization, 1970).

17. Bass, B. M. (1960). *Leadership, Psychology and Organizational Behavior* (New York: Harper, 1960). House, R.J. (1971). "A Path-Goal Theory of Leader Effectiveness," *Administrative Science Quarterly* 16, pp. 321–39. Fiedler, F.E. (1967). *A Theory of Leadership Effectiveness* (New York: McGraw-Hill, 1967).

18. McGregor, D. (1960). *The Human Side of Enterprise* (New York: McGraw-Hill, 1960). McGregor, D. (1966). *Leadership and Motivation* (Cambridge, Massachusetts: MIT Press, 1966). Argryis, C. (1957). *Personality and Organization* (New York: Harper, 1957). Argryis, C. (1962). *Interpersonal Competence and Organizational Effectiveness* (Homewood, Illinois: Irwin-Dorsey, 1962). Argryis, C. (1964). *Integrating the Individual and the Organization* (New York: Wiley, 1964). Blake, R.R., and J.S. Mouton (1964). *The Managerial Grid* (Houston, Texas: Gulf, 1964). Blake, R.R., and Mouton, J.S. (1965). "A 9.9 Approach for Increasing Organizational Productivity," in E.H. Schein and W.G. Bennis (eds.), *Personal and Organizational Change through Group Methods* (New York: Wiley). Hersey, P., and K.H. Blanchard (1969). "Life Cycle Theory of Leadership," *Train, Develop Journal* 23, pp. 26–34. Hersey, P., and K.H. Blanchard (1972). "The Management of Change. Change and the Use of Power," *Train, Develop Journal* 26, pp. 6–10. Hersey, P., and K.H. Blanchard (1977). *The Management of Organizational Behavior* 3rd ed. (Upper Saddle River, N.J.: Prentice Hall).

19. Lord, R.G. (1976). "Group Performance as a Function of Leadership Behavior and Task Structure: Toward an Explanatory Theory," *Organizational Behavior Human Performance* 17, pp. 76–96.

20. Katz, D. and R.L. Kahn, (1966). *The Social Psychology of Organizations* (New York: Wiley, 1966). Bass, B.M., and E.R. Valenzi (1974). "Contingent Aspects of Effective Management Styles," in J.G. Hunt and L.L. Larson (eds.), *Contingency Approaches to Leadership* (Carbondale: Southern Illinois University Press).

21. Katz and Kahn, *The Social Psychology of Organizations*. Bass and Valenzi, "Contingent Aspects of Effective Management Styles."

22. Burns, James McGregor (1978). *Leadership* (New York: Harper and Row, 1978).

23. Greenleaf, Robert K. (1970). *The Servant as Leader* (South Orange, NJ: Seton Hall University, 1970).

24. House, R. J. (1977). "A 1976 Theory of Charismatic Leadership," in J. G. Hunt and L.L. Larson (eds.), *Leadership: The Cutting Edge* (Carbondale: Southern Illinois University Press), pp. 189–207.

25. Lamb, R. (2013). "How Can Managers Use Participative Leadership Effectively?" http://www.task.fm/participative-leadership.

26. Sanfilippo, Marisa (2021). "Shared Leadership: How Modern Businesses

Run Themselves," *Business News Daily*, December 1, 2021, https://www.businessnewsdaily.com/135-shared-leadership-social-media-fuel-business-growth.html.

27. STU Online (2018). "What is Democratic/Participative Leadership? How Collaboration Can Boost Morale," June 1, 2018, https://online.stu.edu/articles/education/democratic-participative-leadership.aspx.

28. Svara, James H. (2007). *The Ethics Primer for Public Administrators in Government and Nonprofit Organizations* (Sudbury, Massachusetts: Jones and Bartlett Publishers, 2007).

29. Denhardt, Robert B. 1993. *The Pursuit of Significance: Strategies for Managerial Success in Public Organizations* (Prospect Heights, Illinois: Waveland Press, 1993).

30. Terry, R.W. (1993), *Authentic Leadership: Courage in Action* (San Francisco, CA: Jossey-Bass, 1993).

31. Goleman, Daniel, Richard Boyatzis, and Annie McKee (2002). *Primal Leadership: Realizing the Power of Emotional Intelligence* (Boston: Harvard Business School Press, 2002). George, Bill (2003). *Authentic Leadership: Rediscovering the Secrets of Creating Lasting Value* (San Francisco: CA: Jossey-Bass, 2003). Luthans, F., and B.J. Avolio (2003). "Authentic Leadership Development," in K.S. Cameron, J.E. Dutton, and R.E. Quinn (eds.), *Positive Organizational Scholarship: Foundations of a New Discipline* (San Francisco, CA: Berrett-Koehler), pp. 241–58. Seligman, M.E.P. (2002). *Authentic Happiness* (New York: Free Press, 2002).

32. Uhl-Bien, M., and R. Marion, eds. (2008). *Complexity and Leadership, Volume I: Conceptual Foundations* (Charlotte, NC: Information Age Publishing, 2008). Lichtenstein, B. B. (2007). "A Matrix of Complexity for Leadership: Fourteen Disciplines of Complex Systems Leadership Theory," in J.K. Hazy, J.A. Goldstein, and B.B. Lichtenstein (eds.), "Complex Systems Leadership Theory: New Perspectives from Complexity Sciences on Social and Organizational Effectiveness," ISCE Publishing, Mansfield, 2007.

33. Pearce, Craig L., and Jay A. Conger (2003). *Shared Leadership: Reframing the Hows and Whys of Leadership* (Thousand Oaks, CA: Sage Publications, 2003). Gronn, P. (2002). "Distributed Leadership as a Unit of Analysis," *Leadership Quarterly* 13, No. 4 (2002): pp 423–51. Fletcher (2004). *The Paradox of Post Heroic Leadership: Gender Matters* (Thousand Oaks, CA: Sage Publications, 2004). Volberda, H.W. (1996). "Toward the Flexible Form: How to Remain Vital in Hypercompetitive Environments," *Organizational Science* 7, No. 4 (1996): 359–87. Marion, R., and M. Uhl-Bien (2001). "Complexity Leadership Theory: Shifting Leadership from the Industrial Age to the Knowledge Era," *The Leadership Quarterly* 18, No. 4 (2001): pp. 298–318.

34. Uhl-Bien and Marion, *Complexity & Leadership, Volume I*.

35. Thompson, James (1967). *Organizations in Action* (New York: McGraw-Hill, 1967). Senge, P.M. (1990). *The Fifth Discipline: The Art and Practice of the*

Learning Organization (New York: Doubleday Currency, 1990). Schein, E.H. (1993). "On Dialogue, Culture, and Organizational Learning," *Organizational Dynamics* 22, No. 2 (1993): pp. 40-51.

36. Wheatley, Margaret (2005). *Finding Our Way: Leadership for an Uncertain Time* (San Francisco, CA: Berrett-Koehler Publishers, 2005).

37. Argyris, C. (1992). *On Organizational Learning* (Cambridge, Massachusetts: Blackwell Business, 1992). Mumford, M.D., and B. Licuanan (2004). "Leading for Innovation: Conclusions, Issues, and Directions," *The Leadership Quarterly* 15, No. 1 (2004): pp. 163–71.

38. Kotter, John P. (1995). "Why Transformation Efforts Fail." Yukl, Gary A. (2002). *Leadership in Organizations* (Upper Saddle River, NJ: Prentice Hall, 2002). Ginter, Peter, and Jack Duncan (1990). "Microenvironmental Analysis for Strategic Management," *Long Range Planning* 23, No. 6 (1990): pp. 91–100.

39. Yukl, *Leadership in Organizations.*

40. Lassey, W. (1976). *Leadership and Social Change* (Los Angeles: University Associates, 1976).

41. Denhardt, Robert B., and Janet Vinzant Denhardt (1999). "Leadership for Change: Case Studies in American Local Government," Price Waterhouse. Denhardt, Janet V., and Kelly B. Campbell (2006). "The Role of Democratic Values in Transformational Leadership," *Administration & Society* 38, No. 5 (2006): pp. 556–72.

42. Aghina, Wouter, Karin Ahlback, Aaron De Smet, et al. (2018). "The Five Trademarks of Agile Organizations," McKinsey & Company, January 22, 2018, https://www.mckinsey.com/business-functions/people-and-organizational-performance/our-insights/the-five-trademarks-of-agile-organizations.

43. Aghina, Ahlback, De Smet, et al. "The Five Trademarks of Agile Organizations."

44. Heidrick & Struggles International, Inc. (2020). "Building a Culture of Operational Excellence in Financial Services," file:///C:/Users/Carol/Downloads/Building_a_culture_of_operational_excellence_in_financial_services.pdf.

45. Torres, Roselinde (2013). "What It Takes to Be a Great Leader," TED Talk, https://www.ted.com/talks/roselinde_torres_what_it_takes_to_be_a_great_leader.

46. Neider, L. L., and C.A. Schriesheim (2011). "The Authentic Leadership Inventory (ALI): Development and Empirical Tests," *The Leadership Quarterly* 22, No. 6 (2011): 1146–1164.

47. Mayer, Roger C., James H. Davis, and F. David Schoorman (1995). "An Integrative Model of Organizational Trust," *Academy of Management Review* 20, No. 3 (1995).

48. Schoorman, David F., Roger C. Mayer, and James H. Davis (2007). "An Integrative Model of Organizational Trust: Past, Present and Future," *Academy of Management Review* 32, No. 2 (April 2007): pp. 344–54.

49. Baird, John, and Edward Sullivan (2022). *Leading with the Heart: Five Conversations That Unlock Creativity, Purpose, and Results* (New York: Harper Business, 2022).

50. Baird and Sullivan, *Leading with the Heart.*

51. "Leading by Convening: A Blueprint for Authentic Engagement," The Wisconsin Department of Public Instruction, https://servingongroups.org/leading-by-convening#:~:text=Leading%20by%20Convening%20(LbC)%3A,together%20%2D%20to%20achieve%20overall%20goals.

52. Szreter, S., and Michael Woolcock (2004). "Health by Association? Social Capital, Social Theory, and the Political Economy of Public Health," *International Journal of Epidemiology* 33, No. 4 (2004): pp. 650–67.

53. Claridge, Tristan (2018). "What Is Linking Social Capital?" Institute for Social Capital, January 7, 2018, https://www.socialcapitalresearch.com/what-is-linking-social-capital/.

54. Schaefer, R.T. (2005). *Sociology*, 9th ed. (New York: McGraw-Hill, 2005).

CHAPTER 7

1. Porter, M. E. 1996. "What Is a Strategy?" *Harvard Business Review,* November-December, 1996, pp. 61–78.

2. Hadaya, Pierre, and James D. Stockmal (2022). "Guide to the Strategy Planning and Management Body of Knowledge, Third Edition," Association for Strategic Planning, now known as the International Association for Strategy Professionals, https://www.strategyassociation.org/page/bok3.

3. Tesla (2022). "Tesla 2021 Annual Report," https://www.tesla.com/ns_videos/2021-tesla-impact-report.pdf.

4. Tesla, "Tesla 2021 Annual Report."

5. Stadler, Christian, Julia Hautz, and Kurt Matzler, (2021). "A User's Guide to Open Strategy," *Harvard Business Review*, November 2, 2021, https://hbr.org/2021/11/balancing-open-innovation-with-protecting-ip.

6. Plymouth State University (2022). "What Is a Wicked Problem?" https://wicked-problem.press.plymouth.edu/chapter/what-is-a-wicked-problem/.

7. Gurteen, David (2022). "Open, Adaptive Strategy: Make Employees Partners in the Strategy Process," Conversational Leadership, https://conversational-leadership.net/open-strategy/.

8. Gates, Linda Parker (2018). "Agile Strategy: Short-Cycle Strategy Development and Execution," Software Engineering Institute, Carnegie Mellon University, June 25, 2018, https://insights.sei.cmu.edu/blog/agile-strategy-short-cycle-strategy-development-and-execution/.

9. Grill-Goodman, Jamie (2021). "10 Retailers Ruling Curbside & BOPS," Retail Info Systems (RIS), January 29, 2021, https://risnews.com/10-retailers-ruling-curbside-bopis.

10. Hadaya and Stockmal, "Guide to the Strategy Planning and Management Body of Knowledge, Third Edition."

11. Preedy, Louise (2022). "How to Host a Large Event in the Metaverse," DXT Technology, June 3, 2022, https://dxc.com/us/en/insights/perspectives/blogs/how-to-host-a-large-event-in-the-metaverse.

12. Hackl, Cathy (2021). "The Future of Leadership & Corporate Narratives with Alvaro Cedeno," Future Insiders, March 14, 2021, https://anchor.fm/cathy-hackl/episodes/. The-Future-of-Leadership--Corporate-Narratives-with-Alvaro-Cedeno-er5hf7.

13. Poore, Carol A. (2021). *Strategic Impact: A Leader's Three-Step, Customizable Framework for the Vital Strategic Plan* (Austin, Texas: Fast Company Press, 2021).

14. The Open Insulin Foundation (2022), https://openinsulin.org/who-we-are/.

15. The Open Insulin Foundation (2022), https://openinsulin.org/.

16. The Open Insulin Foundation (2022), https://openinsulin.org/.

17. International Futures Forum (2022), https://www.internationalfuturesforum.com/.

18. National Technology and Engineering Solutions of Sandia operates Sandia National Laboratories as a contractor for the US Department of Energy's National Nuclear Security Administration (NNSA) and supports numerous federal, state, and local government agencies, companies, and organizations.

19. Ali, Rama, and David Luther (2020). "Scenario Planning: Strategy, Steps and Practical Examples," Netsuite Brainyard, May 14, 2020, https://www.netsuite.com/portal/business-benchmark-brainyard/aboutus.shtml.

20. Chussil, Mark (2022). "What You Can Learn by Simulating Strategies," *Strategy Magazine*, No. 37 (Spring 2022): pp. 10–12.

21. Robinson, John B. (1990). "Futures Under Glass: A Recipe for People Who Hate to Predict," *Futures* 22, No. 8 (1990): pp. 820–42.

22. Shaping Tomorrow (2022), https://www.shapingtomorrow.com/home.

23. Bloomenthal, Andrew (2021). "Competitive Intelligence," Investopedia, July 1, 2021, https://www.investopedia.com/terms/c/competitive-intelligence.asp.

24. Chussil, "What You Can Learn by Simulating Strategies."

25. Proactive Worldwide (2022). "What Is Business Wargaming?" January 20, 2022, https://www.proactiveworldwide.com/resources/market-and-competitive-intelligence-blog/what-is-business-war-gaming/#:~:text=Business%20wargaming%20is%20an%20experiential,before%20making%20full%2Dscale%20investments.

26. Arbor Biotechnologies (2022). "Arbor Biotechnologies to Present at the Bank of America Global Healthcare Conference," May 3, 2022, https://arbor.bio/news.

27. LBL Strategies (2019). "Strategy Implementation in the Public Sector: Initial

Survey Results of Public Sector Leaders," https://www.lblstrategies.com/wp-content/uploads/2019/10/LBL-CS-SEPS_Survey-03.pdf.

28. Gates, Linda Parker (2020). "Show Me Agility: Agile Strategy Execution," Software Engineering Institute, Carnegie Mellon University, November 23, 2020, https://insights.sei.cmu.edu/blog/show-me-agility-agile-strategy-execution/.

29. Poore, Carol A. (2022). "Leveraging '3V' Communication to Support Strategic Management," *Strategy Magazine*, No. 37 (Spring 2022): pp. 22–25.

30. Kaplan, Robert S., and David P. Norton (2005). "The Office of Strategy Management," *Harvard Business Review*, October 2005.

31. Kruse, Kevin (2012). "What Is Employee Engagement?" *Forbes*, June 22, 2012.

32. Poore, "Leveraging '3V' Communication."

33. TEDxSHMS (2022). "Leadership and the Metaverse: Facing the Next Frontier," a presentation given by Marcus Fromm, managing director, Accenture, June 1, 2022, https://www.youtube.com/watch?v=CFXz8NvectI.

CHAPTER 8

1. Accenture (2022). "Meet Me in the Metaverse," https://www.accenture.com/_acnmedia/Thought-Leadership-Assets/PDF-5/Accenture-Meet-Me-in-the-Metaverse-Full-Report.pdf.

2. Masterson, Victoria (2022). "The metaverse Is Coming. Here Are 4 Things Businesses Can Expect," World Economic Forum, April 14, 2022, https://www.weforum.org/agenda/2022/04/accenture-metaverse-technology-vision-2022/.

3. The Meta-Verse research group (2021). *Metaverse Investment Guide: Invest in Virtual Land, Crypto Art, NFT (Non Fungible Token), VR, AR, and Digital Assets. Blockchain Gaming the Future of the Cryptocurrency Economy and the New Digital World.* Mastership Books: London, UK.

4. Meta-Verse (2021). *Metaverse Investment Guide: Invest in Virtual Land, Crypto Art, NFT (Non Fungible Token), VR, AR, and Digital Assets. Blockchain Gaming the Future of the Cryptocurrency Economy and the New Digital World* (London: Mastership Books, 2021).

5. *Merriam Webster Dictionary*, "Community," 2022, https://www.merriam-webster.com/dictionary/community.

6. Field, John (2003). *Social Capital: Key Ideas* (London: Routledge, 2003).

7. Putnam, Robert (2000). *Bowling Alone: The Collapse and Revival of American Community* (New York: Simon & Schuster, 2000). Herreros, Francisco (2004). *The Problem of Forming Social Capital: Why Trust?* (New York: Palgrave Macmillan, 2004).

8. Hanifan, L.J. (1916). "The Rural School Community Centre," *Annals of the American Academy of Political and Social Sciences* 67, pp. 130–38.

9. Lin, Nan (2001). *Social Capital: A Theory of Social Structure and Action* (Cambridge, Massachusetts: Cambridge University Press, 2001).

10. Flap, Henk D., and Beate Volker (2004). *Creation and Returns of Social Capital: A New Research Program* (New York, Routledge, 2004).

11. Flap, Hendrik D., and Nan Dirk De Graaf (1988). "Social Capital and Attained Occupational Status," *Netherlands Journal of Sociology*. Flap, Henk D. (1991). "Social Capital in the Reproduction of Inequality," *Comparative Sociology of Family, Health and Education* 20, No. 6 (1991): 179–202. Flap, Henk D. (1994). "No Man Is An Island: The Research Program of a Social Capital Theory," World Congress of Sociology, Bielefeld, Germany, July 1994.

12. Bourdieu, Pierre (1985). "The Social Space and the Genesis of Groups," *Social Science Information* 24, No. 2 (1985): 195–220. Coleman, James (1988). "Social Capital in the Creation of Human Capital," *American Journal of Sociology* 94, supplement, S95–S120. Coleman, James (1990). *Foundations of Social Theory* (Cambridge, Massachusetts: Harvard University Press, 1990).

13. Putnam, Robert, R. Leonardi, and R. Nanetti (1993). *Making Democracy Work: Civic Traditions in Modern Italy* (Princeton, NJ: Princeton University Press, 1993).

14. Putnam, Leonardi, and Nanetti, *Making Democracy Work*.

15. Putnam, *Bowling Alone*.

16. Shah, Neil (2022). "Major Music Acts Are Seeing 20% No-Show Rates at Concerts," *Wall Street Journal*, December 16, 2021, https://www.wsj.com/articles/major-music-acts-are-seeing-20-no-show-rates-at-concerts-11639663201.

17. Rodgers III, William M., and Lowell Ricketts (2022). "The Great Retirement: Who Are the Retirees?" Federal Reserve Bank of St. Louis, January 4, 2022, https://www.stlouisfed.org/on-the-economy/2022/january/great-retirement-who-are-retirees.

18. Kovacs, Balazs, Nicholas Caplan, Samuel Grob, and Marissa King (2021). "Social Networks and Loneliness during the COVID-19 Pandemic," *Socius: Sociological Research for a Dynamic World* 7, pp. 1–16. American Sociological Association.

19. Pew Research Center (2021). "Social Media Fact Sheet," April 7, 2021, https://www.pewresearch.org/internet/fact-sheet/social-media/; BroadbandSearch, 2022. https://www.broadbandsearch.net/blog/average-daily-time-on-social-media.

20. Heimlich, Russell (2010). "Baby Boomers Retire," Pew Research Center, December 29, 2010, https://www.pewresearch.org/fact-tank/2010/12/29/baby-boomers-retire/.

21. Yasin, Danish (2022). "Gemie: Building the Future of Asian Entertainment in the Metaverse," *CryptoPotato*, March 17, 2022.

22. Kahl, Arvid (2021). "What Founders Can Learn from Web3 Community-Building (and What They Can't)," The Boostrappedfounder.

com, December 30, 2021, https://thebootstrappedfounder.com/ what-founders-can-learn-from-web3-community-building-and-what-they-cant/.

23. Author Sherry Turkle, clinical psychologist and professor of the social studies of science and technology in the program in science, technology, and society at MIT.

24. American Psychological Association (2022). "Is Technology Killing Empathy?" with Sherry Turkle, PhD, *Speaking of Psychology* (podcast), episode 189, May 2022, https://www.apa.org/news/podcasts/speaking-of-psychology/ anti-empathy-machine.

25. Meta Festival (2022). Numerous speakers discussed the importance of the metaverse experience over promoting a brand. If the user has an enjoyable experience, the brand will be elevated.

26. Nagarajan, Amith (2018). *The Open Garden Organization: A Blueprint for Associations in the Digital Age.* (Charleston, SC: Advantage Media Group, 2018).

27. Nagarajan, *The Open Garden Organization.*

28. Mason, Venessa (2020). "Leveraging Tech to Build the Future of Belonging," a presentation at CMX Summit 2020, https://vimeo.com/468729296.

29. Nike (2021). "Nike Creates NIKELAND on Roblox," November 18, 2021, https://news.nike.com/news/five-things-to-know-roblox.

30. Official Peloton member page on Facebook (2022), https://www.facebook.com/ groups/pelotonmembers/about/.

31. Rec Room (2022), https://recroom.com/.

32. Dapper Labs, https://www.dapperlabs.com/newsroom/ wnba-moments-to-debut-on-top-shot.

33. Dapper Labs (2022). "NBA and Dapper Labs to Launch First-Ever NFT Auction on NBA Top Shot, Giving Fans Access to the Ultimate All-Star VIP Experience," February 21, 2022, https://www.dapperlabs.com/newsroom/ nba-and-dapper-labs-to-launch-first-ever-nft-auction-on-nba-top-shot-giving-fans-access-to-the-ultimate-all-star-vip-experience.

34. Dapper Labs, "NBA and Dapper Labs."

35. Tolbert, C.J., and K. Mossberger (2006). "The Effects of E-Government on Trust and Confidence in Government," *Public Administration Review* 66, No. 3 (2006): 354–69, http://www.jstor.org/stable/3843917.

36. Robertson, Scott P. (2018). *Social Media and Civic Engagement: History, Theory, and Practice.* (Morgan & Claypool), www.morganclaypool.com.

37. Greener, Rory (2021). "Seoul Pledges $33.1m to Metaverse Project," *XR Today*, November 2, 2021, https://www.xrtoday.com/virtual-reality/ seoul-pledges-33-1m-to-metaverse-project/.

38. York Regional Police (2022). "Community Outreach," https://www.yrp.ca/ en/community/community-outreach.asp. "York Regional Police Abridged

Business Plan," https://www.yrp.ca/en/about/resources/YorkRegionalPolice_
AbridgedBusinessPlan.pdf.

39. US Department of Transportation, Federal Highway Administration—
Washington, DC (2022). *Innovator Newsletter* 15, No. 89 (March–April
2022), https://www.fhwa.dot.gov/innovation/innovator/issue89/page_02.html.

40. US Department of Transportation, Federal Highway Administration—
Washington, DC.

41. Boise, Idaho, Downtown 11th Street Bikeway Virtual Open House (2021),
https://storymaps.arcgis.com/stories/6ed4f51859f745febfb9f4807691487c.

42. Yasin, "Gemie: Building the Future of Asian Entertainment."

CHAPTER 9

1. Gallup (2022). "State of the Global Workplace 2022 Report."

2. Ruler, Betteke van (2018). "Communication Theory: An Underrated
Pillar on Which Strategic Communication Rests," *International
Journal of Strategic Communication* 12, No. 4 (2018): pp.
367–81, doi: 10.1080/1553118X.2018.1452240.

3. Poore, Carol A. (2022). "Leveraging '3V' Communication to Support Strategic
Management," *Strategy Magazine*, No. 37 (Spring 2022): pp. 22–25.

4. Poore, "Leveraging '3V' Communication."

5. Workshop polls conducted by Carol A. Poore, Ph.D., in March and October
2021 with the Association for Strategic Planning and International Association of
Business Communicators.

6. NFT Best Reviews (2022). "Mercedes Launch G-Class Inspired NFT Collection
on Nifty Gateway," May 10, 2022, https://www.nftbestreviews.com/nft/
mercedes-launch-g-class-inspired-nft-collection-on-nifty-gateway/.

7. Eisenberg, Harris (2014). "Humans Process Visual Data Better,"
Thermopylae Sciences + Technology, https://www.t-sciences.com/news/
humans-process-visual-data-better.

8. North Carolina Museum of Natural Sciences. "Strategic Plan," https://
naturalsciences.org/strategic-plan/.

9. Website review of strategic plan and strategy communication included in Fortune
500 companies in 2021–2022 by Carol A. Poore, Ph.D., https://fortune.com/
global500/2021/search/?fg500_profits=desc.

10. Lempert, Phil (2022). "Walmart Is Joining the Metaverse. Are We Ready?"
Forbes, January 26, 2022, https://www.forbes.com/sites/phillempert/2022/01/26/
walmart-is-joining-the-metaverse-are-we-ready/?sh=75cf75d11ec3.

11. Connected Leadership Study by Brunswick (2019). The Brunswick Group

surveyed 2,047 full- and part-time US workers of companies with more than 1,000 employees. Findings are published here: https://www.brunswickgroup.com/connected-leadership-integrity-i12063/#:~:text=In%202019%20Brunswick%20published%20the,S%26P%20500%20and%20FTSE%20350.&text=The%20survey%20sought%20to%20gauge%20their%20expectations%20for%20CEOs%20on%20social%20media.

12. Workshop polls conducted by Carol A. Poore, Ph.D., in March and October 2021 with the Association for Strategic Planning and International Association of Business Communicators.

APPENDIX 1

1. Imagine 4D, https://imagine-4d.com/news/immersive-experiences-what-are-the-differences-between-2d-3d-4d-and10d/#:~:text=4D%3A%20A%204D%20film%20is,further%20enhances%20the%20immersive%20experience.

2. Wikipedia (2022). "5G," https://en.wikipedia.org/wiki/5G.

3. Shwartz, Steven (2021). *Evil Robots, Killer Computers, and Other Myths* (New York: Fast Company Press, 2021).

4. PTC.com (2022), https://www.ptc.com/en/industries/aerospace-and-defense.

5. Wikipedia (2022). "Avatar (Computing)," https://en.wikipedia.org/wiki/Avatar_(computing).

6. IBM (2022), https://www.ibm.com/topics/what-is-blockchain#:~:text=Blockchain%20defined%3A%20Blockchain%20is%20a,patents%2C%20copyrights%2C%20branding).

7. Wikipedia (2022). "Cryptocurrency," https://en.wikipedia.org/wiki/Cryptocurrency#History.

8. Wikipedia (2022). "Decentralized Autonomous Organization," https://en.wikipedia.org/wiki/Decentralized_autonomous_organization.

9. Wikipedia (2022). "Decentralized Finance," https://en.wikipedia.org/wiki/Decentralized_finance.

10. Wikipedia (2022). "Deepfake," https://en.wikipedia.org/wiki/Deepfake.

11. Wikipedia (2022). "Exchange-Traded Fund," https://en.wikipedia.org/wiki/Exchange-traded_fund.

12. Bechtel, Mike, and Scott Buchholz (2022). "3 Tech Trends That Are Poised to Transform Business in the Next Decade," *Harvard Business Review*, May 17, 2022, https://hbr.org/sponsored/2022/05/3-tech-trends-that-are-poised-to-transform-business-in-the-next-decade.

13. Wikipedia (2022). "Extended Reality," https://en.wikipedia.org/wiki/Extended_reality.

14. The Allen Coral Atlas was created through a partnership with *National Geographic*, Planet, Vulcan Inc., the University of Queensland, and Arizona State University.

15. Wikipedia (2022). "Haptic Technology," https://en.wikipedia.org/wiki/Haptic_technology.

16. Techopedia (2022). "Hologram," https://www.techopedia.com/definition/15888/hologram.

17. Nikolova, Elena (2022). "Employee Intranet: The Key to an Efficient and Happy Workplace," Happeo, July 24, 2022, https://www.happeo.com/blog/employee-intranet.

18. Wikipedia (2022). "Mixed Reality," https://en.wikipedia.org/wiki/Mixed_reality.

19. CoinYuppie (2022). "Research forecast: NFT Market Ready to Become a $13.6 Billion Industry by 2027," Metaverse and NFT News, May 7, 2022, https://coinyuppie.com/research-forecast-nft-market-ready-to-become-a-13-6-billion-industry-by-2027/.

20. Online Gambling (2022), https://www.onlinegambling.com/.

21. Roblox (2022), https://ir.roblox.com/news/news-details/2022/Roblox-Reports-Second-Quarter-2022-Financial-Results/default.aspx.

22. *Fast Company* (2021). "Fast Company Magazine Sphere of Influence, Winter 2021–2022."

23. Wikipedia (2022). "Robotics," https://en.wikipedia.org/wiki/Robotics.

24. DataReportal (2022). "Digital around the World," https://datareportal.com/global-digital-overview.

25. Wikipedia (2022). "Space Tourism," https://en.wikipedia.org/wiki/Space_tourism.

26. Reddit (2022). "What Is Reddit?" https://reddit.zendesk.com/hc/en-us/articles/204511479-What-is-Reddit-.

APPENDIX 2

1. Pennington, Adrian (2022). "Avatar to Web3: An A-Z Compendium of the Metaverse," *NAB Amplify*, https://amplify.nabshow.com/articles/avatar-to-web3-an-a-z-compendium-of-the-metaverse/.

2. The Braintrust Technology Foundation (2021). "Braintrust: The Decentralized Talent Network," white paper, September, 2021, https://www.usebraintrust.com/whitepaper.

3. VitaDAO (2022), https://www.vitadao.com/about.

4. Adobe (2022), https://www.adobe.com/metaverse.html.

5. Reddit (2022). "Bringing Community Ideas to Life with Community

Funds," April 25, 2022, https://www.redditinc.com/blog/bringing-community-ideas-to-life-with-community-funds.

6. Reddit Community Funds (2022). "Announcing the Community Funds Program," https://www.reddit.com/r/reddit/comments/ubq33x/announcing_the_community_funds_program/.

7. GCR—Global Coin Research (2021). "Managing a Web3 Community," December 28, 2021, https://globalcoinresearch.com/2021/12/28/managing-a-web3-community/.

8. GCR—Global Coin Research, "Managing a Web3 Community."

9. Rove (2022), https://rove.to/build-your-metaverse.

10. Rove, https://rove.to/build-your-metaverse.

11. Minecraft (2022), https://www.minecraft.net/en-us/community.

12. Williams, Maxine (2022). "Building the Metaverse with Diversity and Inclusion from the Start," Meta, February 24, 2022, https://about.fb.com/news/2022/02/building-the-metaverse-with-diversity-and-inclusion-from-the-start/.

CAROL A. POORE, Ph.D., MBA

CAROL A. POORE IS PRESIDENT OF Poore and Associates Strategic Planning, providing strategic planning expertise for corporate, nonprofit, and social sector executive teams around the world, expanding organizational capacity and strategic impact.

Author of *Strategic Impact: A Leader's Three-Step Framework for the Customized, Vital Strategic Plan* (Fast Company Press) and *Building Your Career Portfolio* (Cengage), Carol provides inspirational keynotes and professional development workshops, webinars, articles, and interviews focused on leading with innovation, purpose, and strategic impact.

Carol's executive roles have included serving as president and CEO of a healthcare and clinical trials research center, as vice provost at Arizona State University, as vice president of a medical technology incubator, and as a senior strategist at Salt River Project Water and Power (SRP), one of the world's largest public power utilities and suppliers of water based in Phoenix. She was tapped by SRP to launch a subsidiary energy marketing company and has supported the start-up of medical technology companies.

A faculty member at Arizona State University since 2011, Carol teaches graduate and undergraduate courses in leadership for change, public policy, and community development. Her extensive board leadership, as well as her heart for community service and philanthropy, spans hospital and healthcare, bank, municipal, university, nonprofit social services, economic development, and arts and culture organizations.

Carol received her Ph.D. in public administration, her MBA, and her bachelor of science degree in journalism and broadcasting from Arizona State University. Her research focuses on leadership and social capital and its connection to vibrant community development and downtown revitalization. For more information, visit CarolPoore. com, as well as LinkedIn.